SWEET & MAXWELL'S
SOCIAL WORK STATUTES

Edited By

Richard M. Jones, M.A.

Solicitor; C.Q.S.W., Senior Lecturer in Social Work
University College, Cardiff

Second Edition

LONDON
SWEET & MAXWELL
1985

First Edition   1980
Second Edition 1985

Published by
Sweet & Maxwell Limited of
11 New Fetter Lane, London.
Computerset by Burgess & Son (Abingdon) Limited.
Printed by Robert Hartnoll (1985) Limited,
Bodmin, Cornwall.

British Library Cataloguing in Publication Data

Great Britain
  Sweet & Maxwell's social work statutes.—2nd ed.
  1. Public welfare—Law and legislation—England
  I. Jones, Richard M.
  344.204′31′02632   KD3294
  ISBN 0–421–34830–5

SWEET & MAXWELL'S
SOCIAL WORK STATUTES

AUSTRALIA AND NEW ZEALAND
The Law Book Company Ltd.
Sydney : Melbourne : Perth

CANADA AND U.S.A.
The Carswell Company Ltd.
Agincourt, Ontario

INDIA
N.M. Tripathi Private Ltd.
Bombay
and
Eastern Law House Private Ltd.
Calcutta and Delhi
M.P.P. House
Bangalore

ISRAEL
Steimatzky's Agency Ltd.
Jerusalem : Tel-Aviv : Haifa

MALAYSIA : SINGAPORE : BRUNEI
Malayan Law Journal (Pte.) Ltd.
Singapore

PAKISTAN
Pakistan Law House
Karachi

PREFACE

This edition follows its predecessor in attempting to meet the need of social work students and practitioners for a volume that brings together the key Statutes affecting social work practice.

The Adoption Act 1976 is once again reproduced in an unimplemented state because of a failure to bring into force sections 1 and 2 of the Children Act 1975. An end to this scandalous situation came into sight with the Secretary of State for Social Services announcement to the House of Commons on November 22, 1984 that the Government "are discussing with the local authority associations our intention to bring in the only unimplemented sections [of the Children Act 1975], namely those requiring every local authority to provide an adoption service in its area." The custodianship provisions of the 1975 Act will be brought into force on December 1, 1985.

I have attempted to set out the legislation as it applies to England and Wales, amended and brought up to date to August 1, 1985.

R.M.J.

Penarth,
August, 1985

CONTENTS

Children and Young Persons Act 1933

(23 GEO. 5, C. 12)

Special Procedure with regard to Offences specified in First Schedule

Warrant to search for or remove a child or young person

40.—(1) If it appears to a justice of the peace on information on oath laid by any person who, in the opinion of the justice, is acting in the interests of a child or young person, that there is reasonable cause to suspect—
   (*a*) that the child or young person has been or is being assaulted, ill-treated, or neglected in any place within the jurisdiction of the justice, in a manner likely to cause him unnecessary suffering, or injury to health; or
   (*b*) that any offence mentioned in the First Schedule to this Act has been or is being committed in respect of the child or young person,
the justice may issue a warrant authorising any constable named therein to search for the child or young person, and, if it is found that he has been or is being assaulted, ill-treated, or neglected in manner aforesaid, or that any such offence as aforesaid has been or is being committed in respect of him [to take him to a place of safety, or authorising any constable to remove him with or without search to a place of safety, and a child or young person taken to a place of safety in pursuance of such a warrant may be detained there] until he can be brought before a juvenile court.

(2) A justice issuing a warrant under this section may by the same warrant cause any person accused of any offence in respect of the child or young person to be apprehended and brought before a court of summary jurisdiction, and proceedings to be taken against him according to law.

(3) Any constable authorised by warrant under this section to search for any child or young person, or to remove any child or young person with or without search, may enter (if need be by force) any house, building, or other place specified in the warrant, and may remove him therefrom.

(4) Every warrant issued under this section shall be addressed to and executed by a constable, who shall be accompanied by the person laying the information, if that person desires, unless the justice by whom the warrant is issued otherwise directs, and may also, if the justice by whom the warrant is issued so directs, be accompanied by a duly qualified medical practitioner.

(5) It shall not be necessary in any information or warrant under this section to name the child or young person.

AMENDMENT
   In subs. (1) the words in square brackets were substituted by the Children and Young Persons Act 1963, s.64(1), Sched. 3, para. 11.

Principles to be observed by all Courts in dealing with Children and Young Persons

General considerations

44.—(1) Every court in dealing with a child or young person who is brought before it, either as [. . .] an offender or otherwise, shall have regard to the welfare of the child or young person and shall in a proper case take steps for removing him from undesirable surroundings, and for securing that proper provision is made for his education and training.

(2) [*Repealed by the Children and Young Persons Act* 1969, *s.* 72(4), *Sched.* 6]

AMENDMENTS
In subs. (1) the words omitted were repealed by the Children and Young Persons Act 1969, s.72(4), Sched. 6.

Juvenile Offenders

Age of criminal responsibility

50. It shall be conclusively presumed that no child under the age of [ten] years can be guilty of any offence.

AMENDMENTS
In this section "ten" was substituted for "eight" by the Children and Young Persons Act 1963, s.16(1).

Punishment of certain grave crimes

53.—[(1) A person convicted of an offence who appears to the court to have been under the age of eighteen years at the time the offence was committed shall not, if he is convicted of murder, be sentenced to imprisonment for life, nor shall sentence of death be pronounced on or recorded against any such person; but in lieu thereof the court shall (notwithstanding anything in this or in any other Act) sentence him to be detained during Her Majesty's pleasure, and if so sentenced he shall be liable to be detained in such place and under such conditions as the Secretary of State may direct.]

(2) Where a child or young person is convicted on indictment of [any offence punishable in the case of an adult with imprisonment for fourteen years or more, not being an offence the sentence for which is fixed by law], and the court is of opinion that none of the other methods in which the case may legally be dealt with is suitable, the court may sentence the offender to be detained for such period [not exceeding the maximum term of imprisonment with which the offence is punishable in the case of an adult] as may be specified in the sentence; and where such a sentence has been passed the child or young person shall, during that period. [. . .], be liable to be detained in such place and on such conditions as the Secretary of State may direct.

(3) A person detained pursuant to the directions of the Secretary of State under this section shall, while so detained, be deemed to be in legal custody.

(4) [*Repealed by the Criminal Justice Act* 1967, *s.*103(2), *Sched.* 7, *Pt.*I]

AMENDMENTS
Subs. (1) was substituted by the Murder (Abolition of Death Penalty) Act 1965, ss.1(5), 4.
In subs. (2) the words in square brackets were substituted and inserted by the Criminal Justice Act 1961, ss.2(1), 41(1)(3), Sched. 4 and the words omitted were repealed by the Criminal Justice Act 1948, s.83, Sched. 10, Pt. I.

[Power to order parent or guardian to pay fine etc.

55.—(1) Where—
    (*a*) a child or young person is convicted or found guilty of any offence for the commission of which a fine or costs may be imposed or a

compensation order may be made under section 35 of the Powers of Criminal Courts Act 1973; and

(*b*) the court is of opinion that the case would be best met by the imposition of a fine or costs or the making of such an order, whether with or without any other punishment.

it shall be the duty of the court to order that the fine, compensation or costs awarded be paid by the parent or guardian of the child or young person instead of by the child or young person himself, unless the court is satisfied—

(i) that the parent or guardian cannot be found; or

(ii) that it would be unreasonable to make an order for payment, having regard to the circumstances of the case.

(2) An order under this section may be made against a parent or guardian who, having been required to attend, has failed to do so, but, save as aforesaid, no such order shall be made without giving the parent or guardian an opportunity of being heard.

(3) A parent or guardian may appeal to the Crown Court against an order under this section made by a magistrates' court.

(4) A parent or guardian may appeal to the Court of Appeal against an order made under this section by the Crown Court, as if he had been convicted on indictment and the order were a sentence passed on his conviction.]

AMENDMENT
This section was substituted by the Criminal Justice Act 1982, s.26.

Interpretation

107.—(1) In this Act, unless the context otherwise requires, the following expressions have the meanings hereby respectively assigned to them, that is to say,—

["Care order" and "interim order" have the same meaning as in the Children and Young Persons Act 1969].

"Approved school" means a school approved by the Secretary of State under section seventy-nine of this Act.

[*Definition repealed by the Children and Young Persons Act 1969, s. 72(4), Sched. 6.*]

"Chief officer of police" [as regards England has the same meaning as in the Police Act 1964], as regards Scotland has the same meaning as in [the Police (Scotland) Act 1967] and as regards Northern Ireland means a district inspector of the Royal Ulster Constabulary;

"Child" means a person under the age of fourteen years;

["Commission area" has the same meaning as in [the Justices of the Peace Act 1979]];

"Guardian," in relation to a child or young person, includes any person who, in the opinion of the court having cognisance of any case in relation to the child or young person or in which the child or young person is concerned, has for the time being the charge of or control over the child or young person;

[*Definition repealed by the Children and Young Persons Act 1963, s. 64(3), Sched. 5.*]

"Intoxicating liquor" [has the same meaning as in the Licensing Act 1964].

"Legal guardian" in relation to a child or young person means a person appointed, according to law, to be his guardian by deed or will, or by order of a court of competent jurisdiction;

"Managers," in relation to an approved school established or taken over by a local authority or by a joint committee representing two or more local authorities, means the local authority or the joint committee as the case may be, and in relation to any other approved school, means the persons for the time being having the management or control thereof;

"Metropolitan police court area" means the area consisting of the police court divisions for the time being constituted under the Metropolitan Police Courts Acts 1839 and 1840 [and the City of London];

"Place of safety" means [a community home provided by a local authority or a controlled community home, any] police station, or any hospital, surgery, or any other suitable place, the occupier of which is willing temporarily to receive a child or young person;

[*Definition repealed by the Police Act* 1964, *s.* 64(3), *Sched.* 10 *Pt.* I.]

[*Definition repealed by the National Assistance Act* 1948, *s.* 62, *Sched.* 7 *Pt.* III.]

"Prescribed" means prescribed by regulations made by the Secretary of State;

"Public place" includes any public park garden, sea beach or railway station, and any ground to which the public for the time being have or are permitted to have access, whether on payment or otherwise;

"Street" includes any highway and any public bridge, road, lane, footway, square, court, alley or passage, whether a thoroughfare or not;

"Young person" means a person who has attained the age of fourteen years and is under the age of seventeen years.

AMENDMENTS
In this section, the words in square brackets were substituted or added by the Children and Young Persons Act 1969, s. 72(3), Sched. 5 para. 12(1)(2), the Police Act 1964, s. 63, Sched. 9, the Finance Act 1967, s. 5(1)(*e*), the Children and Young Persons Act 1963, s. 64(1), Sched. 3 para. 24, the Police (Scotland) Act 1967, ss. 52, 53, Sched. 4 the Domestic Proceedings and Magistrates' Courts Act 1978, s. 89(2)(*a*), (3), Sched. 2, para. 5, and the Justices of the Peace Act 1979, s. 71(2)(*a*), Sched. 2, para. 2.

SCHEDULE 1

OFFENCES AGAINST CHILDREN AND YOUNG PERSONS, WITH RESPECT TO WHICH SPECIAL PROVISIONS OF THIS ACT APPLY

The murder or manslaughter of a child or young person.
Infanticide
Any offence under sections twenty-seven, [...], or fifty-six of the Offences against the Person Act 1861, and any offence against a child or young person under sections five, forty-two, forty-three [...] of that Act, [...]
[...]
Any offence under sections one, [...], three, four, eleven or twenty-three of this Act.
[Any offence against a child or young person under any of the following sections of the Sexual Offences Act 1956, that is to say, sections two to seven, ten to sixteen, nineteen, twenty, twenty-two to twenty-six and twenty-eight, and any attempt to commit against a child or young person an offence under section two, five, six, seven, ten, eleven, twelve, twenty-two or twenty-three of that Act:
Provided that for the purposes of subsection (2) of section ninety-nine of this Act this entry shall apply so far only as it relates to offences under sections ten, eleven, twelve, fourteen, fifteen, sixteen, twenty and twenty-eight of the Sexual Offences Act 1956, and attempts to commit offences under sections ten, eleven and twelve of that Act.]
Any other offence involving bodily injury to a child or young person.

AMENDMENTS
The words omitted were repealed by the Sexual Offences Act 1956, s. 51, Sched. 4, and the words in square brackets were added by *ibid.*, s. 48. Sched. 3.

National Assistance Act 1948

(11 & 12 GEO. 6, C. 29)

Welfare Services

Welfare arrangements for blind, deaf, dumb and crippled persons, etc.

29.—(1) A local authority [may, with the approval of the Secretary of State, and to such extent as he may direct in relation to persons ordinarily resident in the area of the local authority shall] make arrangements for promoting the welfare of persons to whom this section applies, that is to say persons who are blind, deaf or dumb, [or who suffer from mental disorder of any description] and other persons who are substantially and permanently handicapped by illness, injury, or congenital deformity or such other disabilities as may be prescribed by the Minister.

(2)(3) [*Repealed by the Local Government Act 1972, s. 195(6), Sched. 23, para. 2(4), Sched. 30.*]

(4) Without prejudice to the generality of provisions of subsection (1) of this section, arrangements may be made thereunder—

(*a*) for informing persons to whom arrangements under that subsection relate of the services available for them thereunder;

(*b* for giving persons instruction in their own homes or elsewhere in methods of overcoming the effects of their disabilities;

(*c*) for providing workshops where such persons may be engaged (whether under a contract of service or otherwise) in suitable work, and hostels where persons engaged in the workshops, and other persons to whom arrangements under subsection (1) of this section relate and for whom work or training is being provided in pursuance of the Disabled Persons (Employment) Act 1944, [or the Employment and Training Act 1973] may live;

(*d*) for providing persons to whom arrangements under subsection (1) of this section relate with suitable work (whether under a contract of service or otherwise) in their own homes or elsewhere;

(*e*) for helping such persons in disposing of the produce of their work;

(*f*) for providing such persons with recreational facilities in their own homes or elsewhere;

(*g*) for compiling and maintaining classified registers of the persons to whom arrangements under subsection (1) of this section relate.

(5) [*Repealed by the Health and Social Services and Social Security Adjudications Act 1983, s.30(1), Sched. 10, Pt. I*].

(6) Nothing in the foregoing provisions of this section shall authorise or require—

(*a*) the payment of money to persons to whom this section applies, other than persons for whom work is provided under arrangements made by virtue of paragraph (*c*) or paragraph (*d*) of subsection (4) of this section or who are engaged in work which they are enabled to perform in consequence of anything done in pursuance of arrangements made under this section; or

(*b*) the provision of any accommodation or services required to be provided under the [National Health Service Act 1977] or the National Health Service (Scotland) Act 1947.

(7) A person engaged in work in a workshop provided under paragraph (*c*) of subsection (4) of this section, or a person in receipt of a superannuation allowance granted on his retirement from engagement in any such workshop, shall be deemed for the purposes of this Act to continue to be ordinarily resident in the area in which he was ordinarily resident immediately before he [was accepted for work in that workshop; and for the purposes of this subsection a course of training in such a workshop shall be deemed to be work in that workshop].

AMENDMENTS
    In subs. (1) the words in square brackets were substituted by the Local Government Act 1972, s. 195(6), Sched. 23, para. 2(4) and the Mental Health (Scotland) Act 1960, s. 113(1), Sched. 4.
    In subs. (4)(*c*) the words in square brackets were inserted by the Employment and Training Act 1973, s. 14(1), Sched. 3, para. 3.
    In subs. (6)(*b*) the words in square brackets were substituted by the National Health Service Act 1977, s. 129, Sched. 15, para. 6.
    In subs. (7) the words in square brackets were substituted retrospectively by the National Assistance (Amendment) Act 1959, s. 1(2)(3).

Default powers of Minister

36.—(1) Where the Minister is of opinion, whether on representations made to him or otherwise, that a local authority have failed to discharge any of their functions under this Part of this Act, or have in the discharge thereof failed to comply with any regulations relating thereto, he may after such inquiry as he may think fit make an order declaring the authority to be in default.

(2) An order under the last foregoing subsection shall direct the authority, for the purpose of remedying the default, to discharge such of their functions, in such manner and within such time or times, as may be specified in the order; and if the authority fail to comply with any direction given under this subsection within the time specified in the order, then without prejudice to any other means of enforcing the order the Minister may make an order transferring to himself such of the functions of the authority as he thinks fit.

(3) Any expenses certified by the Minister to have been incurred by him in discharging functions transferred to him under this section shall on demand be paid to him by the authority from which the functions were transferred.

(4) An authority shall have the like power of raising money required for paying expenses certified by the Minister as aforesaid as they have of raising money for paying expenses incurred directly by them, and the payment of any expenses certified as aforesaid shall, to such extent as may be sanctioned by the Minister, be a purpose for which the authority may borrow money in accordance with the statutory provisions relating to borrowing by that authority.

(5) An order under this section may contain such incidental or supplemental provisions as appear to the Minister to be necessary or expedient, including provision for the transfer to the Minister of property and liabilities of the authority in default.

(6) Where any such order is varied or revoked by a subsequent order, the revoking order or a subsequent order may make provision for the re-transfer to the authority in default of any property or liabilities transferred from that authority to the Minister under the first-mentioned order and for the transfer to that authority of any property or liabilities acquired or incurred by the Minister in discharging any of the functions transferred to him.

Removal to suitable premises of persons in need of care and attention

47.—(1) The following provisions of this section shall have effect for the purposes of securing the necessary care and attention for persons who—

(a) are suffering from grave chronic disease or, being aged, infirm or physically incapacitated, are living in insanitary conditions, and

(b) are unable to devote to themselves, and are not receiving from other persons, proper care and attention.

(2) If the medical officer of health certifies in writing to the appropriate authority that he is satisfied after thorough inquiry and consideration that in the interests of any such person as aforesaid residing in the area of the authority, or for preventing injury to the health of, or serious nuisance to, other persons, it is necessary to remove any such person as aforesaid from the premises in which he is residing, the appropriate authority may apply to a court of summary jurisdiction having jurisdiction in the place where the premises are situated for an order under the next following subsection.

(3) On any such application the court may, if satisfied on oral evidence of the allegations in the certificate, and that it is expedient so to do, order the removal of the person to whom the application relates, by such officer of the appropriate authority, as may be specified in the order, to a suitable hospital or other place in, or within convenient distance of, the area of the appropriate authority, and his detention and maintenance therein;

Provided that the court shall not order the removal of a person to any premises, unless either the person managing the premises has been heard in the proceedings or seven clear days' notice has been given to him of the intended application and of the time and place at which it is proposed to be made.

(4) An order under the last foregoing subsection may be made so as to authorise a person's detention for any period not exceeding three months, and the court may from time to time by order extend that period for such further period, not exceeding three months, as the court may determine.

(5) An order under subsection (3) of this section may be varied by an order of the court so as to substitute for the place referred to in that subsection such other suitable place in, or within convenient distance of, the area of the appropriate authority as the court may determine, so however that the proviso to the said subsection (3) shall with the necessary modification apply to any proceedings under this subsection.

(6) At any time after the expiration of six clear weeks from the making of an order under subsection (3) or (4) of this section an application may be made to the court by or on behalf of the person in respect of whom the order was made, and on any such application the court may, if in the circumstances it appears expedient so to do, revoke the order.

(7) No application under this section shall be entertained by the court unless, seven clear days before the making of the application, notice has been given of the intended application and of the time and place at which it is proposed to be made—

(a) where the application is for an order under subsection (3) or (4) of this section, to the person in respect of whom the application is made or to some person in charge of him;

(b) where the application is for the revocation of such an order, to the medical officer of health

(8) Where in pursuance of an order under this section a person is maintained neither in hospital accommodation provided by the Minister of Health under the [National Health Service Act 1977] or by the Secretary of

State under the National Health Service (Scotland) [Act 1978], nor in premises where accommodation is provided by, or by arrangement with, a local authority under Part III of this Act, the cost of his maintenance shall be borne by the appropriate authority.

(9) Any expenditure incurred under the last foregoing subsection shall be recoverable from the person maintained or from any person who for the purposes of this Act is liable to maintain that person; and any expenditure incurred by virtue of this section in connection with the maintenance of a person in premises where accommodation is provided under Part III of this Act shall be recoverable in like manner as expenditure incurred in providing accommodation under the said Part III.

(10) [*Repealed for England and Wales by the National Health Service Reorganisation Act* 1973, *s.* 57, *Sched.* 5.]

(11) Any person who wilfully disobeys, or obstructs the execution of, an order under this section shall be guilty of an offence and liable on summary conviction to a fine not exceeding ten pounds.

(12) For the purposes of this section, the appropriate authorities shall be the councils of [districts and London boroughs and the Common Council of the City of London] [. . .], and in Scotland the councils of [regions and islands areas].

(13) The foregoing provisions of this section shall have effect in substitution for any provisions for the like purposes contained in, or having effect under, any public general or local Act passed before the passing of this Act:

Provided that nothing in this subsection shall be construed as affecting any enactment providing for the removal to, or detention in, hospital of persons suffering from notifiable or infectious diseases.

(14) Any notice under this section may be served by post.

AMENDMENTS
    In subs. (8) the words in square brackets were substituted by the National Health Service Act 1977, s. 129, Sched. 15, para 7 and the National Health Service (Scotland) Act 1978, s. 109, Sched. 16.
    In subs. (12) the words in square brackets were substituted by the Local Government Act 1972, s. 251, Sched. 29, para. 44(1) and the Local Government (Scotland) Act 1973, s. 214, Sched. 27, Pt. II, para. 91. The words omitted were repealed by the London Government Act 1963, s. 93(1), Sched. 18, Pt. II.

Duty of councils to provide temporary protection for property of persons admitted to hospital etc.

48.—(1) Where a person
    (*a*) is admitted as a patient to any hospital, or
    (*b*) is admitted to accommodation provided under Part III of this Act, or
    (*c*) is removed to any other place under an order made under subsection (3) of the last foregoing section,
and it appears to the council that there is danger of loss of, or damage to, any movable property of his by reason of his temporary or permanent inability to protect or deal with the property, and that no other suitable arrangements have been or are being made for the purposes of this subsection, it shall be the duty of the council to take reasonable steps to prevent or mitigate the loss or damage.

(2) For the purpose of discharging the said duty, the council shall have power at all reasonable times to enter any premises which immediately before the person was admitted or removed as aforesaid were his place of residence or usual place of residence, and to deal with any movable property of his in any way which is reasonably necessary to prevent or mitigate loss thereof or damage thereto.

(3) A council may recover from a person admitted or removed as aforesaid, or from any person who for the purposes of this Act is liable to maintain him, any reasonable expenses incurred by the council in relation to him under the foregoing provisions of this section.

(4) In this section the expression "council" means in relation to any property [the council which is the local authority for the purposes of the Local Authority Social Services Act 1970 and] in the area of which the property is for the time being situated.

AMENDMENTS
In subs. (4) the words in square brackets were substituted for England and Wales by the Local Government Act 1972, s.195(6), Sched. 23, para. 2(10).

Provisions as to entry and inspection

55.—(1) A person who proposes to exercise any power of entry or inspection conferred by this Act shall if so required produce some duly authenticated document showing his authority to exercise the power.

(2) Any person who obstructs the exercise of any such power as aforesaid shall be guilty of an offence and liable on summary conviction to a fine not exceeding [£500] in the case of a first offence or [£500] in the case of a second or any subsequent offence.

AMENDMENTS
In subs. (2) the maximum fine was raised by the Criminal Law Act 1977, s.31(1), Sched. 6.

National Assistance (Amendment) Act 1951

(14 & 15 GEO. 6, C. 57)

An Act to amend section forty-seven of the National Assistance Act 1948.
[1st August 1951]

Amendment of 11 & 12 Geo. 6, c. 29, s. 47

1.—(1) An order under subsection (3) of section forty-seven of the National Assistance Act 1948, for the removal of any such person as is mentioned in subsection (1) of that section may be made without the notice required by subsection (7) of that section if it is certified by the medical officer of health and another registered medical practitioner that in their opinion it is necessary in the interest of that person to remove him without delay.

(2) If in any such case it is shown by the applicant that the manager of any such hospital or place as is mentioned in the said subsection (3) agrees to accommodate therein the person in respect of whom the application is made,

the proviso to that subsection (which requires that the manager of the premises to which a person is to be removed must be heard in the proceedings or receive notice of the application) shall not apply in relation to an order for the removal of that person to that hospital or place.

(3) Any such order as is authorised by this section may be made on the application either of the appropriate authority within the meaning of the said section forty-seven or, if the medical officer of health is authorised by that authority to make such applications, by that officer, and may be made either by a court of summary jurisdiction having jurisdiction in the place where the premises are situated in which the person in respect of whom the application is made resides, or by a single justice having such jurisdiction; and the order may, if the court or justice thinks it necessary, be made *ex parte.*

(4) In relation to any such order as is authorised by this section the provisions of the said section forty-seven shall have effect subject to the following modifications:—

    (*a*) in subsection (4) (which specifies the period for which a person may be detained pursuant to an order) for the words "three months" in the first place where those words occur, there shall be substituted the words "three weeks" and subsection (6) (which enables an application to be made for the revocation of an order) shall not apply;

    (*b*) where the order is made by a single justice, any reference in subsection (4) and (5) to the court shall be construed as a reference to a court of summary jurisdiction having jurisdiction in the same place as that justice.

(5) [*Applies to Scotland*]

The Sexual Offences Act 1956

(4 & 5 ELIZ. 2, C. 69)

Power to search for and remove woman detained for immoral purposes

43.—(1) Where it is made to appear any information on oath laid before a justice of the peace by a woman's parent, relative or guardian, or by any other person who in the opinion of the justice is acting in the woman's interests, that there is reasonable cause to suspect—

    (*a*) that the woman is detained in any place within the justice's jurisdiction in order that she may have unlawful sexual intercourse with men or with a particular man; and,

    (*b*) that either she is so detained against her will, or she is under the age of sixteen or is a defective, or she is under the age of eighteen and is so detained against the will of her parent or guardian;

then the justice may issue a warrant authorising a named constable to search for her and to take her to and detain her in a place of safety until she can be brought before a justice of the peace.

(2) A justice before whom a woman is brought in pursuance of the foregoing subsection may cause her to be delivered up to her parent or guardian, or otherwise dealt with as circumstances may permit and require.

(3) A constable authorised by a warrant under this section to search for a woman may enter (if need be, by force) any premises specified in the warrant, and remove the woman from the premises.

(4) A constable executing a warrant issued under this section shall be accompanied by the person applying for the warrant, if that person so desires, unless the justice issuing it otherwise directs.

(5) In this section "guardian" means any person having the lawful care or charge of the woman.

(6) The powers conferred by this section shall be in addition to and not in derogation of those conferred by section forty of the Children and Young Persons Act 1933.

Children and Young Persons Act 1963

(1963 C. 37)

An Act to amend the law relating to children and young persons; and for purposes connected therewith. [31st July 1963]

PART I

CARE AND CONTROL OF CHILDREN AND YOUNG PERSONS

Welfare powers of local authorities

Children and young persons beyond control

3.–(1) No child or young person shall be brought before a juvenile court by his parent or guardian on the ground that he is unable to control him; but where the parent or guardian of a child or young person has, by notice in writing, requested the local authority within whose area the child or young person resides to bring him before a juvenile court under [section 1 of the Children and Young Persons Act 1969] and the local authority refuse to do so or fail to do so within twenty-eight days from the date on which the notice is given the parent or guardian may apply by complaint to a juvenile court of an order directing them to do so.

(2) Where a complaint has been made under this section for an order against a local authority, the local authority shall make available to the court such information as to the home surroundings, school record, health and character of the child or young person as appears to them likely to assist the court and shall for that purpose make such investigations as may be necessary.

(3) On the hearing of a complaint under this section the child or young person shall not be present.

AMENDMENTS
In subs. (1) the words in square brackets were substituted by the Chldren and Young Persons Act 1969, s.72(3), Sched. 5, para. 47.

Children and young persons detained in places of safety

23.—(1) A court or justice of the peace—
 (*a*) [*Repealed by the Children and Young Persons Act* 1969, *s.* 72(4), *Sched.* 6.]
 (*b*) issuing a warrant under section 40 of [the principal Act] authorising a constable to take a child or young person to a place of safety; or

(*c*) ordering the removal of a child or young person to a place of safety under [section 12 of the Foster Children Act 1980] or section 43 of the Adoption Act 1958;

shall specify in the warrant, [. . .] or order a period, which shall not exceed twenty-eight days, beyond which the child or young person must not be detained in a place of safety without being brought before a juvenile court; and accordingly the child or young person shall be brought before a juvenile court not later than the end of that period unless he has been released or received into the care of a local authority.

(2) [*Repealed by the Children and Young Persons Act* 1969, *s.* 72(4), *Sched.* 6.]

(3) A child or young person required to be brought before a juvenile court or a justice of the peace under subsection (1) [. . .] of this section shall (if not otherwise brought before the court or justice) be brought before the court or justice by the local authority in whose area the place of safety is situated; and the person occupying or in charge of a place of safety not provided by that local authority shall as soon as practicable notify that local authority whenever a child or young person [. . .] is taken there as mentioned in subsection (1) [. . .] of this section.

(4) Notwithstanding anything in the preceding provisions of this section, where the person to be brought before a court or justice is under the age of five or cannot be brought before the court or justice by reason of illness or accident, the duty to bring him before the court or justice may be discharged by the making of an application for an order under subsection (5) of this section.

(5) Where a person is brought before a juvenile court or justice of the peace in pursuance of subsection (3) of this section or an application is made in respect of any person to a juvenile court or justice of the peace in pursuance of subsection (4) thereof, the court or justice may either order him to be released or make an interim order [within the meaning of the Children and Young Persons Act 1969].

(6) to (8) [*Repealed by the Children and Young Persons Act* 1969, *s.* 72(4), *Sched.* 6.]

AMENDMENTS

In subs. (1)(*c*), the words in square brackets were substituted by the Foster Children Act 1980, s. 23(2), Sched. 2. In the rest of this section the words in square brackets were substituted by the Children and Young Persons Act 1969, s. 72(3), Sched. 5, para. 48 and the words omitted were repealed by s. 72(4), Sched. 6 of that Act.

Provisions as to persons between the ages of 17 and 18

29.—(1) Where proceedings in respect of a young person are begun [under section 1 of the Children and Young Persons Act 1969 or for an offence] and he attains the age of seventeen before the conclusion of the proceedings, the court may [. . .] deal with the case and make any order which it could have made if he had not attained that age.

(2) [*Repealed by the Children and Young Persons Act* 1969, *s.* 72(3)(4), *Sched.* 5, *para.* 49, *Sched.* 6.]

AMENDMENTS

In subs. (1) the words in square brackets were substituted by the Children and Young Persons Act 1969, s.72(3), Sched. 5, para. 49 and the words omitted were repealed by s.72(4), Sched. 6 of that Act.

Family Law Reform Act 1969

(1969 C. 46)

An Act to amend the law relating to the age of majority, to persons who have not attained that age and to the time when a particular age is attained; to amend the law relating to the property rights of illegitimate children and of other persons whose relationship is traced through an illegitimate link; to make provision for the use of blood tests for the purpose of determining the paternity of any person in civil proceedings; to make provision with respect to the evidence required to rebut a presumption of legitimacy and illegitimacy; to make further provision, in connection with the registration of the birth of an illegimate child, for entering the name of the father; and for concerned purposes. [25th July 1969]

Committal of wards of court to care of local authority and supervision of wards of court

7.—(1) In this section "the court" means any of the following courts in the exercise of its jurisdiction relating to the wardship of children, that is to say, the High Court, [. . .] and "ward of court" means a ward of the court in question.

(2) Where it appears to the court that there are exceptional circumstances making it impracticable or undesirable for a ward of court to be, or to continue to be, under the care of either of his parents or of any other individual the court may, if it thinks fit, make an order committing the care of the ward to a local authority; [and thereupon—

(a) Part III of the Child Care Act 1980 (which relates to the treatment of children in the care of a local authority); and

(b) for the purposes only of contributions by the child himself at a time when he has attained the age of 16, Part V of that Act (which relates to contributions towards the maintenance of children in the care of a local authority).

shall apply, subject to the next following subsection, as if the child had been received by the local authority into their care under section 2 of that Act].

(3) In subsection (2) of this section "local authority" means one of the local authorities referred to in subsection (1) of [section 43 of the Matrimonial Causes Act 1973] (under which a child may be committed to the care of a local authority by a court having jurisdiction to make an order for its custody); and subsections (2) to (6) of that section (ancillary provisions) shall have effect as if any reference therein to that section included a reference to subsection (2) of this section [and as if, in relation to a ward of court, the reference in subsection (5)(b) to sections 24 and 28 of the Child Care Act 1979 included a reference to section 23 of that Act (guarantee of apprenticeship deeds) and section 29 of that Act (visiting and assistance of persons formerly in care)].

(4) Where it appears to the court that there are exceptional circumstances making it desirable that a ward of court (not being a ward who in pursuance of an order under subsection (2) of this section is in the care of a local authority) should be under the supervision of an independent person, the court may, as respects such period as the court thinks fit, order that the ward be under the supervision of a welfare officer or of a local authority; and [section 44(2) of the Matrimonial Causes Act 1973] (ancillary provisions

where a child is placed under supervision by a court having jurisdiction to make an order for its custody) shall have effect as if any reference therein to that section included a reference to this subsection.

(5) The court shall have power from time to time by an order under this section to vary or discharge any previous order thereunder.

AMENDMENTS
    In subs. (1) the words omitted were repealed by the Courts Act 1971, s. 56, Sched. 11, Pt. II.
    In subs. (2) the words in square brackets were substituted by the Health and Social Services and Social Security Adjudications Act 1983, s.9, Sched. 2, para. 9.
    In subss. (3) and (4) the words in square brackets were substituted by the Matrimonial Causes Act 1973, s. 54(1)(*a*), Sched. 2, para. 8 except for the words in the final set of brackets in subs. (3), which were added by the Child Care Act 1980, s. 89(2), Sched. 5.

Children and Young Persons Act 1969

(1969 c. 54)

An Act to amend the law relating to children and young persons; and for purposes connected therewith.   [22nd October 1969]

PART I

CARE AND OTHER TREATMENT OF JUVENILES THROUGH COURT PROCEEDINGS

Care of children and young persons through juvenile courts

Care proceedings in juvenile courts

1.—(1) Any local authority, constable or authorised person who reasonably believes that there are grounds for making an order under this section in respect of a child or young person may, subject to section 2(3) and (8) of this Act, bring him before a juvenile court.

(2) If the court before which a child or young person is brought under this section is of opinion that any of the following conditions is satisfied with respect to him, that is to say—

   (*a*) his proper development is being avoidably prevented or neglected or his health is being avoidably impaired or neglected or he is being ill-treated, or

   (*b*) it is probable that the condition set out in the preceding paragraph will be satisfied in his case, having regard to the fact that the court or another court has found that that condition is or was satisfied in the case of another child or young person who is or was a member of the household to which he belongs; or

[(*bb*) it is probable that the condition set out in paragraph (*a*) of this subsection will be satisfied in his case, having regard to the fact that a person who has been convicted of an offence mentioned in Schedule 1 to the Act of 1933, including a person convicted of such an offence on whose conviction for the offence an order was made under Part I of the Powers of Criminal Courts Act 1973 placing him on probation or discharging him absolutely or conditionally is, or may become, a member of the same household as the child or young person;]

   (*c*) he is exposed to moral danger; or

   (*d*) he is beyond the control of his parent or guardian; or

(e) he is of compulsory school age within the meaning of the Education Act 1944 and is not receiving efficient full-time education suitable to his age, ability and aptitude; or

(f) he is guilty of an offence, excluding homicide,

and also that he is in need of care or control which he is unlikely to receive unless the court makes an order under this section in respect of him, then, subject to the following provisions of this section and sections 2 and 3 of this Act, the court may if it thinks fit make such an order.

(3) The order which a court may make under this section in respect of a child or young person is—

(a) an order requiring his parent or guardian to enter into a recognisance to take proper care of him and exercise proper control over him; or

(b) a supervision order; or

(c) a care order (other than an interim order); or

(d) a hospital order within the meaning of [Part III of the Mental Health Act 1983]; or

(e) a guardianship order within the meaning of that Act.

(4) In any proceedings under this section the court may make orders in pursuance of paragraphs (c) and (d) of the preceding subsection but subject to that shall not make more than one of the orders mentioned in the preceding subsection, without prejudice to any power to make a further order in subsequent proceedings of any description; and if in proceedings under this section the court makes one of those orders and an order so mentioned is already in force in respect of the child or young person in question, the court may discharge the earlier order unless it is a hospital or guardianship order.

(5) An order under this section shall not be made in respect of a child or young person—

(a) in pursuance of paragraph (a) of subsection (3) of this section unless the parent or guardian in question consents;

(b) in pursuance of paragraph (d) or (e) of that subsection under the conditions which, under [section 37 of the said Act of 1983], are required to be satisfied for the making of a hospital or guardianship order in respect of a person convicted as mentioned in that section are satisfied in his case so far as they are applicable;

(c) if he has attained the age of sixteen and is or has been married.

(6) In this section "authorised person" means a person authorised by order of the Secretary of State to bring proceedings in pursuance of this section and any officer of a society which is so authorised, and in sections 2 and 3 of this Act "care proceedings" means proceedings in pursuance of this section and "relevant infant" means the child or young person in respect of whom such proceedings are brought or proposed to be brought.

AMENDMENTS

In subs. (1) paragraph (bb) was substituted by the Health and Social Services and Social Security Adjudications Act 1983, s.9, Sched. 2, para. 10.

In subss. (3) and (5) the words in square brackets were substituted by the Mental Health Act 1983, s.148, Sched. 4, para. 26.

Provisions supplementary to s.1

2.—(1) If a local authority receive information suggesting that there are grounds for bringing care proceedings in respect of a child or young person who resides or is found in their area, it shall be the duty of the authority to cause enquiries to be made into the case unless they are satisfied that such enquiries are unnecessary.

(2) If it appears to a local authority that there are grounds for bringing care proceedings in respect of a child or young person who resides or is found in their area, it shall be the duty of the authority to exercise their power under the preceding section to bring care proceedings in respect of him unless they are satisfied that it is neither in his interest nor the public interest to do so or that some other person is about to do so or to charge him with an offence.

(3) No care proceedings shall be begun by any person unless that person has given notice of the proceedings to the local authority for the area in which it appears to him that the relevant infant resides or, if it appears to him that the relevant infant does not reside in the area of a local authority, to the local authority for any area in which it appears to him that any circumstances giving rise to the proceedings arose; but the preceding provisions of this subsection shall not apply where the person by whom the notice would fall to be given is the local authority in question.

(4) Without prejudice to any power to issue a summons or warrant apart from this subsection, a justice may issue a summons or warrant for the purpose of securing the attendance of the relevant infant before the court in which care proceedings are brought or proposed to be brought in respect of him; but [subsections (3) and (4) of section 55 of the Magistrates' Courts Act 1980] (which among other things restrict the circumstances in which a warrant may be issued) shall apply with the necessary modifications to a warrant under this subsection as they apply to a warrant under that section and as if in subsection (3) after the word "summons" there were inserted the words "cannot be served or".

(5) Where the relevant infant is arrested in pursuance of a warrant issued by virtue of the preceding subsection and cannot be brought immediately before the court aforesaid, the person in whose custody he is—

    (a) may make arrangements for his detention in a place of safety for a period of not more than seventy-two hours from the time of the arrest (and it shall be lawful for him to be detained in pursuance of the arrangements); and

    (b) shall within that period, unless within it the relevant infant is brought before the court aforesaid, bring him before a justice;

and the justice shall either make an interim order in respect of him or direct that he be released forthwith.

(6) [Section 97 of the Magistrates' Courts Act 1980] (under which a summons or warrant may be issued to secure the attendance of a witness) shall apply to care proceedings as it applies to the hearing of a complaint.

(7) In determining whether the condition set out in subsection (2)(b) of the preceding section is satisfied in respect of the relevant infant, it shall be assumed that no order under that section is to be made in respect of him.

(8) In relation to the condition set out in subsection (2)(e) of the preceding section the references to a local authority in that section and subsections (1), (2) and (11)(b) of this section shall be construed as references to a local education authority; and in any care proceedings—

    (a) the court shall not entertain an allegation that that condition is satisfied unless the proceedings are brought by a local education authority; and

    (b) the said condition shall be deemed to be satisfied if the relevant infant is of the age mentioned in that condition and it is proved that he—

        (i) is the subject of a school attendance order which is in force under section 37 of the Education Act 1944 and has not been complied with, or

(ii) is a registered pupil at a school which he is not attending regularly within the meaning of section 39 of that Act, or

(iii) is a person whom another person habitually wandering from place to place takes with him,

unless it is also proved that he is receiving the education mentioned in that condition;

but nothing in paragraph (*a*) of this subsection shall prevent any evidence from being considered in care proceedings for any purpose other than that of determining whether that condition is satisfied in respect of the relevant infant.

(9) If on application under this subsection to the court in which it is proposed to bring care proceedings in respect of a relevant infant who is not present before the court it appears to the court that he is under the age of five and either—

(*a*) it is proved to the satisfaction of the court, on oath or in such other manner as may be prescribed by rules under section 15 of the Justices of the Peace Act 1949, that notice of the proposal to bring the proceedings at the time and place at which the application is made was served on the parent or guardian of the relevant infant at what appears to the court to be a reasonable time before the making of the application; or

(*b*) it appears to the court that his parent or guardian is present before the court

the court if it thinks fit, after giving the parent or guardian if he is present an opportunity to be heard, give a direction under this subsection in respect of the relevant infant; and a relevant infant in respect of whom such a direction is given by a court shall be deemed to have been brought before the court under section 1 of this Act at the time of the direction, and care proceedings in respect of him may be continued accordingly.

(10) If the court before which the relevant infant is brought in care proceedings is not in a position to decide what order, if any, ought to be made under the preceding section in respect of him, [the court may make—

(*a*) an interim order; or

(*b*) an interim hospital order within the meaning of [section 38 of the Mental Health Act 1983],

in respect of him; but an order shall not be made in respect of the relevant infant in pursuance of paragraph (*b*) of this subsection unless the conditions which, under [the said section 38], are required to be satisfied for the making of an interim hospital order in respect of a person convicted as mentioned in that section are satisfied in his case so far as they are applicable.]

(11) If it appears to the court before which the relevant infant is brought in care proceedings that he resides in a petty sessions area other than that for which the court acts, the court shall, unless it dismisses the case and subject to subsection (5) of the following section, direct that he be brought under the preceding section before a juvenile court acting for the petty sessions area in which he resides; and where the court so directs—

(*a*) it may make an interim order in respect of him and, if it does so, shall cause the clerk of the court to which the direction relates to be informed of the case;

(*b*) if the court does not make such an order it shall cause the local authority in whose area it appears to the court that the relevant infant resides to be informed of the case, and it shall be the duty of that authority to give effect to the direction within twenty-one days.

(12) The relevant infant may appeal to [the Crown Court] against any

order made in respect of him under the preceding section except such an order as is mentioned in subsection (3)(*a*) of that section.

(13) Such an order as is mentioned in subsection (3)(*a*) of the preceding section shall not require the parent or guardian in question to enter into a recognisance for an amount exceeding [£1,000] or for a period exceeding three years or, where the relevant infant will attain the age of eighteen in a period shorter than three years, for a period exceeding that shorter period; and [section 120 of the Magistrates' Courts Act 1980] (which relates to the forfeiture of recognisances) shall apply to a recognisance entered into in pursuance of such an order as it applies to a recognisance to keep the peace.

(14) For the purposes of this Act, care proceedings in respect of a relevant infant are begun when he is first brought before a juvenile court in pursuance of the preceding section in connection with the matter to which the proceedings relate.

AMENDMENTS

In subss. (4), (6) and (13) the words in square brackets were substituted by the Magistrates' Courts Act 1980, s.154(1) Sched. 7, para. 78.

In subs. (10) the words in square brackets were substituted by the Mental Health Act 1983, s.148, Sched. 4, para. 26 and the Mental Health (Amendment) Act 1982, s.65, Sched. 3, para. 44.

In subs. (12) the words in square brackets were substituted by the Courts Act 1971, s.56(2), Sched. 9, Pt. I.

In subs. (13) the figure in square brackets was substituted by S.I. 1984 No. 447, art. 2(1), Sched. 1.

Further supplementary provisions relating to s. 1(2)(*f*)

3.—(1) In any care proceedings, no account shall be taken for the purposes of the condition set out in paragraph (*f*) of subsection (2) of section 1 of this Act (hereafter in this section referred to as "the offence condition") of an offence alleged to have been committed by the relevant infant if—

(*a*) in any previous care proceedings in respect of him it was alleged that the offence condition was satisfied in consequence of the offence; or

(*b*) the offence is a summary offence [. . .] and, disregarding section 4 of this Act, the period for beginning summary proceedings in respect of it expired before the care proceedings were begun; or

(*c*) disregarding section 4 of this Act, he would if charged with the offence be entitled to be discharged under any rule of law relating to previous acquittal or conviction.

(2) In any care proceedings the court shall not entertain an allegation that the offence condition is satisfied in respect of the relevant infant unless the proceedings are brought by a local authority or a constable; but nothing in this or the preceding subsection shall prevent any evidence from being considered in care proceedings for any purpose other than that of determining whether the offence condition is satisfied in respect of the relevant infant.

(3) If in any care proceedings the relevant infant is alleged to have committed an offence in consequence of which the offence condition is satisfied with respect to him, the court shall not find the offence condition satisfied in consequence of the offence unless, disregarding section 4 of this Act, it would have found him guilty of the offence if the proceedings had been in pursuance of an information duly charging him with the offence and the court had had jurisdiction to try the information; and without prejudice to the preceding provisions of this subsection the same proof shall be required to substantiate or refute an allegation that the offence condition is

satisfied in consequence of an offence as is required to warrant a finding of guilty or, as the case may be, of not guilty of the offence.

(4) A person shall not be charged with an offence if in care proceedings previously brought in respect of him it was alleged that the offence condition was satisfied in consequence of that offence.

(5) If in any case proceedings in which it is alleged that the offence condition is satisfied in respect of the relevant infant it appears to the court that the case falls to be remitted to another court in pursuance of subsection (11) of the preceding section but that it is appropriate to determine whether the condition is satisfed before remitting the case, the court may determine accordingly; and any determination under this subsection shall be binding on the court to which the case is remitted.

[(6) Where in any care proceedings the court finds the offence condition satisfied with respect to the relevant infant, then, whether or not the court makes an order under section 1 of this Act—

   (a) section 35 of the Powers of Criminal Courts Act 1973 (which relates to compensation for personal injury and loss of or damage to property) shall apply as if the finding were a finding of guilty of the offence; and

   (b) it shall be the duty of the court, subject to subsections (6A) and (6B). of this section, to order that any sum awarded by virtue of this section be paid by the relevant infant's parent or guardian instead of by the relevant infant, unless the court is satisfied—
      (i) that the parent or guardian cannot be found; or
      (ii) that it would be unreasonable to make an order for payment, having regard to the circumstances of the case.

(6A) An order shall not be made in pursuance of the preceding subsection unless the parent or guardian has been given an opportunity of being heard or has been required to attend the proceedings and failed to do so.

(6B) Where the finding that the offence condition is satisfied is made in pursuance of subsection (5) of this section, the powers conferred by subsection (6) of this section shall be exercisable by the court to which the case is remitted instead of by the court which made the finding.]

(7) Where in any care proceedings the court finds the offence condition satisfied with respect to the relevant infant and he is a young person, the court may if it thinks fit and he consents, instead of making such an order as is mentioned in section 1(3) of this Act, order him to enter into a recognisance for an amount not exceeding [£50] and for a period not exceeding one year to keep the peace or to be of good behaviour; and such an order shall be deemed to be an order under section 1 of this Act but no appeal to [the Crown Court] may be brought against an order under this subsection.

(8) Where in any care proceedings the court finds the offence condition satisfied with respect to the relevant infant in consequence of an offence which was not admitted by him before the court, then—

   (a) if the finding is made in pursuance of subsection (5) of this section and the court to which the case is remitted decides not to make any order under section 1 of this Act in respect of the relevant infant; or

   (b) if the finding is not made. in pursuance of that subsection and the court decides as aforesaid,

the relevant infant may appeal to [the Crown Court] against the finding, and in a case falling within paragraph (a) of this subsection any notice of appeal shall be given within [twenty-one] days after the date of the decision mentioned in that paragraph; and a person ordered to pay compensation by virtue of subsection (6) of this section may appeal to [the Crown Court] against the order.

(9) [*Repealed by Courts Act* 1971, *s.* 56(4), *Sched.* 11, *Pt.* IV.]

AMENDMENTS
In subss. (1)(*b*) and (6) the words omitted were repealed by the Criminal Law Act 1977, s.65, Sched. 13.
Subs. (6) was substituted by the Criminal Justice Act 1982, s.27.
In subs. (7), the figure in square brackets was substituted by the Criminal Law Act 1977, s.58(3).
In subss. (7) and (8), the reference to the Crown Court were substituted by the Courts Act 1971, s.56(1)(2), Sched. 8, para. 59(1), Sched. 9, Pt. I.
In subs. (8) "twenty-one" was substituted for "fourteen" by the Crown Court Rules 1982 (S.I. 1982 No. 1109), Sched. 3, Pt. II, para. 6.

Consequential changes in criminal proceedings etc.

Prohibition of criminal proceedings for offences by children

4. A person shall not be charged with an offence, except homicide, by reason of anything done or omitted while he was a child.

Restrictions on criminal proceedings for offences by young persons

5.—(1) A person other than a qualified informant shall not lay an information in respect of an offence if the alleged offender is a young person.

(2) A qualified informant shall not lay an information in respect of an offence if the alleged offender is a young person unless the informant is of opinion that the case is of a description prescribed in pursuance of subsection (4) of this section and that it would not be adequate for the case to be dealt with by a parent, teacher or other person or by means of a caution from a constable or through an exercise of the powers of a local authority or other body not involving court proceedings or by means of proceedings under section 1 of this Act.

(3) A qualified informant shall not come to a decision in pursuance of the preceding subsection to lay an information unless—

(*a*) he has told the appropriate local authority that the laying of the information is being considered and has asked for any observations which the authority may wish to make on the case to the informant; and

(*b*) the authority either have notified the informant that they do not wish to make such observations or have not made any during the period or extended period indicated by the informant as that which in the circumstances he considers reasonable for the purpose or the informant has considered the observations made by the authority during that period;

but the informant shall be entitled to disregard the foregoing provisions of this subsection in any case in which it appears to him that the requirements of the preceding subsection are satisfied and will continue to be satisfied notwithstanding any observations which might be made in pursuance of this subsection.

(4) The Secretary of State may make regulations specifying, by reference to such considerations as he thinks fit, the descriptions of cases in which a qualified informant may lay an information in respect of an offence if the alleged offender is a young person; but no regulations shall be made under

this subsection unless a draft of the regulations has been approved by a resolution of each House of Parliament.

(5) An information laid by a qualified informant in a case where the informant has reason to believe that the alleged offender is a young person shall be in writing and shall—

    (*a*) state the alleged offender's age to the best of the informant's knowledge; and

    (*b*) contain a certificate signed by the informant stating that the requirements of subsections (2) and (3) of this section are satisfied with respect to the case or that the case is one in which the requirements of the said subsection (2) are satisfied and the informant is entitled to disregard the requirements of the said subsection (3).

(6) If at the time when justices begin to inquire into a case, either as examining justices or on the trial of an information, they have reason to believe that the alleged offender is a young person and either—

    (*a*) it appears to them that the person who laid the information in question was not a qualified informant when he laid it; or

    (*b*) the information is not in writing or does not contain such a certificate as is mentioned in subsection (5)(*b*) of this section,

it shall be their duty to quash the information, without prejudice to the laying of a further information in respect of the matter in question; but no proceedings shall be invalidated by reason of a contravention of any provision of this section and no action shall lie, by reason only of such a contravention, in respect of proceedings in respect of which such a contravention has occurred.

(7) Nothing in the preceding provisions of this section applies to an information laid with the consent of the Attorney General or laid by or on behalf or with the consent of the Director of Public Prosecutions.

(8) It shall be the duty of a person who decides to lay an information in respect of an offence in a case where he has reason to believe that the alleged offender is a young person to give notice of the decision to the appropriate local authority unless he is himself that authority.

(9) In this section—

    "the appropriate local authority", in relation to a young person, means the local authority for the area in which it appears to the informant in question that the young person resides or, if the young person appears to the informant not to reside in the area of a local authority, the local authority in whose area it is alleged that the relevant offence or one of the relevant offences was committed; and

    "qualified informant" means a servant of the Crown, a police officer and a member of a designated police force acting in his capacity as such a servant, officer or member, a local authority, the Greater London Council, the council of a county district and any body designated as a public body for the purposes of this section;

and in this subsection "designated" means designated by an order made by the Secretary of State; but nothing in this section shall be construed as preventing any council or other body from acting by an agent for the purposes of this section.

Summary trial of young persons

    6.—[*Repealed by the Magistrates' Courts Act* 1980, *s.* 154(3), *Sched.* 9.]

Alterations in treatment of young offenders etc.

7. (1) [*Repealed by the Criminal Justice Act 1982, s. 78, Sched. 16.*]

(2) [*Repealed by the Powers of Criminal Courts Act 1973, s. 56(2), Sched. 6.*]

(3)–(4) [*Repealed by the Criminal Justice Act 1982, s. 78, Sched. 16.*]

(5) An order sending a person to an approved school shall not be made after such day as the Secretary of State may by order specify for the purposes of this subsection.

(6) [*Repeals sections 54 and 57 of the Children and Young Persons Act 1933.*]

(7) Subject [to subsection (7A) of this section and] to the enactments requiring cases to be remitted to juvenile courts and to section 53(1) of the Act of 1933 (which provides for detention for certain grave crimes), where a child is found guilty of homicide or a young person is found guilty of any offence by or before any court, that court or the court to which his case is remitted shall have power—

> (*a*) if the offence is punishable in the case of an adult with imprisonment, to make a care order (other than an interim order) in respect of him; or
>
> (*b*) to make a supervision order in respect of him; or
>
> (*c*) with the consent of his parent or guardian, to order the parent or guardian to enter into a recognisance to take proper care of him and exercise proper control over him,

and if it makes such an order as is mentioned in this subsection while another such order made by any court is in force in respect of the child or young person, shall also have power to discharge the earlier order; and subsection (13) of section 2 of this Act shall apply to an order under paragraph (*c*) of this subsection as it applies to such an order as is mentioned in that subsection.

[(7A) A court shall not make a care order under subsection (7) of this section in respect of a child or young person unless it is of opinion—

> (*a*) that a care order is appropriate because of the seriousness of the offence; and
>
> (*b*) that the child or young person is in need of care or control which he is unlikely to receive unless the court makes a care order.]

(8) Without prejudice to the power to remit any case to a juvenile court which is conferred on a magistrates' court other than a juvenile court by section 56(1) of the Act of 1933, in a case where such a magistrates' court finds a person guilty of an offence and either he is a young person or was a young person when the proceedings in question were begun it shall be the duty of the court to exercise that power unless the court [if of the opinion that the case is one which can properly be dealt with by means of—

> (*a*) an order discharging him absolutely or conditionally; or
>
> (*b*) an order for the payment of a fine; or
>
> (*c*) an order requiring his parent or guardian to enter into a recognisance to take proper care of him and exercise proper control over him, with or without any other order that the court has power to make when absolutely or conditionally discharging an offender.]

AMENDMENTS

The words in square brackets in subs. (7), and subs. (7A), were inserted by the Criminal Justice Act 1982, s.23.

In subs. (8) the words in square brackets were substituted by the Criminal Justice Act 1972, s.64(7), Sched. 5.

Legal representation

7A.—(1) A court shall not make a care order under section 7(7) of this Act in respect of a child or young person who is not legally represented in that court unless either—

(*a*) he applied for legal aid and the application was refused on the ground that it did not appear that his means were such that he required assistance; or

(*b*) having been informed of his right to apply for legal aid and had the opportunity to do so, he refused or failed to apply.

(2) For the purposes of this section a person is to be treated as legally represented in a court if, he has the assistance of counsel of a solicitor to represent him in the proceedings in that court at some time after he is found guilty and before a care order is made, and in this section "legal aid" means legal aid for the purposes of proceedings in that court, whether the whole proceedings or the proceedings on or in relation to the making of the care order; but in the case of a person committed to the Crown Court for sentence or trial, it is immaterial whether he applied for legal aid in the Crown Court to, or was informed of his right to apply by, that court or the court which committed him.]

AMENDMENT
This section was inserted by the Criminal Justice Act 1982, s.24.

Investigations by local authorities

9.—(1) Where a local authority or a local education authority brings proceedings under section 1 of this Act or proceedings for an offence alleged to have been committed by a young person or are notified that any such proceedings are being brought, it shall be the duty of the authority, unless they are of opinion that it is unnecessary to do so, to make such investigation and provide the court before which the proceedings are heard with such information relating to the home surroundings, school record, health and character of the person in respect of whom the proceedings are brought as appear to the authority likely to assist the court.

(2) If the court mentioned in subsection (1) of this section requests the authority aforesaid to make investigations and provide information or to make further investigations and provide further information relating to the matters aforesaid, it shall be the duty of the authority to comply with the request.

Supervision

Supervision orders

11. Any provision of this Act authorising a court to make a supervision order in respect of any person shall be construed as authorising the court to make an order placing him under the supervision of a local authority designated by the order or of a probation officer; and in this Act "supervision order" shall be construed accordingly and "supervised person" and "supervisor", in relation to a supervision order, mean respectively the person placed or to be placed under supervision by the order and the person under whose supervision he is placed or to be placed by the order.

[Local authority functions under certain supervision orders

11A. The Secretary of State may make regulations with respect to the exercise by a local authority of their functions in a case where a person has been placed under their supervision by an order made under section 1(3)(*b*) or 21(2) of this Act.]

AMENDMENTS
This section was added by the Children Act 1975, s.108(1), Sched. 3, para. 68.

Power to include requirements in supervision orders

12.—(1) A supervision order may require the supervised person to reside with an individual named in the order who agrees to the requirement, but a requirement imposed by a supervision order in pursuance of this subsection shall be subject to any such requirement of the order as is authorised by the following provisions of this section.

[(2) Subject to section 19(12) of this Act, a supervision order may require the supervised person to comply with any directions given from time to time by the supervisor and requiring him to do all or any of the following things—

    (*a*) to live at a place or places specified in the directions for a period or periods so specified;

    (*b*) to present himself to a person or persons specified in the directions at a place or places and on a day or days so specified;

    (*c*) to participate in activities specified in the directions on a day or days so specified;

but it shall be for the supervisor to decide whether and what extent he exercises any power to give directions conferred on him by virtue of this subsection and to decide the form of any directions; and a requirement imposed by a supervision order in pursuance of this subsection shall be subject to any such requirement of the order as is authorised by subsection (4) of this section.

(3) The total number of days in respect of which a supervised person may be required to comply with directions given by virtue of paragraph (*a*), (*b*) or (*c*) of subsection (2) above in pursuance of a supervision order shall not exceed 90 or such lesser number, if any, as the order may specify for the purposes of this subsection; and for the purpose of calculating the total number of days in respect of which such directions may be given the supervisor shall be entitled to disregard any day in respect of which directions were previously given in pursuance of the order and on which the directions were not complied with.

(3A) Subject to subsection (3B) of this section, this subsection applies to—

    (*a*) any supervision order made under section 7(7) of this Act in respect of a child or young person found guilty as there mentioned; and

    (*b*) any supervision order made in respect of a person under section 21(2) of this Act by a court on discharging a care order made in respect of him under the said section 7(7).

(3B) Subsection (3A) of this section does not apply to any supervision order which by virtue of subsection (2) of this section requires the supervised person to comply with directions given by the supervisor.

(3C) Subject to the following provisions of this section and to section 19(13) of this Act, but without prejudice to subsection (4) below, a supervision order to which subsection (3A) of this section applies may require a supervised person—

 (a) to do anything that by virtue of subsection (2) of this section a supervisor has power, or would but for section 19(12) of this Act have power, to direct a supervised person to do;

 (b) to remain for specified periods between 6 p.m. and 6 a.m.—

  (i) at a place specified in the order; or

  (ii) at one of several places so specified;

 (c) to refrain from participating in activities specified in the order—

  (i) on a specified day or days during the period for which the supervision order is in force; or

  (ii) during the whole of that period or a specified portion of it.

(3D) A requirement under subsection (3C)(b) of this section is referred to in this section as a "night restriction".

(3E) The total number of days in respect of which a supervised person may be subject to requirements imposed by virtue of subsection (3C)(a) or (b) of this section shall not exceed 90.

(3F) The court may not include requirements under subsection (3C) of this section in a supervision order unless—

 (a) it has first consulted the supervisor as to—

  (i) the offender's circumstances; and

  (ii) the feasibility of securing compliance with the requirements,

  and is satisfied, having regard to the supervisor's report, that it is feasible to secure compliance with them;

 (b) having regard to the circumstances of the case, it considers the requirements necessary for securing the good conduct of the supervised person or for preventing a repetition by him of the same offence or the commission of other offences; and

 (c) the supervised person or, if he is a child, his parent or guardian, consents to their inclusion.

(3G) The court shall not include in such an order by virtue of subsection (3C) of this section—

 (a) any requirement that would involve the co-operation of a person other than the supervisor and the supervised person unless that other person consents to its inclusion; or

 (b) any requirement requiring the supervised person to reside with a specified individual; or

 (c) any such requirement as is mentioned in subsection (4) of this section.

(3H) The place, or one of the places, specified for the purposes of a night restriction shall be the place where the supervised person lives.

(3J) A night restriction shall not require the supervised person to remain at a place for longer than 10 hours on any one night.

(3K) A night restriction shall not be imposed in respect of any day which falls outside the period of three months beginning with the date when the supervision order is made.

(3L) A night restriction shall not be imposed in respect of more than 30 days in all.

(3M) A supervised person who is required by a night restriction to remain at a place may leave it if he is accompanied—

 (a) by his parent or guardian;

 (b) by his supervisor; or

 (c) by some other person specified in the supervision order.

(3N) For the purposes of this section a night restriction imposed in respect of a period of time beginning in the evening and ending in the morning shall be treated as imposed only in respect of the day upon which the period begins.]

(4) Where a court which proposes to make a supervision order is satisfied, on the evidence of a medical practitioner approved for the purposes of [section 12 of the Mental Health Act 1983], that the mental condition of a supervised person is such as requires and may be susceptible to treatment but is not such as to warrant his detention in pursuance of a hospital order under [Part III] of that Act, the court may include in the supervision order a requirement that the supervised person shall, for a period specified in the order, submit to treatment of one of the following descriptions so specified, that is to say—

(a) treatment by or under the direction of a fully registered medical practitioner specified in the order;

(b) treatment as a non-resident patient at a place specified in the order; or

(c) treatment as a resident patient in a hospital or mental nursing home within the meaning of [the said Act of 1983], but not a special hospital within the meaning of that Act.

(5) A requirement shall not be included in a supervision order in pursuance of the preceding subsection—

(a) in any case, unless the court is satisfied that arrangements have been or can be made for the treatment in question and, in the case of treatment as a resident patient, for the reception of the patient;

(b) in the case of an order made or to be made in respect of a person who has attained the age of fourteen, unless he consents to its inclusion; and a requirement so included shall not in any case continue in force after the supervised person becomes eighteen.

AMENDMENTS

Subss. (2) to (3N) were substituted by the Criminal Justice Act 1982, s.20.

In subs. (4) the words in square brackets were substituted by the Mental Health Act 1983, s.148, Sched. 4, para. 26.

Selection of supervisor

13.—(1) A court shall not designate a local authority as the supervisor by a provision of a supervision order unless the authority agree or it appears to the court that the supervised person resides or will reside in the area of the authority.

(2) A court shall not insert in a supervision order a provision placing a child under the supervision of a probation officer unless the local authority of which the area is named or to be named in the order in pursuance of section 18(2)(a) of this Act so request and a probation officer is already exercising or has exercised, in relation to another member of the household to which the child belongs, duties imposed [on probation officers by paragraph 8 of Schedule 3 to the Powers of Criminal Courts Act 1973 or by rules under paragraph 18(1)(b)] of that Schedule.

(3) Where a provision of a supervision order places a person under the supervision of a probation officer, the supervisor shall be a probation officer appointed for or assigned to the petty sessions area named in the order in pursuance of section 18(2)(a) of this Act and selected under arrangements made by the probation and after-care committee; but if the probation officer

selected as aforesaid dies or is unable to carry out his duties [. . .], another probation officer shall be selected as aforesaid for the purposes of the order.

AMENDMENTS
In subs. (2) the words in square brackets were substituted by the Powers of Criminal Courts Act 1973, s.56(1), Sched. 5.
In subs. (3) the words omitted were repealed by the Criminal Law Act 1977, s.65, Sched. 13.

Duty of supervisor

14. While a supervision order is in force it shall be the duty of the supervisor to advise, assist and befriend the supervised person.

[Refusal to allow supervisor to visit child or young person

14A. Where a supervision order has been made in a case where a condition set out in paragraph (*a*), (*b*), (*bb*) or (*c*) of section 1(2) above is satisfied, a refusal to comply with a requirement imposed under section 18(2)(*b*) below—
(*a*) that the supervisor of a child or young person shall visit him; or
(*b*) that a child or young person shall be medically examined,
shall be treated for the purposes of section 40 of the Children and Young Persons Act 1933 (under which a warrant authorising the search for and removal of a child or young person may be issued on suspicion of unnecessary suffering caused to, or certain offences committed against, the child or young person) as giving reasonable cause for such suspicion.]

AMENDMENT
This section was inserted by the Health and Social Services and Social Security Adjudications Act 1983, s.9, Sched. 2, para. 11.

Variation and discharge of supervision orders

15.—(1) If while a supervision order is in force in respect of a supervised person who has not attained the age of eighteen it appears to a juvenile court, on the application of the supervisor or the supervised person, that it is appropriate to make an order under this subsection, the court may make an order discharging the supervision order or varying it by—
(*a*) cancelling any requirement included in it in pursuance of section 12 or section 18(2)(*b*) of this Act; or
(*b*) inserting in it (either in addition to or in substitution for any of its provisions) any provision which could have been included in the order if the court had then had power to make it and were exercising the power,
and may on discharging the supervision order make a care order (other than an interim order) in respect of the supervised person; but the powers of variation conferred by this subsection do not include power to insert in the supervision order, after the expiration of [three months beginning with the date when the order was originally made], a requirement in pursuance of section 12(4) of this Act, unless [. . .] it is in substitution for such a requirement already included in the order [or power to insert in the supervision order a requirement in pursuance of section 12(3C)(*b*) of this Act in respect of any day which falls outside the period of 3 months beginning with the date when the order was originally made.].

(2) If on an application in pursuance of the preceding subsection, in a case where the supervised person has attained the age of seventeen and the supervision order was not made by virtue of section 1 of this Act or on the

occasion of the discharge of a care order, it appears to the court appropriate to do so it may proceed as if the application were in pursuance of subsection (3) or, if it is made by the supervisor, in pursuance of subsections (3) and (4) of this section and as if in that subsection or those subsections, as the case may be, the word "seventeen" were substituted for the word "eighteen" and the words "a magistrates' court other than" were omitted.

[(2A) If while a supervision order to which section 12(3A) of this Act applies is in force in respect of a person who has not attained the age of eighteen it is proved to the satisfaction of a juvenile court, on the application of the supervisor, that the supervised person has failed to comply with any requirement included in the supervision order in pursuance of section 12 or section 18(2)(*b*) of this Act, the court may, whether or not it also makes an order under subsection (1) of this section—

    (*a*) order him to pay a fine of an amount not exceeding [£100]; or

    (*b*) subject to section 16(10) of this Act, make an attendance centre order in respect of him.]

(3) If while a supervision order is in force in respect of a supervised person who has attained the age of eighteen it appears to a magistrates' court other than a juvenile court, on the application of the supervisor or the supervised person, that it is appropriate to make an order under this subsection, the court may make an order discharging the supervision order or varying it by—

    (*a*) inserting in it a provision specifying the duration of the order or altering or cancelling such a provision already included in it; or

    (*b*) substituting for the provisions of the order by which the supervisor is designated or by virtue of which he is selected such other provisions in that behalf as could have been included in the order if the court had then had power to make it and were exercising the power; or

    (*c*) substituting for the name of an area included in the order in pursuance of section 18(2)(*a*) of this Act the name of any other area of a local authority or petty sessions area, as the case may be, in which it appears to the court that the supervised person resides or will reside; or

    (*d*) cancelling any provision included in the order by virtue of section 18(2)(*b*) of this Act or inserting in it any provision prescribed for the purposes of that paragraph; or

    (*e*) cancelling any requirement included in the order in pursuance of section 12(1) or (2) of this Act.

(4) If while a supervision order is in force in respect of a supervised person who has attained the age of eighteen it is provided to the satisfaction of a magistrates' court other than a juvenile court, on the application of the supervisor, that the supervised person has failed to comply with any requirement included in the supervision order in pursuance of section 12 or section 18(2)(*b*) of this Act, the court may—

    (*a*) whether or not it also makes an order under subsection (3) of this section, order him to pay a fine of an amount not exceeding [£100] or, subject to subsection (10) of the following section, make an attendance centre order in respect of him;

    (*b*) if it also discharges the supervision order, make an order imposing on him any punishment which it could have imposed on him if it had then had power to try him for the offence in consequence of which the supervision order was made and had convicted him in the exercise of that power;

and in a case where the offence in question is of a kind which the court has no power to try or has no power to try without appropriate consents, the punishment imposed by virtue of paragraph (*b*) of this subsection shall not exceed that which any court having power to try such an offence could have imposed in respect of it and shall not in any event exceed imprisonment for a term of six months and a fine of [£2,000].

(5) If a medical practitioner by whom or under whose direction a supervised person is being treated for his mental condition in pursuance of a requirement included in a supervision order by virtue of section 12(4) of this Act is unwilling to continue to treat or direct the treatment of the supervised person or is of opinion—

  (*a*) that the treatment should be continued beyond the period specified in that behalf in the order; or

  (*b*) that the supervised person needs different treatment; or

  (*c*) that he is not susceptible to treatment; or

  (*d*) that he does not require further treatment,

the practitioner shall make a report in writing to that effect to the supervisor; and on receiving a report under this subsection the supervisor shall refer it to a juvenile court, and on such a reference the court may make an order cancelling or varying the requirement.

(6) The preceding provisions of this section shall have effect subject to the provisions of the following section.

AMENDMENTS

   In subs. (1) the words omitted were repealed, and the words in square brackets were substituted, by the Criminal Law Act 1977, s.65, Scheds. 12, 13. The words in square brackets at the end of the subsection were inserted by the Criminal Justice Act 1982, Sched. 14, para. 25.

   Subs. (2A) was inserted by the Criminal Law Act 1977, s.37(2).

   In subss. (2A) and (4) the figures in square brackets were inserted by S.I. 1984 No. 447, art. 2(3), Sched. 3.

Provisions supplementary to s.15

16.—(1) Where the supervisor makes an application or reference under the preceding section to a court he may bring the supervised person before the court, and subject to subsection (5) of this section a court shall not make an order under that section unless the supervised person is present before the court.

(2) Without prejudice to any power to issue a summons or warrant apart from this subsection, a justice may issue a summons or warrant for the purpose of securing the attendance of a supervised person before the court to which any application or reference in respect of him is made under the preceding section; but [subsections (3) and (4) of section 55 of the Magistrates' Courts Act 1980] (which among other things restrict the circumstances in which a warrant may be issued) shall apply with the necessary modifications to a warrant under this subsection as they apply to a warrant under that section and as if in subsection (3) after the word "summons" there were inserted the words "cannot be served or".

(3) Where the supervised person is arrested in pursuance of a warrant issued by virtue of the preceding subsection and cannot be brought immediately before the court referred to in that subsection, the person in whose custody he is—

  (*a*) may make arrangements for his detention in a place of safety for a period of not more than seventy-two hours from the time of the arrest (and it shall be lawful for him to be detained in pursuance of the arrangements); and (*b*) shall within that period, unless within it the relevant infant is brought before the court aforesaid, bring him before a justice;

and the justice shall either direct that he be released forthwith or—

(i) if he has not attained the age of eighteen, make an interim order in respect of him;

(ii) if he has attained that age, remand him.

(4) If on an application to a court under subsection (1) of the preceding section—

(*a*) the supervised person is brought before the court under a warrant issued or an interim order made by virtue of the preceding provisions of this section; or

(*b*) the court considers that it is likely to exercise its powers under that subsection to make an order in respect of the supervised person but, before deciding whether to do so, seeks information with respect to him which it considers is unlikely to be obtained unless the court makes an interim order in respect of him,

the court may make an interim order in respect of the supervised person.

(5) A court may make an order under the preceding section in the absence of the supervised person if the effect of the order is confined to one or more of the following, that is to say—

(*a*) discharging the supervision order;

(*b*) cancelling a provision included in the supervision order in pursuance of section 12 or section 18(2)(*b*) of this Act;

(*c*) reducing the duration of the supervision order or any provision included in it in pursuance of the said section 12;

(*d*) altering in the supervision order the name of any area;

(*e*) changing the supervisor.

(6) A juvenile court shall not—

(*a*) exercise its powers under subsection (1) of the preceding section to make a care order or an order discharging a supervision order or inserting in it a requirement authorised by section 12 of this Act or varying or cancelling such a requirement except in a case where the court is satisfied that the supervised person either is unlikely to receive the care or control he needs unless the court makes the order or is likely to receive it notwithstanding the order;

(*b*) exercise its powers to make an order under subsection (5) of the preceding section except in such a case as is mentioned in paragraph (*a*) of this subsection;

(*c*) exercise its powers under the said subsection (1) to make an order inserting a requirement authorised by section 12(4) of this Act in a supervision order which does not already contain such a requirement unless the court is satisfied as mentioned in the said section 12(4) on such evidence as is there mentioned.

(7) Where the supervised person has attained the age of fourteen, then except with his consent a court shall not make an order under the preceding section containing provisions which insert in the supervision order a requirement authorised by section 12(4) of this Act or which alter such a requirement already included in the supervision order otherwise than by removing it or reducing its duration.

(8) The supervised person may appeal to [the Crown Court] against

(*a*) any order made under the preceding section, except an order made or which could have been made in the absence of the supervised person and an order containing only provisions to which he consented in pursuance of the preceding subsection;

(*b* the dismissal of an application under that section to discharge a supervision order.

(9) Where an application under the preceding section for the discharge of a supervision order is dismissed, no further application for its discharge shall be made under that section by any person during the period of three months beginning with the date of the dismissal except with the consent of a court having jurisdiction to entertain such an application.

(10) In [paragraph (*b*) of subsection (2A) and] paragraph (*a*) of subsection (4) of the preceding section "attendance centre order" means such an order to attend an attendance centre as is mentioned in subsection (1) of section [17 of the Criminal Justice Act 1982]; and the provisions of that section shall accordingly apply for the purposes of [each of those paragraphs] as if for the words from "has power" to "probation order" in subsection (1) there were substituted the words "considers it appropriate to make an attendance centre order in respect of any person in pursuance of [section 15(2A) or (4)]yof the Children and Young Persons Act 1969" and for references to an offender there were substituted references to the supervised person and as if subsection [(13)] were omitted.

(11) In this and the preceding section references to a juvenile court or any other magistrates' court, in relation to a supervision order, are references to such a court acting for the petty sessions area for the time being named in the order in pursuance of section 18(2)(*a*) of this Act; and if while an application to a juvenile court in pursuance of the preceding section is pending the supervised person to whom it relates attains the age of seventeen or eighteen, the court shall deal with the application as if he had not attained the age in question.

AMENDMENTS
In subs. (2), the words in square brackets were substituted by the Magistrates' Courts Act 1980, s.154(1), Sched. 7, para. 81.
In subs. (8) the words in square brackets were substituted by the Courts Act 1971, s.56(2), Sched. 9, Pt. I.
In subs. (10) the words in square brackets were substituted by the Criminal Law Act 1977, s.65, Sched. 12 and the Criminal Justice Act 1982, Sched. 14, para. 26.

Termination of supervision

17. A supervision order shall, unless it has previously been discharged, cease to have effect—

(*a*) in any case, on the expiration of the period of three years, or such shorter period as may be specified in the order, beginning with the date on which the order was originally made;

(*b*) if the order was made by virtue of section 1 of this Act or on the occasion of the discharge of a care order and the supervised person attains the age of eighteen on a day earlier than that on which the order would expire under paragraph (*a*) above, on that earlier day.

Supplementary provisions relating to supervision orders

18.—(1) A court shall not make a supervision order unless it is satisfied that the supervised person resides or will reside in the area of a local authority; and a court shall be entitled to be satisfied that the supervised person will so reside if he is to be required so to reside by a provision to be included in the order in pursuance of section 12(1) of this Act.

(2) A supervision order—

(*a*) shall name the area of the local authority and the petty sessions area in which it appears to the court making the order, or to the court varying any provision included in the order in pursuance of this paragraph, that the supervised person resides or will reside; and

(*b*) may contain prescribed provisions as the court aforesaid considers appropriate for facilitating the performance by the supervisor of his functions under section 14 of this Act, including any prescribed provisions for requiring visits to be made by the supervised person to the supervisor,

and in paragraph (*b*) of this subsection "prescribed" means prescribed by rules under [section 144 of the Magistrates' Courts Act 1980.]

(3) A court which makes a supervision order or an order varying or discharging a supervised order shall forthwith send a copy of its order—

(*a*) to the supervised person and, if the supervised person is a child, to his parent or guardian; and

(*b*) to the supervisor and any person who has ceased to be the supervisor by virtue of the order; and

(*c*) to any local authority who is not entitled by virtue of the preceding paragraph to such a copy and whose area is named in the supervision order in pursuance of the preceding subsection or has ceased to be so named by virtue of the court's order; and

(*d*) where the supervised person is required by the order, or was required by the supervision order before it was varied or discharged, to reside with an individual or to undergo treatment by or under the direction of an individual or at any place, to the individual or the person in charge of that place; and

(*e*) where a petty sessions area named in the order or discharged order in pursuance of subsection (2) of this section is not that for which the court acts, to the clerk to the justices for the petty sessions area so named;

and, in a case falling within paragraph (*e*) of this subsection, shall also send to the clerk to the justices in question such documents and information relating to the case as the court considers likely to be of assistance to them.

[(4) Where a supervision order—

(*a* requires compliance with directions given by virtue of section 12(2) of this Act; or

(*b* includes by virtue of section 12(3C) of this Act a requirement which involves the use of facilities for the time being specified in a scheme in force under section 19 of this Act for an area in which the supervised person resides or will reside,

any expenditure incurred by the supervisor for the purposes of the directions or requirements shall be defrayed by the local authority whose area is named in the order in pursuance of subsection (2) of this section.]

AMENDMENTS
   In subs. (2), the words in square brackets were substituted by the Magistrates' Courts Act 1980, s.154(1), Sched. 7, para. 82.
   Subs. (4) was substituted by the Criminal Justice Act 1982, s.20(2).

[Facilities for the carrying out of supervisors' directions and requirements included in supervision orders by virtue of section 12(3C)

19.—(1) It shall be the duty of a local authority, acting either individually or in association with other local authorities, to make arrangements with such persons as appear to them to be appropriate, for the provision by those persons of facilities for enabling—

(a) directions given by virtue of section 12(2) of this Act to persons resident in their area; and

(b) requirements that may only be included in a supervision order by virtue of section 12(3C) of this Act if they are for the time being specified in a scheme,

to be carried out effectively.

(2) The authority or authorities making any arrangements in accordance with subsection (1) of this section shall consult each relevant probation committee as to the arrangements.

(3) Any such arrangements shall be specified in a scheme made by the authority or authorities making them.

(4) A scheme shall come into force on a date to be specified in it.

(5) The authority or authorities making a scheme shall send copies of it to the clerk to the justices for each petty sessions area of which any part is included in the area to which the scheme relates.

(6) A copy of a scheme shall be kept available at the principal office of every authority who are a party to it for inspection by members of the public at all reasonable hours, and any such authority shall on demand by any person furnish him with a copy of the scheme free of charge.

(7) The authority or authorities who made a scheme may at any time make a further scheme altering the arrangements or specifying arrangements to be substituted for those previously specified.

(8) A scheme which specifies arrangements to be substituted for those specified in a previous scheme shall revoke the previous scheme.

(9) The powers conferred by subsection (7) of this section shall not be exercisable by an authority or authorities unless they have first consulted each relevant probation committee.

(10) The authority or authorities who made a scheme shall send to the clerk to the justices for each petty sessions area of which any part is included in the area for which arrangements under this section have been specified in the scheme notice of any exercise of a power conferred by subsection (7) of this section, specifying the date for the coming into force, and giving details of the effect, of the new or altered arrangements, and the new or altered arrangements shall come into force on that date.

(11) Arrangements shall not be made under this section for the provision of any facilities unless the facilities are approved or are of a kind approved by the Secretary of State for the purposes of this section.

(12) A supervision order shall not require compliance with directions given by virtue of section 12(2) of this Act unless the court making it is satisfied that a scheme under this section is in force for the area where the supervised person resides or will reside; and no such directions may involve the use of facilities which are not for the time being specified in a scheme in force under this section for that area.

(13) Subject to subsection (14) of this section, a supervision order may not include by virtue of subsection 12(3C) of this Act—

(a) any requirement that would involve the supervised person in absence from home—
   (i) for more than 2 consecutive nights; or
   (ii) for more than 2 nights in any one week; or

(b) if the supervised person is of compulsory school age, any requirement to participate in activities during normal school hours,

unless the court making the order is satisfied that the facilities whose use would be involved are for the time being specified in a scheme in force under this section for the area in which the supervised person resides or will reside.

(14) Subsection 13(*b*) of this section does not apply to activities carried out in accordance with arrangements made or approved by the local education authority in whose area the supervised person resides or will reside.

(15) It shall be the duty of every local authority to ensure that a scheme made by them in accordance with this section, either individually or in association with any other local authority, comes into force for their area not later than April 30, 1983 or such later date as the Secretary of State may allow.

(16) In this section "relevant probation committee" means a probation committee for an area of which any part is included in the area to which a scheme under this section relates.

(17) Expressions used in this section and in the Education Act 1944 have the same meanings in this section as in that Act.]

AMENDMENT
　　This section was substituted by the Criminal Justice Act 1982, s.21.

Committal to care of local authorities)

Orders for committal to care of local authorities

20.—(1) Any provision of this Act authorising the making of a care order in respect of any person shall be construed as authorising the making of an order committing him to the care of local authority; and in this Act "care order" shall be construed accordingly and "interim order" means a care order containing provision for the order to expire with the expiration of twenty-eight days, or of a shorter period specified in the order, beginning—

(*a*) if the order is made by a court, with the date of the making of the order; and

(*b*) if it is made by a justice, with the date when the person to whom it relates was first in legal custody in connection with the matter in consequence of which the order is made.

(2) The local authority to whose care a person is committed by a care order shall be—

(*a*) except in the case of an interim order, the local authority in whose area it appears to the court making the order that that person resides or, if it does not appear to the court that he resides in the area of a local authority, any local authority in whose area it appears to the court that any offence was committed or any circumstances arose in consequence of which the order is made; and

(*b*) in the case of an interim order such one of the local authorities mentioned in paragraph (*a*) of this subsection as the court or justice making the order thinks fit (whether or not the person in question appears to reside in their area).

[(2A) In determining the place of residence of any person for the purposes of this section, any period shall be disregarded during which, while in the care of a local authority (whether by virtue of a care order or not), he resided outside the local authority's area.]

(3) Subject to the provisions of the following section, a care order other than an interim order shall cease to have effect—

(*a*) if the person to whom it relates had attained the age of sixteen when the order was originally made, when he attains the age of nineteen; and

(*b*) in any other case, when that person attains the age of eighteen.

(4) A care order shall be sufficient authority for the detention by any local authority or constable of the person to whom the order relates until he is

received into the care of the authority to whose care he is committed by the order.

AMENDMENT
Subs. (2A) was inserted by the Health and Social Services and Social Security Adjudications Act 1983, s.9, Sched. 2, para. 12.

[Power of court to add condition as to charge and control of offender in care

20A.—(1) Where a person to whom a care order relates which was made—

(*a*) by virtue of subsection (3) of section 1 of this Act in a case where the court which made the order was of the opinion that the condition mentioned in subsection (2)(*f*) of that section was satisfied; or

(*b*) by virtue of section 7(7) of this Act.

is convicted or found guilty of an offence punishable with imprisonment in the case of a person over 21, the court which convicts or finds him guilty of that offence may add to the care order a condition under this section that the power conferred by section 21(2) of the Child Care Act 1980 (power of local authority to allow a parent, guardian, relative or friend charge and control) shall for such period not exceeding 6 months as the court may specify in the condition—

(*a*) not be exercisable; or

(*b*) not be exercisable except to allow the person to whom the order relates to be under the charge and control of a specified parent, guardian, relative or friend.

(2) Where—

(*a*) the power conferred by subsection (1) above has been exercised; and

(*b*) before the period specified in the condition has expired the person to whom the care order relates is convicted or found guilty of another offence punishable with imprisonment in the case of a person over 21,

the court may replace the condition with another condition under this section.

(3) A court shall not exercise the powers conferred by this section unless the court is of opinion that it is appropriate to exercise those powers because of the seriousness of the offence and that no other method of dealing with the person to whom the care order relates is appropriate; and for the purpose of determining whether any other method of dealing with him is appropriate the court shall obtain and consider information about the circumstances.

(4) A court shall not exercise the said powers in respect of a person who is not legally represented in that court unless either—

(*a*) he applied for legal aid and the application was refused on the ground that it did not appear his means were such that he required assistance; or

(*b*) having been informed of his right to apply for legal aid and had the opportunity to do so, he refused or failed to apply.

(5) Before adding a condition under this section to a care order a court shall explain to the person to whom the care order relates the purpose and effect of the condition.

(6) At any time when a care order includes a condition under this section—

(*a*) the person to whom the order relates;

(*b*) his parent or guardian, acting on his behalf; or

(*c*) the local authority in whose care he is,

may apply to a juvenile court for the revocation or variation of the condition.

(7) The local authority may appeal to the Crown Court against the imposition of a condition under this section by a magistrates' court or against the terms of such a condition.

(8) For the purposes of this section a person is to be treated as legally represented in a court if, but only if, he has the assistance of counsel or a solicitor to represent him in the proceedings in that court at some time after he is convicted or found guilty and before any power conferred by this section is exercised, and in this section "legal aid" means legal aid for the purposes of proceedings in that court, whether the whole proceedings or the proceedings on or in relation to the exercise of the power; but in the case of a person committed to the Crown Court for sentence or trial, it is immaterial whether he applied for legal aid in the Crown Court to, or was informed of his right to apply by, that court or the court which committed him.]

AMENDMENT
    This section was inserted by the Criminal Justice Act 1982, s.22.

Variation and discharge of care orders

21.—(1) If it appears to a juvenile court, on the application of a local authority to whose care a person is committed by a care order which would cease to have effect by virtue of subsection (3)(*b*) of the preceding section, that he is accommodated in a community home or a home provided by the Secretary of State and that by reason of his mental condition or behaviour it is in his interest or the public interest for him to continue to be so accommodated after he attains the age of eighteen, the court may order that the care order shall continue in force until he attains the age of nineteen; but the court shall not make an order under this subsection unless the person in question is present before the court

(2) If it appears to a juvenile court, on the application of a local authority to whose care a person is committed by a care order or on the application of that person, that it is appropriate to discharge the order, the court may discharge it and on discharging it may, unless it was an interim order and unless the person to whom the discharged order related has attained the age of eighteen, make a supervision order in respect of him

[(2A) A juvenile court shall not make an order under subsection (2) of this section in the case of a person who has not attained the age of 18 and appears to the court to be in need of care or control unless the court is satisfied that, whether through the making of a supervision order or otherwise, he will receive that care of control.

(3) Where an application under [subsection (2) of this section] for the discharge of a care order is dismissed, then—

  (*a*) in the case of an interim order, no further application for its discharge shall be made under that subsection except with the consent of a juvenile court (without prejudice to the power to make an application under subsection (4) of the following section); and

  (*b*) in any other case, no further application for its discharge shall be made under this subsection by any person during the period of three months beginning with the date of the dismissal except with the consent of a juvenile court.

(4) The person to whom the relevant care order relates or related may appeal to [the Crown Court] against an order under subsection (1) of this

section or a supervision order made in pursuance of subsection (2) of this section or the dismissal of an application under the said subsection (2) for the discharge of the care order

(5) The local authority to whose care a person is committed by a care order (other than an interim order) may, within the period of three months beginning with the date of the order, appeal to [the Crown Court] against the provision of the order naming their area on the ground that the time the order was made the person aforesaid resided in the area of another local authority named in the notice of appeal; but no appeal shall be brought by a local authority under this subsection unless they give notice in writing of the proposals to bring it to the other local authority in question before giving notice of appeal

(6) References in this section to a juvenile court, in relation to a care order, are references to a juvenile court acting for any part of the area of the local authority to whose care a person is committed by the order or for the place where that person resides.

AMENDMENTS
Subs. (2A) was inserted, and the words in square brackets in subs. (3) were substituted, by the Children Act 1975, s.108(1), Sched. 3, para. 69.
In subss. (4) and (5), the words in square brackets were substituted by the Courts Act 1971, s.56(2), Sched. 9, Pt. I.

["Termination of care order on adoption etc.

21A.—(1) A care order relating to a person under the age of 18 shall cease to have effect—
  (a) on his adoption;
  (b) if any order under an enactment to which this paragraph applies is made in relation to him;
  (c) if any order similar to an order under section 25 of the Children Act 1975 is made in relation to him in Northern Ireland, the Isle of Man or any of the Channel Islands.

(2) Subsection (1)(b) above applies to the following enactments—
  (a) section 14 and 25 of the Children Act 1975;
  (b) sections 18 and 55 of the Adoption Act 1976; and
  (c) sections 18 and 49 of the Adoption (Scotland) Act 1978.

(3) After the commencement of section 55 of the Adoption Act 1976 subsection (1)(c) above shall have effect with the substitution of subsection '55 of the Adoption Act 1976' for '25 of the Children Act 1975'."]

AMENDMENT
This section was substituted by the Health and Social Services and Social Security Adjudications Act 1983, s.9, Sched. 2, para. 13.

Special provisions relating to interim orders

22.—(1) A juvenile court or a justice shall not make an interim order in respect of any person unless either—
  (a) that person is present before the court or justice; or
  (b) the court or justice is satisfied that he is under the age of five or cannot be present as aforesaid by reasons of illness or accident.

(2) An interim order shall contain provision requiring the local authority to whose care a person is committed by the order to bring that person before a court specified in the order on the expiration of the order or at such earlier

time as the specified court may require, so however that the said provision shall, if the court making the order considers it appropriate so to direct by reason of the fact that that person is under the age of five [or is legally represented] or by reason of illness or accident, require the local authority to bring him before the specified court on the expiration of the order only if the specified court so requires.

(3) A juvenile court acting for the same area as a juvenile court by which or a justice by whom an interim order has been made in respect of any person may, at any time before the expiration of the order, make a further interim order in respect of him; and the power to make an interim order conferred by this subsection is without prejudice to any other power to make such an order.

(4) The High Court may, on the application of a person to whom an interim order relates, discharge the order on such terms as the court thinks fit; but if on such an application the discharge of the order is refused, the local authority to whose care he is committed by the order shall not exercise in his case their powers under [section 21(2) of the Child Care Act 1980] (which enables them to allow a parent or other person to be in charge of him) except with the consent and in accordance with any directions of the High Court.

(5) If a court which has made or, apart from this subsection, would make an interim order in respect of a person who has attained the age of fourteen certifies that he is of so unruly a character that he cannot safely be committed to the care of a local authority and has been notified by the Secretary of State that a remand centre is available for the reception from the court of persons of his class or description, then, subject to the following provisions of this section, the court shall commit him to a remand centre for twenty-eight days or such shorter period as may be specified in the warrant; but in a case where an interim order is in force in respect of the person in question, a warrant under this subsection shall not be issued in respect of him except on the application of the local authority to whose care he is committed by the order and shall not be issued for a period extending beyond the date fixed for the expiration of the order, and on the issue of a warrant under this subsection in such a case the interim order shall cease to have effect.

In this subsection "court" includes a justice.

(6) Subsections (1), (3) and (4) of this section, so much of section 2(11)(*a*) as requires the clerk to be informed and section 21(2) to (4) of this Act shall apply to a warrant under subsection (5) of this section as they apply to an interim order but as if the words "is under the age of five or" in subsection (1) of this section were omitted.

AMENDMENT
The words in square brackets in subs.(2) were inserted by the Health and Social Services and Social Security Adjudication Act 1983, s.9, Sched. 2, para. 14.
The words in square brackets in subs.(4) were substituted by the Child Care Act 1980, s.89(2), Sched. 5.

Remand to care of local authorities etc.

23.—(1) Where a court—
  (*a*) remands or commits for trial a child charged with homicide or remands a child convicted of homicide; or
  (*b*) remands a young person charged with or convicted of one or more offences or commits him for trial or sentence,

and he is not released on bail, then, subject to the following provisions of this section, the court shall commit him to the care of a local authority in whose area it appears to the court that he resides or that the offence or one of the offences was committed.

(2) If the court aforesaid certifies that a young person is of so unruly a character that he cannot safely be committed to the care of a local authority under the preceding subsection, then if the court has been notified by the Secretary of State that a remand centre is available for the reception from the court of persons of his class or description, it shall commit him to a remand centre and, if it has not been so notified, it shall commit him to a prison.

(3) If, on the application of the local authority to whose care a young person is committed by a warrant under subsection (1) of this section, the court by which he was so committed or any magistrates' court having jurisdiction in the place where he is for the time being certifies as mentioned in subsection (2) of this section, the provisions of the said subsection (2) relating to committal shall apply in relation to him and he shall cease to be committed in pursuance of the said subsection (1).

(4) The preceding provisions of this section shall have effect subject to the provisions of [section 37 of the Magistrates' Courts Act 1980] (which related to committal to quarter sessions with a view to a [youth custody sentence]).

(5) In this section "court" and "magistrates' court" include a justice; and notwithstanding anything in the preceding provisions of this section, [section 128(7) of the Magistrates' Courts Act 1980] (which provides for remands to the custody of a constable for periods not exceeding three clear days) shall have effect in relation to a child or young person as if for the reference to three clear days there were substituted a reference to twenty-four hours.

AMENDMENT

In subss. (4) and (5), the words in square brackets were substituted by the Magistrates' Courts Act 1980, s.154(1), Sched. 7, para. 83 and the Criminal Justice Act 1982, Sched. 14, para. 27.

Detention

Detention of child or young person in place of safety

28.—(1) If, upon an application to a justice by any person for authority to detain a child or young person and take him to a place of safety, the justice is satisfied that the applicant has reasonable cause to believe that—

(a) any of the conditions set out in section 1(2)(a) to (e) of this Act is satisfied in respect of the child or young person; or

(b) an appropriate court would find the condition set out in section 1(2)(b) of this Act satisfied in respect of him; or

(c) the child or young person is about to leave the United Kingdom in contravention of section 25 of the Act of 1933 (which regulates the sending abroad of juvenile entertainers),

the justice may grant the application; and the child or young person in respect of whom an authorisation is issued under this subsection may be detained in a place of safety by virtue of the authorisation for twenty-eight days beginning with the date of authorisation, or for such shorter period beginning with that date as may be specified in the authorisation.

(2) Any constable may detain a child or young person as respects whom the constable has reasonable cause to believe that any of the conditions set

out in section 1(2)(*a*) to (*d*) of this Act is satisfied or that an appropriate court would find the condition set out in section 1(2)(*b*) of this Act satisfied or that an offence is being committed under section 10(1) of the Act of 1933 (which penalises a vagrant who takes a juvenile from place to place).

(3) A person who detains any person in pursuance of the preceding provisions of this section shall, as soon as practicable after doing so, inform him of the reason for his detention and take such steps as are practicable for informing his parent or guardian of his detention and of the reason for it.

(4) A constable who detains any person in pursuance of subsection (2) of this section or who arrests a child without a warrant otherwise than for homicide shall as soon as practicable after doing so secure that the case is enquired into by a police officer not below the rank of inspector or by the police officer in charge of a police station, and that officer shall on completing the enquiry either—

(*a*) release the person in question; or

(*b*) if the officer considers that he ought to be further detained in his own interests or, in the case of an arrested child, because of the nature of the alleged offence, make arrangements for his detention in a place of safety and inform him, and take such steps as are practicable for informing his parent or guardian, of his right to apply to a justice under subsection (5) of this section for his release;

and subject to the said subsection (5) it shall be lawful to detain the person in question in accordance with any such arrangements.

(5) It shall not be lawful for a child arrested without a warrant otherwise than for homicide to be detained in consequence of the arrest or such arrangements as aforesaid, or for any person to be detained by virtue of subsection (2) of this section or any such arrangements, after the expiration of the period of eight days beginning with the day on which he was arrested or, as the case may be, on which his detention in pursuance of the said subsection (2) began; and if during that period the person in question applies to a justice for his release, the justice shall direct that he be released forthwith unless the justice considers that he ought to be further detained in his own interests or, in the case of an arrested child, because of the nature of the alleged offence.

(6) If while a person is detained in pursuance of this section an application for an interim order in respect of him is made to a magistrates' court or a justice, the court or justice shall either make or refuse to make the order and, in the case of a refusal, may direct that he be released forthwith.

Release or further detention of arrested child or young person

29.—(1) Where a person is arrested with or without a warrant and cannot be brought immediately before a magistrates' court, then if either—

(*a*) he appears to be a child and his arrest is for homicide; or

(*b*) he appears to be a young person and his arrest is for any offence the police officer in charge of the police station to which he is brought or another police officer not below the rank of inspector shall forthwith enquire into the case and, subject to subsection (2) of this section, shall release him unless—

(i) the officer considers that he ought in his own interests to be further detained; or

(ii) the officer has reason to believe that he has committed homicide or another grave crime or that his release would defeat the ends of justice or that if he were released (in a case where he was arrested without a warrant) he would fail to appear to answer to any charge which might be made.

[(2) Where a parent or guardian enters into a recognisance to secure that the child or young person appears at the hearing of the charge, the recognisance may, if the said officer thinks fit, be conditioned for the attendance of the parent or guardian at the hearing in addition to the person arrested.]

(3) An officer who enquires into a case in pursuance of subsection (1) of this section and does not release the person to whom the enquiry relates shall, unless the officer certifies that it is impracticable to do so or that he is of so unruly a character as to make it inappropriate to do so, make arrangements for him to be taken into the care of a local authority and detained by the authority, and it shall be lawful to detain him in pursuance of the arrangements; and a certificate made under this subsection in respect of any person shall be produced to the court before which that person is first brought thereafter.

(4) Where an officer decides in pursuance of subsection (1) of this section not to release a person arrested without a warrant and it appears to the officer that a decision falls to be taken in pursuance of section 5 of this Act whether to lay an information in respect of an offence alleged to have been committed by that person, it shall be the duty of the officer to inform him that such a decision falls to be taken and to specify the offence.

(5) A person detained by virtue of subsection (3) of this section shall be brought before a magistrates' court within seventy-two hours from the time of his arrest unless within that period a police officer not below the rank of inspector certifies to a magistrates' court that by reason of illness or accident he cannot be brought before a magistrates' court within that period.

(6) [*Repealed by the Bail Act* 1976, *s.* 12(2), *Sched.* 3.]

AMENDMENTS
Subs. (2) was substituted by the Bail Act 1976, s.12(1), Sched. 2, para. 47.

Detention of young offenders in community homes

30.—(1) The power to give directions under section 53 of the Act of 1933 (under which young offenders convicted on indictment of certain grave crimes may be detained in accordance with directions given by the Secretary of State) shall include power to direct detention by a local authority specified in the directions in a home so specified which is a community home provided by the authority or a controlled community home for the management, equipment and maintenance of which the authority are responsible; but a person shall not be liable to be detained in the manner provided by this section after he attains the age of nineteen.

(2) It shall be the duty of a local authority specified in directions given in pursuance of this section to detain the person to whom the directions relate in the home specified in the directions subject to and in accordance with such instructions relating to him as the Secretary of State may give to the authority from time to time; and the authority shall be entitled to recover from the Secretary of State any expenses reasonably incurred by them in discharging that duty.

[Conflict of interest between parent and child or young person

Conflict of interest between parent and child or young person

32A.—(1) If before or in the course of proceedings in respect of a child or young person—

 (*a*) in pursuance of section 1 of this Act, or

 (*b*) on an application under section 15(1) of this Act for the discharge of a relevant supervision order or a supervision order made under section 21(2) of this Act on the discharge of a relevant care order; or

 (*c*) on an application under section 21(2) of this Act for the discharge of a relevant care order or a care order made under section 15(1) of this Act on the discharge of a relevant supervision order; or

 (*d*) on an appeal to the Crown Court under section 2(12) of this Act, or

 (*e*) on an appeal to the Crown Court under section 16(8) of this Act against the dismissal of an application for the discharge of a relevant supervision order or against a care order made under section 15(1) on the discharge of—

  (i) a relevant supervision order; or

  (ii) a supervision order made under section 21(2) on the discharge of a relevant care order; or

 (*f*) on an appeal to the Crown Court under section 21(4) of this Act against the dismissal of an application for the discharge of a relevant care order or against a supervision order made under section 21(2) on the discharge of—

  (i) a relevant care order; or

  (ii) a care order made under section 15(1) on the discharge of a relevant supervision order,

it appears to the court that there is or may be a conflict, on any matter relevant to the proceedings, between the interests of the child or young person and those of his parent or guardian, the court may order that in relation to the proceedings the parent or guardian is not to be treated as representing the child or young person or as otherwise authorised to act on his behalf.

(2) If an application such as is referred to in subsection (1)(*b*) or (*c*) of this section is unopposed, the court, unless satisfied that to do so is not necessary for safeguarding the interests of the child or young person, shall order that in relation to proceedings on the application no parent or guardian of his shall be treated as representing him or as otherwise authorised to act on his behalf; but where the application was made by a parent or guardian on his behalf the order shall not invalidate the application.

(3) Where an order is made under subsection (1) or (2) of this section for the purposes of proceedings on an application within subsection (1)(*a*), (*b*) or (*c*) of this section, that order shall also have effect for the purposes of any appeal to the Crown Court arising out of those proceedings.

(4) The power of the court to make orders for the purposes of an application within subsection (1)(*a*), (*b*) or (*c*) of this section shall also be exercisable, before the hearing of the application, by a single justice.

(5) In this section—

 "relevant care order" means a care order made under section 1 of this Act;

 "relevant supervision order" means a supervision order made under section 1 of this Act.]

AMENDMENTS
This section was inserted by the Children Act 1975, s.64.

[Safeguarding of interests of young person where section 32A order made

32B.—(1) Where the court makes an order under section 32A(2) of this Act the court, unless satisfied that to do so is not necessary for safeguarding the interests of the child or young person, shall in accordance with rules of court appoint a guardian ad litem of the child or young person for the purposes of the proceedings

In this subsection 'court' includes a single justice.

(2) Rules of court shall provide for the appointment of a guardian ad litem of the child or young person for the purposes of any proceedings to which an order under section 32A(1) of this Act relates.

(3) A guardian ad litem appointed in pursuance of this section shall be under a duty to safeguard the interests of the child or young person in the manner prescribed by rules of court.]

AMENDMENTS
This section was inserted by the Children Act 1975, s.64.

Interpretation and ancillary provisions

70.—(1) in this Act, unless the contrary intention appears, the following expressions have the following meanings;—

"the Act of 1933" means the Children and Young Persons Act 1933;

"the Act of 1963" means the Children and Young Persons Act 1963;

"approved school order", "guardian" and "place of safety" have the same meanings as in the Act of 1933;

"care order" has the meaning assigned to it by section 20 of this Act;

"child", except in Part II (including Schedule 3) and section 27, 63, 64 and 65 of this Act, means a person under the age of fourteen, and in that Part (including that Schedule) and those sections means a person under the age of eighteen and a person who has attained the age of eighteen and is the subject of a care order;

[. . .]

"interim order" has the meaning assigned to it by section 20 of this Act;

"local authority" [except in relation to proceedings under section 1 of this Act instituted by a local education authority, means the council of a non-metropolitan county or of a metropolitan district] or London borough or the Common Council of the City of London;

"petty sessions area" has the same meaning as in the [the Magistrates' Courts Act 1980] except that, in relation to a juvenile court constituted for the metropolitan area within the meaning of Part II of Schedule 2 to the Act of 1963, it means such a division of that area as is mentioned in paragraph 14 of that Schedule;

[. . .]

"police officer" means a member of a police force;

[. . .]

[. . .]

"reside" means habitually reside, and cognate expressions shall be construed accordingly except in section 12(4) and (5) of this Act;

"supervision order", "supervised person" and "supervisor" have the meanings assigned to them by section 11 of this Act;

[...]
[...]
[...]

"young person" means a person who has attained the age of fourteen
and is under the age of seventeen;

and it is hereby declared that, in the expression "care or control", "care"
includes protection and guidance and "control" includes discipline.

(2) Without prejudice to any power apart from this subsection to bring
proceedings on behalf of another person, any power to make an application
which is exercisable by a child or young person by virtue of section 15(1),
21(2), 22(4) or (6) or 28(5) of this Act shall also be exercisable on his behalf
by his parent or guardian; and in this subsection "guardian" includes any
person who was a guardian of the child or young person in question at the
time when any supervision order, care order or warrant to which the
application related was originally made.

(3) In section 99(1) of the Act of 1933 (under which the age which a court
presumes or declares to be the age of a person brought before it is deemed to
be his true age for the purposes of that Act) the references to that Act shall
be construed as including references to this Act.

(4) Subject to the following subsection, any reference in this Act to any
enactment is a reference to it as amended, and includes a reference to it as
applied, by or under any other enactment including this Act.

(5) Any reference in this Act to an enactment of the Parliament of
Northern Ireland shall be construed as a reference to that enactment as
amended by any Act of that Parliament, whether passed before or after this
Act, and to any enactment of that Parliament for the time being in force
which re-enacts the said enactment with or without modifications.

AMENDMENTS

   In subs.(1), the definitions omitted were repealed by the Child Care Act 1980, Sched. 6
   In the definition of "local authority" the words in square brackets were substituted by the
Local Government Act 1972, s.195(6), Sched. 23, para. 16
   In the definition of "petty sessions area", the words in square brackets were substituted by the
Magistrates' Courts Act 1980, s.154(1), Sched. 7, para. 85.

Chronically Sick and Disabled Persons Act 1970

(1970 c. 44)

An Act to make further provision with respect to the welfare of chronically
sick and disabled persons; and for connected purposes.   [29th May 1970]

Welfare and housing

Information as to need for and existence of welfare services

   1.—(1) It shall be the duty of every local authority having functions under
section 29 of the National Assistance Act 1948 to inform themselves of the
number of persons to whom that section applies within their area and of the
need for the making by the authority of arrangements under that section for
such persons.

   (2) Every such local authority—

   (*a*) shall cause to be published from time to time at such times and in
        such manner as they consider appropriate general information as to
        the services provided under arrangements made by the authority

under the said section 29 which are for the time being available in their area; and

(*b*) shall ensure that any such person as aforesaid who uses any of those services is informed of any other of those services which in the opinion of the authority is relevant to his needs.

(3) This section shall come into operation on such date as the Secretary of State may by order made by statutory instrument appoint.

Provision of welfare services

2.—(1) Where a local authority having functions under section 29 of the National Assistance Act 1948 are satisfied in the case of any person to whom that section applies who is ordinarily resident in their area that it is necessary in order to meet the needs of that person for that authority to make arrangements for all or any of the following matters, namely—

(*a*) the provision of practical assistance for that person in his home;

(*b*) the provision for that person of, or assistance to that person in obtaining, wireless, television, library or similar recreational facilities;

(*c*) the provision for that person of lectures, games, outings or other recreational facilities outside his home or assistance to that person in taking advantage of educational facilities available to him;

(*d*) the provision for that person of facilities for, or assistance in, travelling to and from his home for the purpose of participating in any services provided under arrangements made by the authority under the said section 29 or, with the approval of the authority, in any services provided otherwise than as aforesaid which are similar to services which could be provided under such arrangements;

(*e*) the provision of assistance for that person in arranging for the carrying out of any works of adaptation in his home or the provision of any additional facilities designed to secure his greater safety, comfort or convenience;

(*f*) facilitating the taking of holidays by that person, whether at holiday homes or otherwise and whether provided under arrangements made by the authority or otherwise;

(*g*) the provision of meals for that person whether in his home or elsewhere;

(*h*) the provision for that person of, or assistance to that person in obtaining, a telephone and any special equipment necessary to enable him to use a telephone,

then, [...] subject to the provisions of section 35(2) of that Act (which requires local authorities to exercise their functions under Part III of that Act [...] in accordance with the provisions of any regulations made for the purpose) [and to the provisions of section 7(1) of the Local Authority Social Services Act 1970 (which requires local authorities in the exercise of certain functions, including functions under the said section 29, to act under the general guidance of the Secretary of State)] it shall be the duty of that authority to make those arrangements in exercise of their functions under the said section 29.

(2) [*Repealed by the Local Government Act* 1972, *s.* 272(1), *Sched.* 30.]

AMENDMENTS
In subs. (1) the words omitted were repealed by the Local Government Act 1972, s.272(1), Sched. 30 and the Local Authority Social Services Act 1970, s.14(1), Sched. 2, para. 12(1). The words in square brackets were substituted by the Local Authority Social Services Act 1970, *ibid.*

Guardianship of Minors Act 1971

(1971 c. 3)

An Act to consolidate certain enactments relating to the guardianship and
custody of minors.   [17th February 1971]

General principles

Principle on which questions relating to custody, upbringing etc. of minors are to be decided

1. Where in any proceedings before any court (whether or not a court as
defined in section 15 of this Act)—

(*a*) the [legal custody] or upbringing of a minor; or

(*b*) the administration of any property belonging to or held on trust for a
minor, or the application of the income thereof,

is in question, the court, in deciding that question, shall regard the welfare of
the minor as the first and paramount consideration, and shall not take into
consideration whether from any other point of view the claim of the father,
[. . .] in respect of such [legal custody], upbringing, administration or
application is superior to that of the mother, or the claim of the mother is
superior to that of the father.

AMENDMENTS

In this section the words omitted were repealed by the Guardianship Act 1973, s.9(1), Sched.
3. The words in square brackets were substituted by the Domestic Proceedings and Magistrates'
Courts Act 1978, s.36.

Matrimonial Causes Act 1973

(1970 c. 18)

Power to commit children to care of local authority

43.—(1) Where the court has jurisdiction by virtue of this Part of this Act
to make an order for the custody of a child and it appears to the court that
there are exceptional circumstances making it impracticable or undesirable
for the child to be entrusted to either of the parties to the marriage or to any
other individual, the court may if it thinks fit make an order committing the
care of the child to the council of a county other than a metropolitan county,
or of a metropolitan district or London borough or the Common Council of
the City of London (hereafter in this section referred to as "the local
authority"); [and thereupon—

(*a*) Part III of the Child Care Act 1980 (which relates to the treatment of
children in the care of a local authority); and

(*b*) for the purposes of contributions by the child himself at a time when
he has attained the age of 16, Part V of that Act (which relates to
contributions towards the maintenance of children in the care of a
local authority).

shall apply, subject to the provisions of this section, as if the child had been received by the local authority into their care under section 2 of that Act.]

(2) The authority specified in an order under this section shall be the local authority for the area in which the child was, in the opinion of the court, resident before the order was made committing the child to the care of a local authority, and the court shall before making an order under this section hear any representations from the local authority, including any representations as to the making of a financial provision order in favour of the child.

(3) While an order made by virtue of this section is in force with respect to a child, the child shall continue in the care of the local authority notwithstanding any claim by a parent or other person.

(4) An order made by virtue of this section shall cease to have effect as respects any child when he becomes eighteen, and the court shall not make an order committing a child to the care of a local authority under this section after he has become seventeen.

[(5) In the application of Part III of the Child Care Act 1979 by virtue of this section—

> (a) the exercise by the local authority of their powers under sections 18, 21 and 22 of that Act (which among other things relate to the accommodation and welfare of a child in the care of a local authority) shall be subject to any directions given by the court; and
>
> (b) section 24 of that Act (which relates to arrangements for the emigration of such a child) and section 28 of that Act (which relates to the aftercare of a child in the care of a local authority under section 2 of that Act) shall not apply.]

(6) It shall be the duty of any parent or guardian of a child committed to the care of a local authority under this section to secure that the local authority are informed of his address for the time being, and a person who knowingly fails to comply with this subsection shall be liable on summary conviction to a fine not exceeding ten pounds.

(7) The court shall have power from time to time by an order under this section to vary or discharge any provision made in pursuance of this section.

(8) [*Repealed by the Child Care Act* 1980, *s.* 89(3), *Sched.* 6.]

(9) Subject to the following provisions of this subsection, until April 1, 1974 subsection (1) above shall have effect as if for the words "other than a metropolitan county, or of a metropolitan district" there were substituted the words "county borough".

An order (or orders) made under section 273(2) of the Local Government Act 1972 (orders bringing provisions of that Act into force before April 1, 1974) may appoint an earlier date (or, as the case may be, different dates for different purposes or areas) on which subsection (1) above shall cease to have effect as mentioned above.

AMENDMENT
    The words in square brackets in subsection (1) were substituted by the Child Care Act 1980, Sched. 5 and the Health and Social Services and Social Security Adjudication Act 1983, s.9, Sched. 2, para. 20. Subs. (5) was substituted by *ibid.*

Power to provide for supervision of children

44.—(1) Where the court has jurisdiction by virtue of this Part of this Act to make an order for the custody of a child and it appears to the court that there are exceptional circumstances making it desirable that the child should be under the supervision of an independent person, the court may, as respects any period during which the child is, in exercise of that jurisdiction, committed to the [care of any person] order that the child be under the supervision of an officer appointed under this section as a welfare officer or under the supervision of a local authority.

(2) Where the court makes an order under this section for supervision by a welfare officer, the officer responsible for carrying out the order shall be such probation officer as may be selected under arrangements made by the Secretary of State; and where the order is for supervision by a local authority, that authority shall be the council of a county other than a metropolitan county, or of a metropolitan district or London borough selected by the court and specified in the order or, if the Common Council of the City of London is so selected and specified, that Council.

(3) The court shall not have power to make an order under this section as respects a child who in pursuance of an order under section 43 above is in the care of a local authority.

(4) Where a child is under the supervision of any person in pursuance of this section the jurisdiction possessed by a court to vary any financial provision order in the child's favour or any order made with respect to his custody or education under this Part of this Act shall, subject to any rules of court, be exercisable at the instance of that court itself.

(5) The court shall have power from time to time by an order under this section to vary or discharge any provision made in pursuance of this section.

(6) Subject to the following provisions of this subsection, until 1st April 1974 subsection (2) above shall have effect as if for the words "other than a metropolitan county, or of a metropolitan district" there were substituted the words "county borough".

An order (or orders) made under section 273(2) of the Local Government Act 1972 may appoint an earlier date (or, as the case may be, different dates for different purposes or areas) on which subsection (2) above shall cease to have effect as mentioned above.

AMENDMENTS
    In subs. (1) the words in square brackets were substituted by the Children Act 1975, s. 108(1), Sched. 3, para. 78.

Powers of Criminal Courts Act 1973

(1973 c. 62)

An Act to consolidate certain enactments relating to the powers of courts to deal with offenders and defaulters, to the treatment of offenders and to arrangements for persons on bail.   [25th October 1973]

Deferment of sentence

1.—(1) Subject to the provisions of this section, the Crown Court or a magistrates' court may defer passing sentence on an offender for the purpose of enabling the court [or any other court to which it falls to deal with him to have regard, in dealing with him], to his conduct after conviction (including, where appropriate, the making by him of reparation for his offence) or to any change in his circumstances.

(2) Any deferment under this section shall be until such date as may be

specified by the court, not being more than six months after the date [on which the deferment is announced by the court]; and [, subject to subsection (8A) below,] where the passing of sentence has been deferred under this section it shall not be further deferred thereunder.

(3) The power conferred by this section shall be exercisable only if the offender consents and the court is satisfied, having regard to the nature of the offence and the character and circumstances of the offender, that it would be in the interests of justice to exercise the power.

(4) A court which under this section has deferred passing sentence on an offender may [deal with] him before the expiration of the period of deferment if during that period he is convicted in Great Britain of any offence.

[(4A) If an offender on whom a court has under this section deferred passing sentence in respect of one or more offences is during the period of deferment convicted in England or Wales of any offence ('the subsequent offence'), then, without prejudice to subsection (4) above, the court which (whether during that period or not) passes sentence on him for the subsequent offence may also, if this has not already been done, [deal with] him for the first-mentioned offence or offences:

Provided that—

  (a) the power conferred by this subsection shall not be exercised by a magistrates' court if the court which deferred passing sentence was the Crown Court; and

  (b) the Crown Court, in exercising that power in a case in which the court which deferred passing sentence was a magistrates' court, shall not pass any sentence which could not have been passed by a magistrates' court in exercising it.]

(5) Where a court which under this section has deferred passing sentence on an offender proposes to [deal with] him, whether on the date originally specified by the court or by virtue of subsection (4) above before that date, [or where the offender does not appear on the date so specified, the court,] may issue a summons requiring him to appear before the court, or may issue a warrant for his arrest.

[(6) It is hereby declared that in deferring the passing of sentence under this section a magistrates' court is to be regarded as exercising the power of adjourning the trial which is conferred by [section 10(1) of the Magistrates' Courts Act 1980], and that accordingly [sections 11(1) and 13(1), (2) and (5) of that Act] (non-appearance of the accused) [apply] (without prejudice to subsection (5) above) if the offender does not appear on the date specified in pursuance of subsection (2) above.

(6A) Notwithstanding any enactment, a court which under this section defers passing sentence on an offender shall not on the same occasion remand him.]

(7) Nothing in this section shall affect the power of the Crown Court to bind over an offender to come up for judgment when called upon or the power of any court to defer passing sentence for any purpose for which it may lawfully do so apart from this section.

[(8) The power of a court under this section to deal with an offender in a case where the passing of sentence has been deferred thereunder—

  (a) includes power to deal with him in any way in which the court which deferred passing sentence could have dealt with him; and

  (b) without prejudice to the generality of the foregoing, in the case of a magistrates' court, includes the power conferred by section 37 or 38 of the Magistrates' Courts Act 1980 to commit him to the Crown Court for sentence.

(8A) Where, in a case where the passing of sentence on an offender in respect of one or more offences has been deferred under this section, a magistrates' court deals with him by committing him to the Crown Court under section 37 or 38 of the Act of 1980, the power of the Crown Court to deal with him includes the same power to defer passing sentence on him as if he had just been convicted of the offence or offences on indictment before the court.]

AMENDMENTS
In this section, the words in square brackets were substituted, subss. (4A), (6A), (8) and (8A) were inserted and subs. (6) was substituted, by the Criminal Law Act 1977, s. 65, Sched. 12 and the Criminal Justice Act 1982, s. 63. The words in square brackets in subs. (6) were substituted by the Magistrates' Courts Act 1980, s. 154(1), Sched. 7, para. 19.

Absolute and conditional discharge

7.—(1) Where a court by or before which a person is convicted of an offence (not being an offence the sentence for which is fixed by law) is of opinion, having regard to the circumstances including the nature of the offence and the character of the offender, that it is inexpedient to inflict punishment and that a probation order is not appropriate, the court may make an order discharging him absolutely, or, if the court thinks fit, discharging him subject to the condition that he commits no offence during such period, not exceeding three years from the date of the order, as may be specified therein.

(2) An order discharging a person subject to such a condition is in this Act referred to as "an order for conditional discharge", and the period specified in any such order (subject to section 8(1) of this Act) as "the period of conditional discharge".

(3) Before making an order for conditional discharge the court shall explain to the offender in ordinary language that if he commits another offence during the period of conditional discharge he will be liable to be sentenced for the original offence.

(4) Where, under the following provisions of this Part of this Act, a person conditionally discharged under this section is sentenced for the offence in respect of which the order for conditional discharge was made, that order shall cease to have effect.

[(5) The Secretary of State may by order direct that subsection (1) above shall be amended by substituting, for the maximum period specified in that subsection as originally enacted or as previously amended under this subsection, such period as may be specified in the order.]

AMENDMENTS
Subs. (5) was inserted by the Criminal Law Act 1977, s. 57(2).

Community service orders

Community service orders in respect of convicted persons

14.—(1) Where a person of or over [sixteen] years of age is convicted of an offence punishable with imprisonment, the court by or before which he is convicted may, instead of dealing with him in any other way (but subject to subsection (2) below) make an order (in this Act referred to as "a community service order") requiring him to perform unpaid work in accordance with the subsequent provisions of this Act [. . .].

The reference in this subsection to an offence punishable with imprisonment shall be construed without regard to any prohibition or restriction imposed by or under any enactment on the imprisonment of young offenders.

[(1A) The number of hours which a person may be required to work under a community service order shall be specified in the order and shall be in the aggregate—

(*a*) not less than 40; and

(*b*) not more—

(i) in the case of an offender aged sixteen, than 120; and

(ii) in other cases, than 240.]

[(2) A court shall not make a community service order in respect of any offender unless the offender consents and after considering a report by a probation officer or by a social worker of a local authority social services department about the offender and his circumstances and, if the court thinks it necessary, hearing a probation officer or a social worker of a local authority social services department, the court is satisfied that the offender is a suitable person to perform work under such an order.

(2A) Subject to sections 17A and 17B below,—

(*a*) a court shall not make a community service order in respect of any offender who is of or over seventeen years of age unless the court is satisfied that provision for him to perform work under such an order can be made under the arrangements for persons to perform work under such orders which exist in the petty sessions area in which he resides or will reside; and

(*b*) a court shall not make a community service order in respect of an offender who is under seventeen years of age unless—

(i) it has been notified by the Secretary of State that arrangements exist for persons of the offender's age who reside in the petty sessions area in which the offender resides or will reside to perform work under such orders; and

(ii) it is satisfied that provision can be made under the arrangements for him to do so.]

(3) Where a court makes community service orders in respect of two or more offences of which the offender has been convicted by or before the court, the court may direct that the hours of work specified in any of those orders shall be concurrent with or additional to those specified in any other of those orders, but so that the total number of hours which are not concurrent shall not exceed the maximum [specified in paragraph (*b*)(i) or (ii) of subsection (1A) above].

(4) A community service order shall specify the petty sessions area in which the offender resides or will reside; and the functions conferred by the subsequent provisions of this Act on the relevant officer shall be discharged by a probation officer appointed for or assigned to the area for the time being specified in the order (whether under this subsection or by virtue of section 17(5) of this Act), or by a person appointed for the purposes of those provisions by the probation and after-care committee for that area.

(5) Before making a community service order the court shall explain to the offender in ordinary language—

(*a*) the purpose and effect of the order (and in particular the requirements of the order as specified in section 15 of this Act);

(*b*) the consequences which may follow under section 16 if he fails to comply with any of those requirements; and

(*c*) that the court has under section 17 the power to review the order on the application either of the offender or of a probation officer.

(6) The court by which a community service order is made shall forthwith give copies of the order to a probation officer assigned to the court and he shall give a copy to the offender and to the relevant officer; and the court shall, except where it is itself a magistrates' court acting for the petty sessions area specified in the order, send to the clerk to the justices for the petty sessions area specified in the order a copy of the order, together with such documents and information relating to the case as it considers likely to be of assistance to a court acting for that area in exercising its functions in relation to the order.

(7) The Secretary of State may by order direct that [subsection (1A) above shall be amended by substituting for the maximum number of hours for the time being specified in paragraph (*b*)(i) or (ii) of that subsection], such number of hours as may be specified in the order.

(8) Nothing in subsection (1) above shall be construed as preventing a court which makes a community service order in respect of any offence from making an order for costs against, or imposing any disqualification on, the offender or from making in respect of the offence an order under section 35, 39, 43 or 44 of this Act, or under section 28 of the Theft Act 1968.

AMENDMENTS
   The amendments to this section were made by the Criminal Justice Act 1982, s.68(1), Sched. 12, para. 1.

Obligations of person subject to community service order

15.—(1) An offender in respect of whom a community service order is in force shall—
   (*a*) report to the relevant officer and subsequently from time to time notify him of any change of address; and
   (*b*) perform for the number of hours specified in the order such work at such times as he may be instructed by the relevant officer.

(2) Subject to section 17(1) of this Act, the work required to be performed under a community service order shall be performed during the period of twelve months beginning with the date of the order [; but, unless revoked, the order shall remain in force until the offender has worked under it for the number of hours specified in it.]

(3) The instructions given by the relevant officer under this section shall, so far as practicable, be such as to avoid any conflict with the offender's religious beliefs and any interference with the times, if any, at which he normally works or attends a school or other educational establishment.

AMENDMENT
   In subs. (2) the words in square brackets were added by the Criminal Law Act 1977, s.65, Sched. 12.

Breach of requirements of community service order

16.—(1) If at any time while a community service order is in force in respect of an offender it appears on information to a justice of the peace acting for the petty sessions area for the time being specified in the order that the offender has failed to comply with any of the requirements of section 15 of this Act (including any failure satisfactorily to perform the work which he has been instructed to do), the justice may issue a summons requiring the offender to appear at the place and time specified therein, or may, if the information is in writing and on oath, issue a warrant for his arrest.

(2) Any summons or warrant issued under this section shall direct the offender to appear to be brought before a magistrates' court acting for the petty sessions area for the time being specified in the community service order.

(3) If it is proved to the satisfaction of the magistrates' court before which an offender appears or is brought under this section that he has failed without reasonable excuse to comply with any of the requirements of section 15 the court may, without prejudice to the continuance of the order, impose on him a fine not exceeding £50 or may—

(a) if the community service order was made by a magistrates' court, revoke the order and deal with the offender, for the offence in respect of which the order was made, in any manner in which he could have been dealt with for that offence by the court which made the order if the order had not been made;

(b) if the order was made by the Crown Court, commit him to custody or release him on bail until he can be brought or appear before the Crown Court.

(4) A magistrates' court which deals with an offender's case under subsection (3)(b) above shall send to the Crown Court a certificate signed by a justice of the peace certifying that the offender has failed to comply with the requirements of section 15 in the respect specified in the certificate, together with such other particulars of the case as may be desirable; and a certificate purporting to be so signed shall be admissible as evidence of the failure before the Crown Court.

(5) Where by virtue of subsection (3)(b) above the offender is brought or appears before the Crown Court and it is proved to the satisfaction of the court that he has failed to comply with any of the requirements of section 15, that court may either—

(a) without prejudice to the continuance of the order, impose on him a fine not exceeding £50; or

(b) revoke the order and deal with him, for the offence in respect of which the order was made, in any manner in which he could have been dealt with for that offence by the court which made the order if the order had not been made.

(6) A person sentenced under subsection (3)(a) above for an offence may appeal to the Crown Court against the sentence.

(7) In proceedings before the Crown Court under this section any question whether the offender has failed to comply with the requirements of section 15 shall be determined by the court and not by the verdict of a jury.

(8) A fine imposed under this section shall be deemed for the purposes of any enactment to be a sum adjudged to be paid by a conviction.

The Children Act 1975

(C. 72)

Custodianship orders

Custodianship orders

33.—(1) An authorised court may on the application of one or more persons qualified under subsection (3) make an order vesting the legal custody of a child in the applicant or, as the case may be, in one or more of the applicants if the child is in England or Wales at the time the application is made.

(2) An order under subsection (1) may be referred to as a custodianship order, and the person in whom legal custody of the child is vested under the order may be referred to as the custodian of the child.

(3) The persons qualified to apply for a custodianship order are—

    (*a*) a relative or step-parent of the child—

        (i) who applies with the consent of a person having legal custody of the child, and

        (ii) with whom the child has had his home for the three months preceding the making of the application;

    (*b*) any person—

        (i) who applies with the consent of a person having legal custody of the child, and

        (ii) with whom the child has had his home for a period or periods before the making of the application which amount to at least twelve months and include the three months preceding the making of the application;

    (*c*) any person with whom the child has had his home for a period or periods before the making of the application which amount to at least three years and include the three months preceding the making of the application.

(4) The mother or father of the child is not qualified under any paragraph of subsection (3).

(5) A step-parent of the child is not qualified under any paragraph of subsection (3) if in proceedings for divorce or nullity of marriage the child was named in an order made under paragraph (*b*) or (*c*) of section 41(1) (arrangements for welfare of children of family) of the Matrimonial Causes Act 1973.

(6) If no person has legal custody of the child, or the applicant himself has legal custody or the person with legal custody cannot be found, paragraphs (*a*) and (*b*) of subsection (3) apply with the omission of sub-paragraph (i).

(7) The Secretary of State may by order a draft of which has been approved by each House of Parliament amend subsection (3)(*c*) to substitute a different period for the period of three years mentioned in that paragraph (or the period which, by a previous order under this subsection, was substituted for that period).

(8) Subsection (5) does not apply—

    (*a*) if the parent other than the one the step-parent married is dead or cannot be found, or

    (*b*) if the order referred to in subsection (5) was made under subsection (1)(*c*) of section 41 of the Matrimonial Causes Act 1973 and it has since been determined that the child was not a child of the family to whom that section applied.

(9) For the avoidance of doubt, it is hereby declared that the provisions of section 1 of the Guardianship of Minors Act 1971 apply to applications made under this Part of this Act.

(10) This section and sections 34 to 46 do not apply to Scotland.

Access and maintenance

34.—(1) An authorised court may, on making a custodianship order or while a custodianship order is in force, by order—

    (*a*) on the application of the child's mother or father, make such provision as it thinks fit requiring access to the child to be given to the applicant;

(b) on the application of the custodian, require the child's mother or father (or both) to make to the applicant such periodical payments towards the maintenance of the child as it thinks reasonable;

(c) on the application of the child's mother or father, revoke an order requiring the applicant to contribute towards the child's maintenance made (otherwise than under this section) by any court;

(d) on the application of the child's mother or father or the custodian, vary an order made (otherwise than under this section) by any court requiring the mother or father to contribute towards the child's maintenance—

    (i) by altering the amount of the contributions;

    (ii) by substituting the custodian for the person to whom the contributions were ordered to be made.

(2) References in subsection (1) to the child's mother or father include any person in relation to whom the child was treated as a child of the family (as defined in section 52(1) of the Matrimonial Causes Act 1973) but the court in deciding whether to make an order under subsection (1)(b) against a person who is not the child's mother or father shall have regard (among the circumstances of the case)—

(a) to whether that person had assumed any responsibility for the child's maintenance and, if he did, to the extent to which and the basis on which he did so, and to the length of time during which he discharged that responsibility;

(b) to the liability of any other person to maintain that child.

(3) No order shall be made under subsection (1)(b) requiring the father of an illegitimate child to make any payments to the child's custodian.

(4) Subsections (2), (3), (4) and (6) (orders as to supervision, local authority care, maintenance etc. of children) of section 2 of the Guardianship Act 1973 and sections 3 and 4 of that Act (supplementary provisions) shall apply to an application for a custodianship order as they apply to an application under section 9 of the Guardianship of Minors Act 1971, subject to the following modifications, that is to say—

(a) in section 2(2)(b) and (4)(a) of the Guardianship Act 1973 any reference to a parent of the minor to whom the order relates shall be construed as including a reference to any other individual;

(b) section 3(3) of that Act shall have effect as if the words "or the custodian" were inserted after the words "application of either parent".

(5) A local authority may make contributions to a custodian towards the cost of the accommodation and maintenance of the child, except where the custodian is the husband or wife of a parent of the child.

Revocation and variation of orders

35.—(1) An authorised court may by order revoke a custodianship order on the application of—

(a) the custodian, or

(b) the mother or father, or a guardian, of the child, or

(c) any local authority in England or Wales.

(2) The court shall not proceed to hear an application made by any person for the revocation of a custodianship order where a previous such application made by the same person was refused by that or any other court unless—

(a) in refusing the previous application the court directed that this subsection should not apply; or

(b) it appears to the court that because of a change in circumstances or for any other reason it is proper to proceed with the application.

(3) The custodian of a child may apply to an authorised court for the revocation or variation of any order made under section 34 in respect of that child.

(4) Any other person on whose application an order under section 34 was made, or who was required by such an order to contribute towards the maintenance of the child, may apply to an authorised court for the revocation or variation of that order.

(5) Any order made under section 34 in respect of a child who is the subject of a custodianship order shall cease to have effect on the revocation of the custodianship order.

(6) A custodianship order made in respect of a child, and any order made under section 34 in respect of the child, shall cease to have effect when the child attains the age of 18 years.

Care etc. of child on revocation of custodianship order

36.—(1) Before revoking a custodianship order the court shall ascertain who would have legal custody of the child, if, on the revocation of the custodianship order, no further order were made under this section.

(2) If the child would not be in the legal custody of any person, the court shall, if it revokes the custodianship order, commit the care of the child to a specified local authority.

(3) If there is a person who would have legal custody of the child on the revocation of the custodianship order, the court shall consider whether it is desirable in the interests of the welfare of the child for the child to be in the legal custody of that person and—

(a) if the court is of the opinion that it would not be so desirable, it shall on revoking the custodianship order commit the care of the child to a specified local authority;

(b) if it is of the opinion that while it is desirable for the child to be in the legal custody of that person, it is also desirable in the interests of the welfare of the child for him to be under the supervision of an independent person, the court shall, on revoking the custodianship order, order that the child shall be under the supervision of a specified local authority or of a probation officer.

(4) Before exercising its functions under this section the court shall, unless it has sufficient information before it for the purpose, request—

(a) a local authority to arrange for an officer of the authority, or

(b) a probation officer,

to make to the court a report, orally or in writing, on the desirability of the child returning to the legal custody of any individual, and it shall be the duty of the local authority or probation officer to comply with the request.

(5) Where the court makes an order under subsection (3)(a) the order may require the payment by either parent to the local authority, while it has the care of the child, of such weekly or other periodical sum towards the maintenance of the child as the court thinks reasonable.

(6) Sections 3 and 4 of the Guardianship Act 1973 (which contain supplementary provisions relating to children who are subject to supervi-

sion, or in the care of local authority, by virtue of orders made under section 2 of that Act) apply in relation to an order under this section as they apply in relation to an order under section 2 of that Act.

(7) Subsections (2) to (6) of section 6 of the Guardianship Act 1973 shall apply in relation to reports which are requested by magistrates' courts under this section as they apply to reports under subsection (1) of that section.

Custodianship order on application for adoption or guardianship

37.—(1) Where on an application for an adoption order by a relative of the child or by the husband or wife of the mother or father of the child, whether alone or jointly with his or her spouse, the requirements of section 12 or, where the application is for a Convention adoption order, section 24(6) are satisfied, but the court is satisfied—

(a) that the child's welfare would not be better safeguarded and promoted by the making of adoption order in favour of the applicant, than it would be by the making of a custodianship order in his favour, and

(b) that it would be appropriate to make a custodianship order in the applicant's favour,

the court shall direct the application to be treated as if it had been made by the applicant under section 33, but if the application was made jointly by the father or mother of the child and his or her spouse, the court shall direct the application to be treated as if made by the father's wife or the mother's husband alone.

(2) Where on an application for an adoption order made—

(a) by a person who is neither a relative of the child nor the husband or wife of the mother or of the child; or

(b) by a married couple [neither of whom is a relative of the child or the husband or wife of the mother or father of the child],

the said requirements are satisfied but the court is of opinion that it would be more appropriate to make a custodianship order in favour of the applicant, it may direct the application to be treated as if it had been made by the applicant under section 33.

(3) Where on an application under section 9 (orders for custody and maintenance on application of mother or father) of the Guardianship of Minors Act 1971 the court is of opinion that legal custody should be given to a person other than the mother or father, it may direct the application to be treated as if it had been made by that person under section 33.

(4) Where a direction is given under this section the applicant shall be treated (if such is not the case) as if he were qualified to apply for a custodianship order and this Part, except section 40, shall have effect accordingly.

(5) Subsection (1) does not apply to an application made by a step-parent whether alone or jointly with another person in any case where the step-parent is prevented by section 33(5) from being qualified to apply for a custodianship order in respect of the child.

(6) Subsections (1) and (2) do not apply to an application for an adoption order made by the child's mother or father alone.

AMENDMENT
In subs. (2)(*b*) the words in square brackets were substituted by the Health and Social Services and Social Security Adjudications Act 1983, s.9, Sched. 2, para. 23.

Disputes between joint custodians

38. If two persons have a parental right or duty vested in them jointly by a custodianship order by virtue of section 44(2) but cannot agree on its exercise or performance, either of them may apply to an authorised court, and the court may make such order regarding the exercise of the right or performance of the duty as it thinks fit.

Reports by local authorities and probation officers

39.—(1) A court dealing with an application made under this Part, or an application which is treated as if made under section 33, may request—

    (*a*) a local authority to arrange for an officer of the authority, or

    (*b*) a probation officer,

to make to the court a report, orally or in writing, with respect to any specified matter which appears to the court to be relevant to the application, and it shall be the duty of the local authority or probation officer to comply with the request.

(2) Subsections (2) to (6) of section 6 of the Guardianship Act 1973 shall apply in relation to reports which are requested by magistrates' courts under this section as they apply to reports under subsection (1) of that section.

Notice of application to be given to local authority

40.—(1) A custodianship order shall not be made unless the applicant has given notice of the application for the order to the local authority in whose area the child resides within the seven days following the making of the application, or such extended period as the court or local authority may allow.

(2) On receipt of a notice given by the applicant under subsection (1) the local authority shall arrange for an officer of the authority to make a report to the court (so far as is practicable) on the matters prescribed under subsection (3) and on any other matter which he considers to be relevant to the application.

(3) The Secretary of State shall by regulations prescribe matters which are to be included in a report under subsection (2) and, in particular, but without prejudice to the generality of the foregoing, the prescribed matters shall include—

    (*a*) the wishes and feelings of the child have regard to his age and understanding and all other matters relevant to the operation of section 1 (principle on which questions relating to custody are to be decided) of the Guardianship of Minors Act 1971 in relation to the application;

    (*b*) the means and suitability of the applicant;

    (*c*) information of a kind specified in the regulations relating to members of the applicant's household;

    (*d*) the wishes regarding the application, and the means, of the mother and father of the child.

(4) Subsections (2), (3) and 3A) of section 6 of the Guardianship Act 1973 shall apply to a report under this section which is submitted to a magistrates' court.

Restriction on removal of child where applicant has provided home for three years

41.—(1)While an application for a custodianship order in respect of a child made by the person with whom the child has at the time the application is made had his home for a period (whether continuous or not) amounting to at least three years is pending, another person is not entitled, against the will of the applicant, to remove the child from the applicant's [actual] custody except with the leave of a court or under authority conferred by any enactment or on the arrest of the child.

(2) In any case where subsection (1) applies, and

    (*a*) the child was in the care of a local authority before he began to have his home with the applicant, and

    (*b*) the child remains in the care of a local authority,

the authority in whose care the child is shall not remove the child from the applicant's [actual] custody except with the applicant's consent or the leave of a court.

(3) Any person who contravenes subsection (1) commits an offence and shall be liable on summary conviction to imprisonment for a term not exceeding three months or a fine not exceeding £400 or both.

(4) The Secretary of State may by order a draft of which has been approved by each House of Parliament amend subsection (1) to substitute a different period for the period mentioned in that subsection (or the period which, by a previous order under this subsection, was substituted for that period).

AMENDMENTS
In subss.(1) and (2) the words in square brackets were inserted by the Health and Social Services and Social Security Adjudications Act 1983, s.9, Sched. 2, para. 60.

Effect of custodianship order on existing custody

44.—(1) While a custodianship order has effect in relation to a child the right of any person other than the custodian to legal custody of the child is suspended, but, subject to any further order made by any court, revives on the revocation of the custodianship order.

(2) Subsection (1) does not apply where the person already having custody is a parent of the child and the person who becomes custodian under the order is the husband or wife of the parent; and in such a case the spouses have the legal custody jointly.

Certificates of unruly character

69. The court shall not certify under section 22(5) or section 23(2) or (3) of the Children and Young Persons Act 1969 (committals to remand centres or prison) that a child is of so unruly a character that he cannot safely be committed to the care of a local authority unless the conditions prescribed by order made by the Secretary of State are satisfied in relation to that child.

In this section, "court" includes a justice.

Explanation of concepts

Parental rights and duties

85.—(1) In this Act, unless the context otherwise requires, "the parental rights and duties" means as respects a particular child (whether legitimate or not), all the rights and duties which by law the mother and father have in relation to a legitimate child and his property; and references to a parental right or duty shall be construed accordingly and shall include a right of access and any other element included in a right or duty.

(2) Subject to section 1(2) of the Guardianship Act 1973 (which relates to separation agreements between husband and wife), a person cannot surrender or transfer to another any parental right or duty he has as respects a child.

(3) Where two or more persons have a parental right or duty jointly, any one of them may exercise or perform it in any manner without the other or others if the other or, as the case may be, one or more of the others have not signified disapproval of its exercise or performance in that manner.

(4) From the death of a person who has a parental right or duty jointly with one other person, or jointly with two or more other persons, that other person has the right or duty exclusively or, as the case may be, those other persons have it jointly.

(5) Where subsection (4) does not apply on the death of a person who has a parental right or duty, that right or duty lapses, but without prejudice to its acquisition by another person at any time under any enactment.

(6) Subsections (4) and (5) apply in relation to the dissolution of a body corporate as they apply in relation to death of an individual.

(7) Except as otherwise provided by or under any enactment, while the mother of an illegitimate child is living she has the parental rights and duties exclusively.

Legal custody

86. In this Act, unless the context otherwise requires, "legal custody" means, as respects a child, so much of the parental rights and duties as relate to the person of the child (including the place and manner in which his time is spent); but a person shall not by virtue of having legal custody of a child be entitled to effect or arrange for his emigration from the United Kingdom unless he is a parent or guardian of the child.

Actual custody

87.—(1) A person has actual custody of a child if he has actual possession of his person, whether or not that possession is shared with one or more other persons.

(2) While a person not having legal custody of a child has actual custody of the child he has the like duties in relation to the child as a custodian would have by virtue of his legal custody.

(3) In this Act, unless the context otherwise requires, references to the person with whom a child has his home refer to the person who, disregarding absence of the child at a hospital or boarding school and any other temporary absence, has actual custody of the child.

Panel for guardians ad litem and reporting officers

103.—(1) The Secretary of State may by regulations make provision for the establishment of [one or more panels] of persons from whom—

    (*a*) guardians *ad litem* and reporting officers may in accordance with rules or rules of court be appointed for the purposes of—

        (i) section 20 of this Act;

        (ii) section 32B of the Children and Young Persons Act 1969

        (iii) section 7 of the Child Care Act 1980];

        [(iv) section 12F of the Child Care Act 1980;]

    (*b*) [*Applies to Scotland.*]

[(2) Regulations under subsection (1) may provide—

    (*a*) for the defrayment by local authorities of expenses incurred by members of a panel established by virtue of that subsection; and

    (*b*) for a payment by local authorities of fees and allowances for members of such a panel.]

    (3) [*Applies to Scotland.*]

AMENDMENT

Para. (1)(*a*)(iii) was substituted by the Child Care Act 1980, s.89(2), Sched. 5.

Para. (1)(*a*)(iv) was inserted by the Health and Social Services and Social Security Adjudications Act 1983, s.6, Sched. 1, Pt. II. The other words in square brackets in subs. (1) and subs. (2) were substituted by *ibid.*, s.9, Sched. 2, para. 29.

Adoption Act 1976

(1976 c. 36)

An Act to consolidate the enactments having effect in England and Wales in relation to adoption.   **[22nd July 1976]**

GENERAL NOTE

This Act is a consolidating measure which brings together the law on adoption as found in the Adoption Acts 1958, 1960, 1964 and 1968 and in the Children Act 1975.

COMMENCEMENT

This Act will be implemented as soon as sections 1 and 2 of the 1975 Act are brought into force.

Table of Derivations

The following abbreviations are used in this Table:

1958 = The Adoption Act 1958
    (7 & 8 Eliz. 2, c. 5)
1960 = The Adoption Act 1960
    (1960 c. 59)
1964 = The Adoption Act 1964
    (1964 c. 57)
1968 = The Adoption Act 1968
    (1968 c. 53)
1975 = The Children Act 1975
    (1975 c. 72)

ADOPTION ACT 1958

1958	1976	1958	1976	1958	1976
s. 9(3)(4)	s. 66(1)(2)(6)	s. 29(3)–(5).	11	s. 44(2)	36(2)
(5)	66(5)	32(1)	9(1)(2)	45	37(1)
19	40(1)(2)	(1A)	9(1)(2)	46	37(2)
20	50	(2)	9(4)	47	37(4)
20A	51	(3)	9(3)	48	37(3)
21(1)	Sch. 1, para. 1(1)	(4)	67(5)	50	57
(4)–(6)	Sch. 1, para. 1(3)–(5)	33	10	51	58
24(1)–(3)	Sch. 1, para. 4(1)–(3)	34	27	52	56
(4)	Sch. 1, para. 2(1)	34A	28	54(1)	68
(6)	Sch. 1, para. 4(4)	(7)	67(3)	55	69
(7)	Sch. 1, para. 4(6)	35	30	56(1)	67(1)(2)
26(1)	s. 52(1)	36(1)	31(1)	(2)	67(6)
(2)	Sch. 1, para. 6	(2)	31(2)(3)	57(1)	72(1)
(3)	s. 52(4)	36(3)	22(4)	(2)	72(3)
27	Sch. 1, para. 5(1)	37(1)	32(1)(2)	(4)	72(4)
29(1)	s. 11	(3)	32(3)	Sch. 5,	
(2A	s. 11	(4)	32(4)	para. 5	Sch. 2, para. 8
		38	33(1)	para. 6	Sch. 2, para. 5(2)(3)
		39	33(2)	para. 7	Sch. 2, para. 5(4)
		40(4), (6)	35(1)	para. 10	Sch. 2, para. 4
		(5)	35(2)		
		43(1)–(4)	34		
		44(1)*(a)(b)*	36(1)*(a)(b)*		
		(d)	s. 36(1)*(c)*		

ADOPTION ACT 1960

1960	1976
s. 1(1)	s. 52(2)
(3)	52(4)

ADOPTION ACT 1964

1964	1976
s. 1(5)	s. 59(3)
2	60
3	Sch. 1, para. 2(2)–(5)

ADOPTION ACT 1968

1968	1976	1968	1976	1968	1976
s. 4(3)	s. 72(2)	s. 8(2)	Sch. 1, para. 3	s. 11(1)	ss. 71(1), 72(1)
5(1)	59(1)	(4)	Sch. 1, para. 5(2)	(2)	s. 72(4)
6(1)	53(1)	9(1)–(4)	s. 70	12(2)	67(1)(2)
(3)–(5)	53(2)–(5)	(5)	40(3)	(3)	67(4)
7	54	10	71(2)	(4)	67(5)
8(1)	Sch. 1. para. 1(2)				

CHILDREN ACT 1975

PART I

THE ADOPTION SERVICE

The Adoption Service

Establishment of Adoption Service

1.—(1) It is the duty of every local authority to establish and maintain within their area a service designed to meet the needs, in relation to adoption, of—

(a) children who have been or may be adopted,

(b) parents and guardians of such children, and

(c) persons who have adopted or may adopt a child,

and for that purpose to provide the requisite facilities, or secure that they are provided by approved adoption societies.

(2) The facilities to be provided as part of the service maintained under subsection (1) include—

(a) temporary board and lodging where needed by pregnant women, mother or children;

(b) arrangements for assessing children and prospective adopters, and placing children for adoption;

(c) counselling for persons with problems relating to adoption.

(3) The facilities of the service maintained under subsection (1) shall be provided in conjunction with the local authority's other social services and approved adoption societies in their area, so that help may be given in a co-ordinated manner without duplication, omission or avoidable delay.

(4) The services maintained by local authorities under subsection (1) may be collectively referred to as "Adoption Service," and a local authority or approved adoption society may be referred to as an adoption agency.

Local authorities' social services

2. The social services referred to in section 1(3) are the functions of a local authority which stand referred to the authority's social services committee, including, in particular but without prejudice to the generality of the foregoing, a local authority's functions relating to—

(*a*) the promotion of the welfare of children by diminishing the need to receive children into care or keep them in care, including (in exceptional circumstances) the giving of assistance in cash;

(*b*) the welfare of children in the care of local authority;

(*c*) the welfare of children who are foster children within the meaning of [the Foster Children Act 1980];

(*d*) children who are subject to supervision orders made in matrimonial proceedings;

(*e*) the provision of residential accommodation for expectant mothers and young children and of day-care facilities.

(*f*) the regulation and inspection of nurseries and child minders;

(*g*) care and other treatment of children through court proceedings.

AMENDMENT
The words in square brackets in (*c*) were substituted by the Foster Children Act 1980, s.23(2), Sched. 2.

Welfare of children

Duty to promoted welfare of child

6. In reaching any decision relating to the adoption of a child a court or adoption agency shall have regard to all the circumstances, first consideration being given to the need to safeguard and promote the welfare of the child throughout his childhood; and shall so far as practicable ascertain the wishes and feelings of the child regarding the decision and give due consideration to them, having regard to his age and understanding.

Religious upbringing of adopted child

7. An adoption agency shall in placing a child for adoption have regard (so far as is practicable) to any wishes of a child's parents and guardians as to the religious upbringing of the child.

Restriction on arranging adoptions and placing of children

11.—(1) A person other than an adoption agency shall not make arrangements for the adoption of a child, or place a child for adoption, unless—

(*a*) the proposed adopter is a relative of the child, or

(*b*) he is acting in pursuance of an order of the High Court.

(2) An adoption society approved as respects Scotland under section 4 of the Children Act 1975, but which is not approved under section 3 of this Act, shall not act as an adoption society in England and Wales except to the extent that the society considers it necessary to do so in the interests of a person mentioned in section 1 of that Act.

(3) A person who—

(*a*) takes part in the management or control of a body of persons which exists wholly or partly for the purpose of making arrangements for the adoption of children and which is not an adoption agency; or (*b*) contravenes subsection (1); or

(*c*) receives a child placed with him in contravention of subsection (1),

shall be guilty of an offence and liable on summary conviction to imprisonment for a term not exceeding 3 months or to a fine not exceeding £400 or to both.

(4) In any proceedings for an offence under paragraph (*a*) of subsection (3), proof of things done or of words written, spoken or published (whether or not in the presence of any party to the proceedings) by any person taking part in the management or control of a body of persons, or in making arrangements for the adoption of children on behalf of the body, shall be admissible as evidence of the purpose for which that body exists.

(5) Section 26 shall apply where a person is convicted of a contravention of subsection (1) as it applies where an application for an adoption order is refused.

PART II

ADOPTION ORDERS

The making of adoption orders

Adoption orders

12.—(1) An adoption order is an order vesting the parental rights and duties relating to a child in the adopters, made on their application by an authorised court.

(2) The order does not affect the parental rights and duties so far as they relate to any period before the making of the order.

(3) The making of an adoption order operates to extinguish—

(*a*) any parental right or duty relating to the child which—

(i) is vested in a person (not being one of the adopters) who was the parent or guardian of the child immediately before the making of the order, or

(ii) is vested in any other person by virtue of the order of any court; and

(*b*) any duty arising by virtue of an agreement or the order of a court to make payments, so far as the payments are in respect of the child's maintenance for any period after the making of the order or any other matter comprised in the parental duties and relating to such a period.

(4) Subsection (3)(*b*) does not apply to a duty arising by virtue of an agreement—

(*a*) which constitutes a trust, or

(*b*) which expressly provides that the duty is not to be extinguished by the making of an adoption order.

(5) An adoption order may not be made in relation to a child who is or has been married.

(6) An adoption order may contain such terms and conditions as the court thinks fit.

(7) An adoption order may be made notwithstanding that the child is already an adopted child.

Child to live with adopters before order made

13.—(1) Where—

(*a*) the applicant, or one of the applicants, is a parent, step-parent or relative of the child, or

(*b*) the child was placed with the applicants by an adoption agency or in pursuance of an order of the High Court,

an adoption order shall not be made unless the child is at least 19 weeks old and at all times during the preceding 13 weeks had his home with the applicants or one of them.

(2) Where subsection (1) does not apply, an adoption order shall not be made unless the child is at least 12 months old and at all times during the preceding 12 months had his home with the applicants or one of them.

(3) An adoption order shall not be made unless the court is satisfied that sufficient opportunities to see the child with the applicant, or, in the case of an application by a married couple, both applicants together in the home environment have been afforded—

(*a*) where the child was placed with the applicant by an adoption agency, to that agency, or

(*b*) in any other case, to the local authority within whose area the home is.

Adoption by married couple

14.—(1) Subject to section 37(1) of the Children Act 1975 (which provides for the making of a custodianship order instead of an adoption order in certain cases) an adoption order may be made on the application of a married couple where each has attained the age of 21 years but an adoption order shall not otherwise be made on the application of more than one person.

(2) An adoption order shall not be made on the application of a married couple unless—

(*a*) at least one of them is domiciled in a part of the United Kingdom, or in the Channel Islands or the Isle of Man, or

(*b*) the application is for a Convention adoption order and section 17 is complied with.

(3) If the married couple consist of a parent and step-parent of the child, the court shall dismiss the application if it considers the matter would be better dealt with under section 42 (orders for custody etc.) of the Matrimonial Causes Act 1973.

Adoption by one person

15.—(1) Subject to section 37(1) of the Children Act 1975 (which provides for the making of a custodianship order instead of an adoption order in certain cases) an adoption order may be made on the application of one person where he has attained the age of 21 years and—

(*a*) is not married, or

(*b*) is married and the court is satisfied that—

(i) his spouse cannot be found, or

(ii) the spouses have separated and are living apart, and the separation is likely to be permanent, or

(iii) his spouse is by reason of ill-health, whether physical or mental, incapable of making an application for an adoption order.

(2) An adoption order shall not be made on the application of one person unless—

(a) he is domiciled in a part of the United Kingdom, or in the Channel Islands or the Isle of Man, or

(b) the application is for a Convention adoption order and section 17 is complied with.

(3) An adoption order shall not be made on the application of the mother or father of the child alone unless the court is satisfied that—

(a) the other natural parent is dead or cannot be found, or

(b) there is some other reason justifying the exclusion of the other natural parent,

and where such an order is made the reason justifying the exclusion of the other natural parent shall be recorded by the court.

(4) If the applicant is a step-parent of the child, the court shall dismiss the application if it considers the matter would be better dealt with under section 42 (orders for custody etc.) of the Matrimonial Causes Act 1973.

Parental agreement

16.—(1) An adoption order shall not be made unless—

(a) the child is free for adoption by virtue of an order made in England and Wales under section 18 or made in Scotland under section 14 of the Children Act 1975 (freeing children for adoption in Scotland); or

(b) in the case of each parent or guardian of the child the court is satisfied that—

(i) he freely, and with full understanding of what is involved agrees unconditionally to the making of an adoption order (whether or not he knows the identity of the applicants), or

(ii) his agreement to the making of the adoption order should be dispensed with on a ground specified in subsection (2).

(2) The grounds mentioned in subsection (1)(b)(iii) are that the parent or guardian—

(a) cannot be found or is incapable of giving agreement;

(b) is withholding his agreement unreasonably;

(c) has persistently failed without reasonable cause to discharge the parental duties in relation to the child;

(d) has abandoned or neglected the child;

(e) has persistently ill-treated the child;

(f) has seriously ill-treated the child (subject to subsection (5)).

(3) Subsection (1) does not apply in any case where the child is not a United Kingdom national and the application for the adoption order is for a Convention adoption order.

(4) Agreement is ineffective for the purposes of subsection (1)(b)(i) if given by the mother less than six weeks after the child's birth.

(5) Subsection (2)(f) does not apply unless (because of the ill-treatment or for other reasons) the rehabilitation of the child within the household of the parent or guardian is unlikely.

Freeing for adoption

Freeing child for adoption

18.—(1) Where, on an application by an adoption agency, an authorised court is satisfied in the case of each parent or guardian of the child that—

(*a*) he freely, and with full understanding of what is involved, agrees generally and unconditionally to the making of an adoption order, or

(*b*) his agreement to the making of an adoption order should be dispensed with on a ground specified in section 16(2),

the court shall make an order declaring the child free for adoption.

(2) No application shall be made under subsection (1) unless—

(*a*) it is made with the consent of a parent or guardian of a child, or

(*b*) the adoption agency is applying for dispensation under subsection (1)(*b*) of the agreement of each parent or guardian of the child, and the child is in the care of the adoption agency.

(3) No agreement required under subsection (1)(*a*) shall be dispensed with under subsection (1)(*b*) unless the child is already placed for adoption or the court is satisfied that it is likely that the child will be placed for adoption.

(4) An agreement by the mother of the child is ineffective for the purposes of this section if given less than 6 weeks after the child's birth.

(5) On the making of an order under this section, the parental rights and duties relating to the child vest in the adoption agency, and subsections (2) and (3) of section 12 apply as if the order were an adoption order and the agency were the adopters.

(6) Before making an order under this section, the court shall satisfy itself, in relation to each parent or guardian [of the child who can be found], that he has been given an opportunity of making, if he so wishes, a declaration that he prefers not to be involved in future questions concerning the adoption of the child; and any such declaration shall be recorded by the court.

(7) Before making an order under this section in the case of an illegitimate child whose father is not its guardian, the court shall satisfy itself in relation to any person claiming to be the father that either—

(*a*) he has no intention of applying for custody of the child under section 9 of the Guardianship of Minors Act 1971, or

(*b*) if he did apply for custody under that section the application would be likely to be refused.

AMENDMENT

In subs.(6) the words in square brackets were substituted by the Health and Social Services and Social Security Adjudications Act 1983, s.9, Sched. 2, para. 31.

Progress reports to former parent

19.—(1) This section and section 20 apply to any person ("the former parent") who was required to be given an opportunity of making a declaration under section 18(6) but did not do so.

(2) Within the 14 days following the date 12 months after the making of the order under section 18 the adoption agency in which the parental rights and duties were vested on the making of the order, unless it has previously by notice to the former parent informed him that an adoption order has been made in respect of the child, shall by notice to the former parent inform him—

(*a*) whether an adoption order has been made in respect of the child, and (if not)

(*b*) whether the child has his home with a person with whom he has been placed for adoption.

(3) If at the time when the former parent is given notice under subsection (2) an adoption order has not been made in respect of the child, it is thereafter the duty of the adoption agency to give notice to the former parent

of the making of an adoption order (if and when made), and meanwhile to give the former parent notice whenever the child is placed for adoption or ceases to have home with a person with whom he has been placed for adoption.

(4) If at any time the former parent by notice makes a declaration to the adoption agency that he prefers not to be involved in future questions concerning the adoption of the child—

    (*a*) the agency shall secure that the declaration is recorded by the court which made the order under section 18, and

    (*b*) the agency is released from the duty of complying further with subsection (3) as respects that former parent.

Revocation of s.18 order

20.—(1) The former parent, at any time more than 12 months after the making of the order under section 18 when—

    (*a*) no adoption order has been made in respect of the child, and

    (*b*) the child does not have his home with a person with whom he has been placed for adoption,

may apply to the court which made the order for a further order revoking it on the ground that he wishes to resume the parental rights and duties.

(2) While the application is pending the adoption agency having the parental rights and duties shall not place the child for adoption without the leave of the court.

(3) Where an order freeing a child for adoption is revoked under this section—

    (*a*) the parental rights and duties relating to the child are vested in the individual or, as the case may be, the individuals in whom they vested immediately before that order was made;

    (*b*) if the parental rights and duties, or any of them, vested in a local authority or voluntary organisation immediately before the order freeing the child for adoption was made, those rights and duties are vested in the individual, or as the case may be, the individuals in whom they vested immediately before they were vested in the authority or organisation; and

    (*b*) any duty extinguished by virtue of section 12(3)(*b*) is forthwith revived,

but the revocation does not affect any right or duty so far as it relates to any period before the date of the revocation.

(4) Subject to subsection (5), if the application is dismissed on the ground that to allow it would contravene the principle embodied in section 6—

    (*a*) the former parent who made the application shall not be entitled to make any further application under subsection (1) in respect of the child and

    (*b*) the adoption agency is released from the duty of complying further with section 19(3) as respects that parent.

(5) Subsection (4)(*a*) shall not apply where the court which dismissed the application gives leave to the former parent to make a further application under subsection (1), but such leave shall not be given unless it appears to the court that because of a change in circumstances or for any other reason it is proper to allow the application to be made.

Supplemental

Notification to local authority of adoption application

22.—(1) An adoption order shall not be made in respect of a child who was not placed with the applicant by an adoption agency unless the applicant has, at least 3 months before the date of the order, given notice to the local authority within whose area he has his home of his intention to apply for the adoption order.

(2) On receipt of such a notice the local authority shall investigate the matter and submit to the court a report of their investigation.

(3) Under subsection (2), the local authority shall in particular investigate,—

(a) so far as is practicable, the suitability of the applicant, and any other matters relevant to the operation of section 6 in relation to the application; and

(b) whether the child was placed with the application in contravention of section 11.

(4) A local authority which receives notice under subsection (1) in respect of a child whom the authority know to be in the care of another local authority shall, not more than 7 days after the receipt of the notice, inform that other local authority in writing, that they have received the notice.

Reports where child placed by agency

23. Where an application for an adoption order relates to a child placed by an adoption agency, the agency shall submit to the court a report on the suitability of the applicants and any other matters relevant to the operation of section 6, and shall assist the court in any manner the court may direct.

Restrictions on making adoption orders

24.—(1) The court shall not proceed to hear an application for an adoption order in relation to a child where a previous application for a British Adoption order made in relation to the child by the same persons was refused by any court unless—

(a) in refusing the previous application the court directed that this subsection should not apply, or

(b) it appears to the court that because of a change in circumstances or for any other reason it is proper to proceed with the application.

(2) The court shall not make an adoption order in relation to a child unless it is satisfied that the applicants have not, as respects the child, [contravened] section 57.

AMENDMENT
   In subs.(2) the word in square brackets was substituted by the Health and Social Services and Social Security Adjudications Act 1983, s.9, Sched. 2, para.32.

Interim orders

25.—(1) Where on an application for an adoption order the requirements of sections 16(1) and 22(1) are complied with, the court may postpone the determination of the application and make an order vesting the legal custody of the child in the ' applicants for a probationary period not exceeding 2 years upon such terms for the maintenance of the child and otherwise as the court thinks fit.

(2) Where the probationary period specified in an order under subsection (1) is less than 2 years, the court may by a further order extend the period to a duration not exceeding 2 years in all.

Care etc. of child on refusal of adoption order

26.—(1) Where on an application for an adoption order in relation to a child [...] the court refuses to make the adoption order then—

(*a*) if it appears to the court that there are exceptional circumstances making it desirable that the child should be under the supervision of an independent person, the court may order that the child shall be under the supervision of a specified local authority or under the supervision of a probation officer;

(*b*) if it appears to the court that there are exceptional circumstances making it impracticable or undesirable for the child to be entrusted to either of the parents or to any other individual, the court may by order commit the child to the care of a special local authority.

(2) Where the court makes an order under subsection (1)(*b*) the order may require the payment by either parent to the local authority, while it has the care of the child, of such weekly or other periodical sum towards the maintenance of the child as the court thinks reasonable.

(3) Sections 3 and 4 of the Guardianship Act 1973 (which contain supplementary provisions relating to children who are subject to supervision, or in the care of local authority, by virtue of orders made under section 2 of that Act) apply in relation to an order under this section as they apply in relation to an order under section 2 of that Act.

AMENDMENT

In subs. (1), the words omitted were repealed by the Domestic Proceedings and Magistrates' Courts Act 1978, s.72(2).

PART III

CARE AND PROTECTION OF CHILDREN AWAITING ADOPTION

Restrictions on removal of children

Restrictions on removal where adoption agreed or application made under s.18

27.—(1) While an application for an adoption order is pending in a case where a parent or guardian of the child has agreed to the making of the adoption order (whether or not he knows the identity of the applicant), the parent or guardian is not entitled, against the will of the person with whom the child has his home, to remove the child from the [actual] custody of that person except with the leave of the court.

(2) While an application is pending for an order freeing a child for adoption and—

(*a*) the child is in the care of the adoption agency making the application, and

(*b*) the application was not made with the consent of each parent or guardian of the child,

no parent or guardian of the child is entitled, against the will of the person with whom the child has his home, to remove the child from the [actual] custody of that person except with the leave of the court.

(3) Any person who contravenes subsection (1) or (2) shall be guilty of an offence and liable on summary conviction to imprisonment for a term not exceeding 3 months or a fine not exceeding £400 or both.

(4) (5) [*Repealed by the Health and Social Services and Social Security Adjudications Act* 1983 *s.*30(1), *Sched.* 10, *Pt. I.*]

AMENDMENTS
   In subss. (1) and (2) the words in square brackets were substituted by the Health and Social Services and Social Security Adjudications Act 1983, s.9, Sched. 2, para. 60.

Restrictions on removal where applicant has provided home for 5 years

28.—(1) While an application for an adoption order in respect of a child made by the person with whom the child has had his home for the 5 years preceding the application is pending, no person is entitled, against the will of the applicant, to remove the child from the applicant's [actual] custody except with the leave of the court or under authority conferred by any enactment or on the arrest of the child.

(2) Where a person ("the prospective adopter") gives notice to the local authority within whose area he has his home that he intends to apply for an adoption order in respect of a child who for the preceding 5 years has had his home with the prospective adopter, no person is entitled, against the will of the prospective adopter, to remove the child from the prospective adopter's [actual] custody, except with the leave of a court or under authority conferred by any enactment or on the arrest of the child, before—

(*a*) the prospective adopter applies for the adoption order, or

(*b*) the period of 3 months from the receipt of the notice by the local authority expires.

whichever occurs first.

(3) In any case where subsection (1) or (2) applies and—

(*a*) the child was in the care of a local authority before he began to have his home with the applicant or, as the case may be, the prospective adopter, and

(*b*) the child remains in the care of [a local authority].

the authority [in whose care the child is] shall not remove the child from the actual custody of the applicant or of the prospective adopter except in accordance with section 30 or 31 or with leave of a court.

(4) In subsections (2) and (3) "a court" means a court with jurisdiction to make adoption orders.

(5) A local authority which receives such notice as is mentioned in subsection (2) in respect of a child whom the authority know to be in the care of another local authority or a voluntary organisation shall, not more than 7 days after the receipt of the notice, inform that other authority or the organisation, in writing, that they have received the notice.

(6) Subsection (2) does not apply to any further notice served by the prospective adopter on any local authority in respect of the same child during the period referred to in paragraph (*b*) of that subsection or within 28 days after its expiry.

(7) Any person who contravenes subsection (1) or (2) shall be guilty of an offence and liable on summary conviction to imprisonment for a term not exceeding 3 months or a fine not exceeding £400 or both.

(8) (9) [*Repealed by the Health and Social Services and Social Security Adjudications Act* 1983, *s.*30(1), *Sched.* 10, *Pt. I.*]

(10) The Secretary of State may by order amend subsection (1) or (2) to substitute a different period for the period of 5 years mentioned in that subsection (or the period which, by a previous order under this subsection, was substituted for that period).

AMENDMENTS
In subss. (1) and (2) the words in square brackets were inserted by the Health and Social Services and Social Security Adjudications Act 1983, s.9, Sched. 2, para. 60.
In subs. (3)(b) the words in square brackets were substituted by the Domestic Proceedings and Magistrates' Courts Act 1978, s.89(2)(a), Sched. 2, para. 50.

Return of a child taken away in breach of s.27 or 28

29.—(1) An authorised court may on the application of a person from whose custody a child has been removed in breach of section 27 or 28 [or section 27 or 28 of the Adoption (Scotland) Act 1978] order the person who has so removed the child to return the child to the applicant.

(2) An authorised court may on the application of a person who has reasonable grounds for believing that another person is intending to remove a child from the applicant's custody in breach of section 27 or 28 [or section 27 or 28 of the Adoption (Scotland) Act 1978] by order direct that other person not to remove the child from the applicant's custody in breach of section 27 or 28.

(3) If, in the case of an order made by the High Court under subsection (1), the High Court or, in the case of an order made by a county court under subsection (1), a county court is satisfied that the child has not been returned to the applicant, the court may make an order authorising an officer of the court to search such premises as may be specified in the order for the child and, if the officer finds the child, to return the child to the applicant.

(4) If a justice of the peace is satisfied by information on oath that there are reasonable grounds for believing that a child to whom an order under subsection (1) relates is in premises specified in the information, he may issue a search warrant authorising a constable to search the premises for the child; and if a constable acting in pursuance of a warrant under this section finds the child, he shall return the child to the person on whose application the order under subsection (1) was made.

(5) An order under subsection (3) may be enforced in like manner as a warrant for committal.

AMENDMENTS
In subss. (1) and (2) the words in square brackets were inserted by the Health and Social Services and Social Security Adjudications Act 1983, s.9, Sched. 2, para. 34.

Protected children

Meaning of "protected child"

32.—(1) Where a person gives notice in pursuance of section 22(1) to the local authority within whose area he lives of his intention to apply for an adoption order in respect of a child, the child is for the purposes of this Part a protected child while he has his home with that person.

(2) A child shall be deemed to be a protected child for the purposes of this Part if he is a protected child within the meaning of section 37 of the Adoption Act 1958.

(3) A child is not a protected child by reason of any such notice as is mentioned in subsection (1) while—

(a) he is in the care of any person in any such school, home or institution as is mentioned in [section 2(2) of the Foster Children Act 1980]; or

(b) he is resident in a residential home for mentally disordered persons as defined by [section 1(3) of the Residential Homes Act 1980]; or

(c) he is liable to be detained or subject to guardianship under [the Mental Health Act 1983].

(4) A protected child ceases to be a protected child—

    (*a*) on the appointment of a guardian for him under the Guardian-ship of Minors Act 1971;

    (*b*) on the notification to the local authority for the area where the child has his home that the application for an adoption order has been withdrawn;

    (*c*) on the making of any of the following orders in respect of the child—

        (i) an adoption order;

        (ii) an order under section 26;

        (iii) a custodianship order;

        (iv) an order under section 42, 43 or 44 of the Matrimonial Causes Act 1973; or

    (*d*) on his attaining the age of 18 years.

whichever first occurs.

Duty of local authorities to secure well-being of protected children

33.—(1) It shall be the duty of every local authority to secure that protected children within their area are visited from time to time by officers of the authority, who shall satisfy themselves as to the well-being of the children and give such advice as to their care and maintenance as may appear to be needed.

(2) Any officer of a local authority authorised to visit protected children may, after producing, if asked to do so, some duly authenticated document showing that he is so authorised, inspect any premises in the area of the authority in which such children are to be or are being kept.

Removal of protected children from unsuitable surroundings

34.—(1) If a juvenile court is satisfied, on the complaint of a local authority, that a protected child is being kept or is about to be received by any person who is unfit to have his care or in any premises or any environment detrimental or likely to be detrimental to him, the court may make an order for his removal to a place of safety until he can be restored to a parent, relative or guardian of his, or until other arrangements can be made with respect to him; and on proof that there is imminent danger to the health or well-being of the child the power to make an order under this section may be exercised by a justice of the peace acting on the application of a person authorised to visit protected children.

(2) An order under this section may be executed by any person authorised to visit protected children or by any constable.

(3) A local authority may receive into their care under [section 2 of the Child Care Act 1980] any child removed under this section, whether or not the circumstances of the child are such that they fall within paragraphs (*a*) to (*c*) of subsection (1) of that section and notwithstanding that he may appear to the local authority to be over the age of 17 years.

(4) Where a child is removed under this section the local authority shall, if

practicable, inform a parent or guardian of the child, or any person who acts as his guardian.

AMENDMENT
The words in square brackets in subs. (3) were substituted by the Child Care Act 1980, s.89(2), Sched. 5.

Notices and information to be given to local authorities

35.—(1) Where a person who has a protected child in his actual custody changes his permanent address he shall, not less than 2 weeks before the change, or, if the change is made in an emergency, not later than one week after the change, give notice specifying the new address to the local authority in whose area his permanent address is before the change, and if the new address is in the area of another local authority, the authority to whom the notice is given shall inform that other local authority and give them such of the following particulars as are known to them, that is to say—

(*a*) the name, sex and date and place of birth of a child;

(*b*) the name and address of every person who is a parent or guardian or acts as a guardian of the child or from whom the child was received.

(2) If a protected child dies, the person in whose actual custody he was at his death shall within 48 hours give notice of the child's death to the local authority.

Offences relating to protected children

36.—(1) A person shall be guilty of an offence if—

(*a*) being required, under section 35 to give any notice or information, he fails to give the notice within the time specified in that provision or fails to give the information within a reasonable time, or knowingly makes or causes or procures another person to make any false or misleading statement in the notice of information;

(*b*) he refuses to allow the visiting of a protected child by a duly authorised officer of a local authority or the inspection, under the power conferred by section 33(2) of any premises;

(*c*) he refuses to comply with an order under section 34 for the removal of any child or obstructs any person in the execution of such an order.

(2) A person guilty of an offence under this section shall be liable on summary conviction to imprisonment for a term not exceeding 3 months or a fine not exceeding £400 or both.

Miscellaneous provisions relating to protected children

37.—(1) For the purposes of section 40 of the Children and Young Persons Act 1933, under which a warrant authorising the search for and removal of a child may be issued on suspicion of unnecessary suffering caused to, or certain offences committed against, the child, any refusal to allow the visiting of a protected child or the inspection of any premises by a person authorised to do so under section 33 shall be treated as giving reasonable cause for such a suspicion.

(2) A person who maintains a protected child shall be deemed for the purposes of the Life Assurance Act 1774 to have no interest in the life of the child.

(3) An appeal shall lie to the Crown Court against any order made under section 34 by a juvenile court or a justice of the peace.

(4) Subsection (2) of section 47 of the Children and Young Persons Act 1933 (which restricts the time and place at which a sitting of a juvenile court may be held and the persons who may be present at such a sitting) shall not apply to any sitting of a juvenile court in any proceedings under section 34.

PART IV

STATUS OF ADOPTED CHILDREN

Meaning of "adoption" in Part IV

    38.—(1) In this Part "adoption" means adoption—
      (*a*) by an adoption order;
      (*b*) by an order made under the Children Act 1975, the Adoption Act 1958, the Adoption Act 1950 or any enactment repealed by the Adoption Act 1950;
      (*c*) by an order made in Scotland, Northern Ireland, the Isle of Man or in any of the Channel Islands;
      (*d*) which is an overseas adoption; or
      (*e*) which is an adoption recognised by the law of England and Wales and effected under the law of any other country,
and cognate expressions shall be construed accordingly.

    (2) The definition of adoption includes, where the context admits, an adoption effected before the passing of the Children Act 1975, and the date of an adoption effected by an order is the date of the making of the order.

Status conferred by adoption

    39.—(1) An adopted child shall be treated in law—
      (*a*) where the adopters are a married couple, as if he had been born as a child of the marriage (whether or not he was in fact born after the marriage was solemnized);
      (*b*) in any other case, as if he had been born to the adopter in wedlock (but not as a child of any actual marriage of the adopter).

    (2) An adopted child shall, subject to subsection (3), be treated in law as if he were not the child of any person other than the adopters or adopter.

    (3) In the case of a child adopted by one of its natural parents as sole adoptive parent, subsection (2) has no effect as respects entitlement to property depending on relationship to that parent, or as respects anything else depending on that relationship.

    (4) It is hereby declared that this section prevents an adopted child from being illegitimate.

    (5) This section has effect—
      (*a*) in the case of an adoption before January 1, 1976, from that date, and
      (*b*) in the case of any other adoption, from the date of the adoption.

    (6) Subject to the provisions of this Part, this section—
      (*a*) applies for the construction of enactments or instruments passed or made before the adoption or later, and so applies subject to any contrary indication; and

(*b*) has effect as respects things done, or events occurring, after the adoption, or after December 31, 1975, whichever is the later.

Miscellaneous enactments

47.—(1) Section 39 does not apply for the purposes of the table of kindred and affinity in Schedule 1 to the Marriage Act 1949 or sections 10 and 11 (incest) of the Sexual Offences Act 1956.

(2) [. . .] section 39 does not apply for the purposes of any provision of—

(*a*) [the British Nationality Act 1981],

(*b*) the Immigration Act 1971,

(*c*) any instrument having effect under an enactment within paragraph (*a*) or (*b*), or

(*d*) any other provision of the law for the time being in force which determines [British citizenship, British Dependent Territories citizenship or British Overseas citizenship].

(3) Section 39 shall not prevent a person being treated as a near relative of a deceased person for the purposes of section 32 of the Social Security Act 1975 (payment of death grant), if apart from section 39 he would be so treated.

(4) Section 39 does not apply for the purposes of section 70(3)(*b*) or section 73(2) of the Social Security Act 1975 (payment of industrial death benefit to or in respect of an illegitimate child of the deceased and the child's mother).

(5) Subject to regulations made under section 72 of the Social security Act 1975 (entitlement of certain relatives of deceased to industrial death benefit), section 39 shall not affect the entitlement to an industrial death benefit of a person who would, apart from section 39, be treated as a relative of a deceased person for the purposes of the said section 72.

AMENDMENT

In subs. (2) the words in square brackets were substituted by the British Nationality Act 1981, s.52(6), Sched. 7. The words omitted were repealed by *ibid.* s. 52(8), Sched. 9.

Disclosure of birth records of adopted children

51.—(1) Subject to subsections (4) and (6), the Registrar General shall on an application made in the prescribed manner by an adopted person a record of whose birth is kept by the Registrar General and who has attained the age of 18 years supply to that person on payment of the prescribed fee (if any) such information as is necessary to enable that person to obtain a certified copy of the record of his birth.

(2) On an application made in the prescribed manner by an adopted person under the age of 18 years, a record of whose birth is kept by the Registrar General and who is intending to be married in English or Wales, and on payment of the prescribed fee (if any), the Registrar General shall inform the applicant whether or not it appears from information contained in the registers of live births or other records that the applicant and the person whom he intends to marry may be within the prohibited degrees of relationship for the purposes of the Marriage Act 1949.

(3) It shall be the duty of the Registrar General and each local authority and approved adoption society to provide counselling for adopted persons who apply for information under subsection (1).

(4) Before supplying any information to an applicant under subsection (1) the Registrar General shall inform the applicant that counselling services are available to him—

(a) at the General Register Office; or

(b) from the local authority for the area where the applicant is at the time the application is made; or

(c) from the local authority for the area where the court sat which made the adoption order relating to the applicant; or

(d) if the applicant's adoption was arranged by an adoption society which is approved under section 3 of this Act or under section 4 of the Children Act 1975, from that society.

(5) If the applicant chooses to receive counselling from a local authority or an adoption society under subsection (4) the Registrar General shall send to the authority or society of the applicant's choice the information to which the applicant is entitled under subsection (1).

(6) The Registrar General shall not supply a person who was adopted before November 12, 1975 with any information under subsection (1) unless that person has attended an interview with a counsellor either at the General Register Office or in pursuance of arrangements made by the local authority or adoption society from whom the applicant is entitled to receive counselling in accordance with subsection (4).

(7) In this section, "prescribed" means prescribed by regulations made by the Registrar General.

Prohibition on certain payments

57.—(1) Subject to the provisions of this section, it shall not be lawful to make or give to any person any payment or reward for or in consideration of—

(a) the adoption by that person of a child;

(b) the grant by that person of any agreement or consent required in connection with the adoption of a child;

(c) the transfer by that person of the actual custody of a child with a view to the adoption of the child; or

(d) the making by that person of any arrangements for the adoption of a child.

(2) Any person who makes or gives, or agrees or offers to make or give, any payment or reward prohibited by this section, or who receives or agrees to receive or attempts to obtain any such payment or rewards, shall be guilty of an offence and liable on summary conviction to imprisonment for a term not exceeding 3 months or to a fine not exceeding £400 or to both; and the court may order any child in respect of whom the offence was committed to be removed to a place of safety until he can be restored to his parents or guardian or until other arrangements can be made for him.

(3) This section does not apply to any payment made to an adoption agency by a parent or guardian of a child or by a person who adopts or proposes to adopt a child, being a payment in respect of expenses reasonably incurred by the agency in connection with the adoption of the child, or to any payment or reward authorised by the court to which an application for an adoption order in respect of a child is made.

[(3A) This section does not apply to—

(a) any payment made by an adoption agency to a person who has applied or proposes to apply to a court for an adoption order or an order under section 55 (adoption of children abroad), being a payment of or towards any legal or medical expenses incurred or to be incurred by that person in connection with the application; or

(b) any payment made by an adoption agency to another adoption agency in consideration of the placing of a child in the actual custody of any person with a view to the child's adoption; or

(c) any payment made by an adoption agency to a voluntary organisation for the time being approved for the purposes of this paragraph by the Secretary of State as a fee for the services of that organisation in putting that adoption agency into contact with another adoption agency with a view to the making of arrangements between the adoption agencies for the adoption of a child.

In paragraph (c) 'voluntary organisation' means a body, other than a public or local authority, the activities of which are not carried on for profit.]

(4) If an adoption agency submits to the Secretary of State a scheme for the payment by the agency of allowances to persons who have adopted or intend to adopt a child where arrangements for the adoption were made, or are to be made, by that agency, and the Secretary of State approves the scheme, this section shall not apply to any payment made in accordance with the scheme.

(5) The Secretary of State, in the case of a scheme approved by him under subsection (4), may at any time—

(a) make, or approve the making by the agency of, alterations to the scheme;

(b) revoke the scheme.

(6) The Secretary of State shall, within seven years of the date on which section 32 of the Children Act 1975 came into force and, thereafter, every five years, publish a report on the operation of the schemes since that date or since the publication of the last report.

(7) Subject to the following subsection, subsection (4) of this section shall expire on the seventh anniversary of the date on which section 32 of the Children Act 1976 came into force.

(8) The Secretary of State may by order made by statutory instrument at any time before the said anniversary repeal subsection (7) of this section.

(9) An order under subsection (8) of this section shall not be made unless a report has been published under subsection (6) of this section.

(10) Notwithstanding the expiry of subsection (4) of this section or the revocation of a scheme approved under this section, subsection (1) of this section shall not apply in relation to any payment made, whether before or after the expiry of subsection (4) or the revocation of the scheme, in accordance with a scheme which was approved under this section to a person to whom such payments were made—

(a) where the scheme was not revoked, before the expiry of subsection (4), or

(b) if the scheme was revoked, before the date of its revocation.

AMENDMENT
Subs. (3A) was inserted by the Criminal Law Act 1977, s.65, Sched. 12.

Restriction on advertisements

58.—(1) It shall not be lawful for any advertisement to be published indicating—

(*a*) that the parent or guardian of a child desires to cause a child to be adopted; or

(*b*) that a person desires to adopt a child; or

(*c*) that any person (not being an adoption agency) is willing to make arrangements for the adoption of a child.

(2) Any person who causes to be published or knowingly publishes an advertisement in contravention of the provisions of this section shall be guilty of an offence and liable on summary conviction to a fine not exceeding £400.

Guardians *ad litem* and reporting officers

65.—(1) For the purpose of any application for an adoption order or an order freeing a child for adoption or an order under section 20 or 55 rules shall provide for the appointment, in such cases as are prescribed—

(*a*) of a person to act as guardian *ad litem* of the child upon the hearing of the application, with the duty of safeguarding the interests of the child in the prescribed manner;

(*b*) of a person to act as reporting officer for the purpose of witnessing agreements to adoption and performing such other duties as the rules may prescribe.

(2) A person who is employed—

(*a*) in the case of an application for an adoption order, by the adoption agency by whom the child was placed; or

(*b*) in the case of an application for an order freeing a child for adoption, by the adoption agency by whom the application was made; or

(*c*) in the case of an application under section 20, by the adoption agency with the parental rights and duties relating to the child,

shall not be appointed to act as guardian *ad litem* or reporting officer for the purposes of the application but, subject to that, the same person may if the court thinks fit be both guardian *ad litem* and reporting officer.

Interpretation

72.—(1) In this Act, unless the context otherwise requires—

"adoption agency" in sections 11, 13, 18 to 23 and 27 to 32 includes an adoption agency within the meaning of section 1 of the Children Act 1975 (adoption agencies in Scotland);

"adoption order" means an order under section 12(1) and, in sections 12(3) and (4), 18 to 21 [27 and 28] and 30 to 32 includes an order under section 8 of the Children Act 1975 (adoption orders in Scotland);

"adoption society" means a body of persons whose functions consist of or include the making of arrangements for the adoption of children;

"approved adoption society" means an adoption society approved under Part I;

"authorised court" shall be construed in accordance with section 62;

body of persons" means any body of persons, whether incorporated or unincorporated;

"British adoption order" means an adoption order, an order under section 8 of the Children Act 1975 (adoption orders in Scotland), or any provision for the adoption of a child effected under the law of Northern Ireland or any British territory outside the United Kingdom;

"British territory" means, for the purposes of any provision of this Act, any of the following countries, that is to say, Great Britain, Northern Ireland, the Channel Islands, the Isle of Man and a colony, being a country designated for the purposes of that provision by order of the Secretary of State or, if no country is so designated, any of those countries;

"child", except where used to express a relationship, means a person who has not attained the age of 18 years;

"the Convention" means the Convention relating to the adoption of children concluded at the Hague on November 15, 1965 and signed on behalf of the United Kingdom on that date;

"Convention adoption order" means an adoption order made in accordance with section 17(1);

"Convention country" means any country outside British territory, being a country for the time being designated by an order of the Secretary of State as a country in which, in his opinion, the Convention is in force;

"existing", in relation to an enactment or other instrument, means one passed or made at any time before January 1, 1976;

"guardian" means—
- (b) a person appointed by deed or will in accordance with the provisions of the Guardianship of Infants Acts 1886 and 1925 or the Guardianship of Minors Act 1971 or by a court of competent jurisdiction to be the guardian of the child, and
- (b) in the case of an illegitimate child, includes the father where he has custody of the child by virtue of an order under section 9 of the Guardianship of Minors Act 1971, or under section 2 of the Illegitimate Children (Scotland) Act 1930.

"internal law" has the meaning assigned by section 71;

"local authority" means the council of a county (other than a metropolitan county), a metropolitan district, a London borough or the Common Council of the City of London and, in sections 13, 22, 28 to 31, 35(1) and 51, includes a regional or islands council;

"notice" means a notice in writing;

"order freeing a child for adoption" means an order under section 18 [and in section 27(2) includes an order under section 18 of the Adoption (Scotland) Act 1978 (order freeing a child for adoption made in Scotland)];

"overseas adoption" has the meaning assigned by subsection (2);

"place of safety" means a community home provided by a local authority, a controlled community home, police station, or any hospital, surgery or other suitable place the occupier of which is willing temporarily to receive a child;

"prescribed" means prescribed by rules;

"regulated adoption" means an overseas adoption of a description designated by an order under subsection (2) as that of an adoption regulated by the Convention;

"relative" in relation to a child means a grandparent, brother, sister, uncle or aunt, whether of the full blood or half-blood or by affinity and includes, where the child is illegitimate, the father of the child and any person who would be a relative within the meaning of this definition if the child were the legitimate child of his mother and father;

"rules" means rules made under section 66(1) or made by virtue of section 66(2) under [section 144 of the Magistrates' Courts Act 1980];

"specified order" means any provision for the adoption of a child effected under enactments similar to section 12(1) and 17 in force in Northern Ireland or any British territory outside the United Kingdom;

"United Kingdom national" means, for the purposes of any provision of this Act, a citizen of the United Kingdom and colonies satisfying such conditions, if any, as the Secretary of State may by order specify for the purposes of that provision;

"voluntary organisation" means a body other than a public or local authority the activities of which are not carried on for profit.

Short title, commencement and extent

74.—(1) This Act may be cited as the Adoption Act 1976.

(2) This Act shall come into force on such date as the Secretary of State may by order appoint and different dates may be appointed for different provisions.

(3) This Act, except sections 22, 23, 51 and 73(2), this section and Part II of Schedule 3, shall not extend to Scotland and the said Part II shall not extend to England and Wales.

(4) This Act, [. . .], section 1(3) of the Adoption Act 1964 and sections 9(5) and 14 of the Adoption Act 1968, shall not extend to Northern Ireland.

AMENDMENT
In subs. (4) the words omitted were repealed by the British Nationality Act 1981, s.52(8), Sched. 9.

Child Care Act 1980

(C. 5)

An Act to consolidate certain enactments relating to the care of children by local authorities or voluntary organisations and certain other enactments relating to the care of children.   [31st January 1980]

PART I

POWERS AND DUTIES OF LOCAL AUTHORITIES IN RELATION TO THE WELFARE AND CARE OF CHILDREN

General duty of local authorities to promote welfare of children

Duty of local authorities to promote welfare of children

1.—(1) It shall be the duty of every local authority to make available such advice, guidance and assistance as may promote the welfare of children by diminishing the need to receive children into or keep them in care under this

Act or to bring children before a juvenile court; and any provisions made by a local authority under this subsection may, if the local authority think fit, include provision for giving assistance in kind or, in exceptional circumstances, in cash.

(2) In carrying out their duty under subsection (1) above, a local authority may make arrangements with voluntary organisations or other persons for the provision by those organisations or other persons of such advice, guidance or assistance as is mentioned in that subsection.

(3) Where any provision which may be made by a local authority under subsection (1) above is made (whether by that or any other authority) under any other enactment, the local authority shall not be required to make the provision under this section but shall have power to do so.

(4) In this section "child" means a person under the age of eighteen.

Duty of local authorities to assume care of orphans and deserted children etc.

Duty of local authority to provide for orphans, deserted children etc.

2.—(1) Where it appears to a local authority with respect to a child in their area appearing to them to be under the age of seventeen—

(b) that he has neither parent nor guardian or has been and remains abandoned by his parents or guardian or is lost; or

(b) that his parents or guardian are, for the time being or permanently, prevented by reason of mental or bodily disease or infirmity or other incapacity or any other circumstances from providing for his proper accommodation, maintenance and upbringing; and

(c) in either case, that the intervention of the local authority under this section is necessary in the interests of the welfare of the child.

it shall be the duty of the local authority to receive the child into their care under this section.

Where a local authority have received a child into their care under this section, it shall, subject to the provisions of this Part of this Act, be their duty to keep the child in their care so long as the welfare of the child appears to them to require it and the child has not attained the age of eighteen.

Nothing in this section shall authorise a local authority to keep a child in their care under this section if any parent or guardian desires to take over the care of the child, and the local authority shall, in all cases where it appears to them consistent with the welfare of the child so to do, endeavour to secure that the care of the child is taken over either—

(a) by a parent or guardian of his, or

(b) by a relative or friend of his, being, where possible, a person of the same religious persuasion as the child or who gives an undertaking that the child will be brought up in that religious persuasion.

(4) Where a local authority receive into their care under this section a child who is then ordinarily resident in the area of another local authority—

(a) that other local authority may at any time not later than three months after the determination (whether by agreement between the authorities or in accordance with the following provisions of this subsection) of the ordinary residence of the child, or with the concurrence of the first mentioned authority at any subsequent time, take over the care of the child; and

(b) the first mentioned authority may recover from the other authority any expenses duly incurred by them under Part III of this Act in respect of the child (including any expenses so incurred after he has ceased to be a child and, if the other authority takes over the care of him, including also any travelling or other expenses incurred in connection with the taking over).

Any question arising under this subsection as to the ordinary residence of a child shall be determined by the Secretary of State and in this subsection any reference to another local authority includes a reference to a local authority within the meaning of the Social Work (Scotland) Act 1968.

(5) In determining for the purposes of subsection (4) above the ordinary residence of any child, any period during which he resides in any place—

(b) as an inmate of a school or other institution, or

(b) in accordance with the requirements of a supervision order or probation order or of a supervision requirement, or

(c) in accordance with the conditions of a recognisance, or

(d) while boarded out under this Act, the Children and Young Persons (Scotland) Act 1937 or Part II of the Social Work (Scotland) Act 1968 by a local authority or education authority,

shall be disregarded.

(6) Any reference in this section to the parents or guardian of a child shall be construed as a reference to all the persons who are parents of the child or who are guardians of the child.

Assumption by local authority of parental rights and duties

3.—(1) Subject to the provisions of this Part of this Act, if it appears to a local authority in relation to any child who is in their care under section 2 of this Act—

(a) that his parents are dead and he has no guardian or custodian; or

(b) that a parent of his—

(i) has abandoned him, or

(ii) suffers from some permanent disability rendering him incapable of caring for the child, or

(iii) while not falling within sub-paragraph (ii) of this paragraph, suffers from a mental disorder (within the meaning of [the Mental Health Act 1983]), which renders him unfit to have the care of the child, or

(iv) is of such habits or mode of life as to be unfit to have the care of the child, or

(v) has so consistently failed without reasonable cause to discharge the obligations of a parent as to be unfit to have the care of the child; or

(c) that a resolution under paragraph (b) of this subsection is in force in relation to one parent of the child who is, or is likely to become, a member of the household comprising the child and his other parent; or

(d) that throughout the three years preceding the passing of the resolution the child has been in the care of a local authority under section 2 of this Act, or partly in the care of a local authority and partly in the care of a voluntary organisation,

the local authority may resolve that there shall vest in them the parental rights and duties with respect to that child, and, if the rights and duties were vested in the parent on whose account the resolution was passed jointly with another person, they shall also be vested in the local authority jointly with that other person.

[(2) If the local authority know the whereabouts of the person whose parental rights and duties have vested in them by virtue of a resolution passed under subsection (1)(*b*), (*c*) or (*d*) above, they shall forthwith after it is passed serve notice in writing of its passing on him.]

(3) Every notice served by a local authority under subsection (2) above shall inform the person on whom the notice is served of his right to object to the resolution and the effect of any objection made by him.

(4) If, not later than one month after notice is served on a person under subsection (2) above, he serves a counter-notice in writing on the local authority objecting to the resolution, the resolution shall, subject to the provisions of subsections (5) and (6) below, lapse on the expiry of fourteen days from the service of the counter-notice.

(5) Where a counter-notice has been served on a local authority under subsection (4) above, the authority may not later than fourteen days after the receipt by them of the counter-notice complain to a juvenile court having jurisdiction in the area of the authority, and in that event the resolution shall not lapse until the determination of the complaint.

(6) On hearing a complaint made under subsection (5) above the court may if it is satisfied—

(*a*) that the grounds mentioned in subsection (1) above on which the local authority purported to pass the resolution were made out, and

(*b*) that at the time of the hearing there continue to be grounds on which a resolution under that subsection could be founded, and

(*c*) that it is in the interests of the child to do so,

order that the resolution shall not lapse by reason of the service of the counter-notice.

(7) Any notice under this section (including a counter-notice) may be served by post, so however that a notice served by a local authority under subsection (2) above shall not be duly served by post unless it is sent by registered post or recorded delivery service.

(8) Where, after a child has been received into the care of a local authority under section 2 of this Act, the whereabouts of any parent of his have remained unknown for twelve months, then, for the purposes of this section, the parent shall be deemed to have abandoned the child.

(9) The Secretary of State may by order a draft of which has been approved by each House of Parliament amend subsection (1)(*d*) above by substituting a different period for the period mentioned in that paragraph (or the period which, by a previous order under this subsection, was substituted for that period).

(10) In this section—

"parent", except in subsection (1)(*a*), includes a guardian or custodian;

"parental rights and duties", in relation to a particular child, does not include

(*a*) the right to consent or refuse to consent to the making of an application under section 18 of the Adoption Act 1976 (orders freeing a child for adoption in England and Wales) or section 18 of the Adoption (Scotland) Act 1978 (orders freeing a child for adoption in Scotland), and

(*b*) the right to agree or refuse to agree to the making of an adoption order or an order under section 55 of the Adoption Act 1976 (orders in England and Wales authorising adoption abroad) or section 49 of the Adoption (Scotland) Act 1978 (orders in Scotland authorising adoption abroad).

AMENDMENT
In subs. (1)(*b*)(iii) the words in square brackets were substituted by the Mental Health Act 1983, s.148, Sched. 4, para. 50. Subs. (2) was substituted by the Health and Social Services and Social Security Adjudications Act 1983, s.9, Sched. 2, para. 46.

Effect of resolution under s.3

4.—(1) While a resolution passed under subsection (1)(*b*), (*c*) or (*d*) of section 3 of this Act is in force with respect to a child, section 2(3) of this Act shall not apply in relation to the person who, but for the resolution, would have the parental rights and duties in relation to the child.

(2) A resolution under section 3 of this Act shall not relieve any person from any liability to maintain, or contribute to the maintenance of, the child.

(3) A resolution under section 3 of this Act shall not authorise a local authority to cause a child to be brought up in any religious creed other than that in which he would have been brought up but for the resolution.

Duration and rescission of resolutions under s.3

5.—(1) Subject to the provisions of this Part of this Act, a resolution under section 3 of this Act shall continue in force until the child with respect to whom it was passed attains the age of 18.

(2) A resolution under section 3 of this Act shall cease to have effect if—

(*a*) the child is adopted;

(*b*) an order in respect of the child is made under section 18 or 55 of the Adoption Act 1976 or section 18 or 49 of the Adoption (Scotland) Act 1978; or

(*c*) a guardian of the child is appointed under section 5 of the Guardianship of Minors Act 1971.

(3) A resolution under section 3 of this Act may be rescinded by resolution of the local authority if it appears to them that the rescinding of the resolution will be for the benefit of the child.

(4) On a complaint being made—

(*a*) in the case of a resolution passed by virtue of section 3(1)(*a*) of this Act, by a person claiming to be a parent, guardian or custodian of the child;

(*b*) in the case of a resolution passed by virtue of section 3(1)(*b*), (*c*) or (*d*) of this Act, by the person who, but for the resolution, would have the parental rights and duties in relation to the child,

a juvenile court having jurisdiction where the complainant resides, if satisfied that there was no ground for the making of the resolution or that the resolution should in the interests of the child be determined, may by order determine the resolution, and the resolution shall thereupon cease to have effect.

Appeal to the High Court

6. An appeal shall lie to the High Court from the making by a juvenile court of an order under section 3(6) or 5(4) of this Act or from the refusal by a juvenile court to make such an order.

Guardians ad litem and reports in care proceedings

7.—(1) In any proceedings under section 3(6) or 5(4) or 6 of this Act a juvenile court or the High Court may, where it considers it necessary in order to safeguard the interests of the child to whom the proceedings relate, by order make the child a party to the proceedings and appoint, subject to rules of court, a guardian ad litem of the child for the purposes of the proceedings.

(2) A guardian ad litem appointed in pursuance of this section shall be under a duty to safeguard the interests of the child in the manner prescribed by rules of court.

(3) Section 6 of the Guardianship Act 1973 shall apply in relation to complaints under section 3(6) or 5(4) of this Act as it applies in relation to applications under section 3(3) of the said Act of 1973.

Application of Part I in relation to children subject to orders of court

8.—(1) The reception of a child into their care by a local authority under section 2 of this Act, and the passing of a resolution with respect to him under section 3 of this Act, shall not affect any supervision order or probation order previously made with respect to him by any court.

(2) Where an order of any court is in force giving the custody of a child to any person, the foregoing provisions of this Part of this Act shall have effect in relation to the child as if for references to the parents or guardian of the child or to a parent or guardian of his there were substituted references to that person.

Duty of parents to maintain contact with local authorities having their children in care

9.—(1) The parent of a child who is in the care of a local authority under section 2 of this Act shall secure that the appropriate local authority are informed of the parent's address for the time being.

(2) Where under section 2(4) of this Act a local authority take over the care of a child from another local authority, that other authority shall where possible inform the parent of the child that the care of the child has been so taken over.

(3) For the purposes of subsection (1) above, the appropriate local authority shall be the authority in whose care the child is for the time being; but where under section 2(4) of this Act a local authority have taken over the care of a child from another authority, then unless and until a parent is informed that the care of a child has been so taken over the appropriate local authority shall in relation to that parent continue to be the authority from whom the care of the child was taken over.

(4) Any parent who knowingly fails to comply with subsection (1) above shall be guilty of an offence and liable on summary conviction to a fine not exceeding £10.

(5) It shall be a defence in any proceeding under subsection (4) above to prove that the defendant was residing at the same address as the other parent of the child and had reasonable cause to believe that the other parent had informed the appropriate authority that both parents were residing at that address.

Provisions as to children subject to care order etc.

Powers and duties of local authorities with respect to children committed to their care

10.—(1) It shall be the duty of a local authority to whose care a child is committed by a care order or by a warrant under section 23(1) of the

Children and Young Persons Act 1969 (which relates to remands in the care of local authorities) to receive the child into their care and, notwithstanding any claim by his parent or guardian, to keep him in their care while the order or warrant is in force.

(2) A local authority shall, subject to the following provisions of this section, have the same powers and duties with respect to a person in their care by virtue of a care order or such a warrant as his parent or guardian would have apart from the order or warrant ...].

(3) A local authority shall not cause a child in their care by virtue of a care order to be brought up in any religious creed other than that in which he would have been brought up apart from the order.

(4) It shall be the duty of a local authority to comply with any provision included in an interim order in pursuance of section 22(2) of the Children and Young Persons Act 1969 and, in the case of a person in their care by virtue of section 23 of that Act, to permit him to be removed from their care in due course of law.

[(5) This section does not give a local authority—

(a) the right to consent or refuse to consent to the making of an application under section 18 of the Adoption Act 1976 or section 18 of the Adoption (Scotland) Act 1978; or

(b) the right to agree or refuse to agree to the making of an adoption order or an order under section 55 of the Adoption Act 1976 or section 49 of the Adoption (Scotland) Act 1978.]

AMENDMENT

In subs. (2) the words in square brackets were substituted by the Criminal Justice Act 1982, Sched. 14, para. 44 and the words omitted were repealed by the Health and Social Services and Social Security Adjudications Act 1983, s.30, Sched. 10, Pt. I. Subs.(5) was inserted by *ibid.*, s.9, Sched. 2, para. 47.

Appointment of visitor for child subject to care order

11.—(1) If a child who is subject to a care order and has attained the age of five is accommodated in a community home or other establishment which he has not been allowed to leave during the preceding three months for the purpose of ordinary attendance at an educational institution or at work and it appears to the local authority to whose care he is committed by the order that—

(a) communication between him and his parent or guardian has been so infrequent that it is appropriate to appoint a visitor for him; or

(b) he has not lived with or visited or been visited by either of his parents or his guardian during the preceding twelve months,

it shall be the duty of the authority to appoint an independent person to be his visitor for the purposes of this subsection; and a person so appointed shall—

(i) have the duty of visiting, advising and befriending the child to whom the care order relates; and

(ii) be entitled to exercise on behalf of that child his powers under section 21(2) of the Children and Young Persons Act 1969 (which relates to the discharge of care orders); and

(iii) be entitled to recover from the authority who appointed him any expenses reasonably incurred by him for the purposes of his functions under this subsection.

(2) A person's appointment as a visitor in pursuance of subsection (1) above shall be determined if the care order in question ceases to be in force or he gives notice in writing to the authority who appointed him that he

resigns the appointment or the authority give him notice in writing that they terminate it; but the determination of such an appointment shall not prejudice any duty under subsection (1) above to make a further appointment.

(3) In this section "independent person" means a person satisfying such conditions as may be prescribed by regulations made by the Secretary of State with a view to securing that he is independent of local authority in question and unconnected with any community home.

Supplementary provisions relating to children subject to care order etc.

12.—(1) While a care order other than an interim order is in force in respect of a child who has not attained the age of eighteen, it shall be the duty of his parent to keep the local authority to whose care he is committed by the order informed of the parent's address; and if the parent knows of the order and fails to perform his duty under this subsection, the parent shall be guilty of an offence and liable on summary conviction to a fine not exceeding £10 unless he shows that at the material time he was residing at the address of the other parent and had reasonable cause to believe that the other parent had kept the authority informed of their address.

(2) The functions conferred on a local authority by sections 10 and 11 of this Act in respect of any child are additional to the functions which are conferred on the authority in respect of the child by Part III of this Act.

[PART IA

ACCESS TO CHILDREN IN CARE]

[Children to whom Part IA applies

12A.—(1) Subject to subsection (2) below, this Part of this Act applies to any child in the care of a local authority in consequence—

(*a*) of a care order (including an interim order);

(*b*) of an order under section 2(1) of the Matrimonial Proceedings (Magistrates' Courts) Act 1960;

(*c*) of committal under section 23(1) of the Children and Young Person Act 1969;

(*d*) of an order under section 2(2)(*b*) of the Guardianship Act 1973;

(*e*) of an order under section 17(1)(*b*) of the Children Act 1975 or section 26(1)(*b*) of the Adoption Act 1976 (order on refusal of adoption order);

(*f*) of an order under section 36(2) or (3)(*a*) of the Children Act 1975 (order on revocation of custodianship order);

(*g*) of an order under section 10(1) of the Domestic Proceedings and Magistrates' Courts Act 1978; or

(*h*) of a resolution under section 3 above.

This Part of this Act does not apply to a child in the care of a local authority in consequence of an order made by the High Court.]

AMENDMENT
This section was inserted by the Health and Social Services and Social Security Adjudications Act 1983, s.6, Sched. 1.

[Termination of access

12B.—(1) A local authority may not terminate arrangements for access to a child to whom this Part of this Act applies by its parents, guardian or custodian, or refuse to make such arrangements unless they have first given the parent, guardian or custodian notice of termination or refusal in a form prescribed by order made by the Secretary of State.

(2) A notice under this section shall contain a statement that the parent, guardian or custodian has a right to apply to a court for an order under section 12C below.

(3) A notice terminating access shall state that access will be terminated as from the date of service of the notice.

(4) A local authority are not to be taken to terminate access for the purpose of this section in a case where they propose to substitute new arrangements for access for existing arrangements.

(5) A local authority are not to be taken to refuse to make arrangements for access for the purposes of this section in a case where they postpone access for such reasonable period as appears to them to be necessary to enable them to consider what arrangements for access (if any) are to be made.

(6) A notice under this section may be served on a parent, guardian or custodian either by delivering it to him or by leaving it at his proper address or by sending it by post.

(7) For the purposes of this section, and of section 7 of the Interpretation Act 1978 in its application to this section, the proper address of a person shall be his last known address.]

AMENDMENT

This section was inserted by the Health and Social Services and Social Security Adjudications Act 1983, s.6, Sched. 1.

[Access orders—general

12C.—(1) A parent, guardian or custodian on whom a notice under section 12B above is served may apply for an order under this section (in this Part of this Act referred to as an "access order").

(2) An application under subsection (1) above shall be made by way of complaint to an appropriate juvenile court.

(3) An access order shall be an order requiring the authority to allow the child's parent, guardian or custodian access to the child subject to such conditions as the order may specify with regard to commencement, frequency, duration or place of access or to any other matter for which it appears to the court that provision ought to be made in connection with the requirement to allow access.

(4) A juvenile court is an appropriate juvenile court for the purposes of this Part of the Act if it has jurisdiction in the area of the authority serving the notice under section 12B above.

(5) An appeal shall lie to the High Court against any decision of a juvenile court under this Part of this Act.]

AMENDMENT

This section was inserted by the Health and Social Services and Social Security Adjudications Act 1983, s.6, Sched. 1.

[Variation and discharge of access orders

12D.—(1) Where an access order has been made—

(*a*) the parent, guardian or custodian named in the order; or

(*b*) the local authority,

may apply for the variation or discharge of the order.

(2) An application under this section shall be made by way of complaint to an appropriate juvenile court.]

AMENDMENT

This section was inserted by the Health and Social Services and Social Security Adjudications Act 1983, s.6, Sched. 1.

[Emergency orders

12E.—(1) A qualified justice of the peace may make an order under this subsection where he is satisfied that continued access to a child by its parent, guardian or custodian in accordance with the terms of an access order will put the child's welfare seriously at risk.

(2) Subject to subsection (3) below, an order under subsection (1) above shall be an order suspending the operation of an access order for 7 days beginning with the date of the order under subsection (1) above, or for such shorter period beginning with that date as may be specified in that order.

(3) If during the period for which the operation of the access order is suspended the local authority make an application for its variation or discharge to an appropriate juvenile court, its operation shall be suspended until the date on which the application to vary or discharge it is determined or abandoned.

(4) An application for an order under subsection (1) above may be made ex parte.

(5) A justice of the peace is a qualified justice of the peace for the purposes of this section if he is a member of a juvenile court panel formed under Schedule 2 to the Children and Young Persons Act 1933.]

AMENDMENT

This section was inserted by the Health and Social Services and Social Security Act 1983, s.6, Sched. 1.

[Safeguarding of interest of child

12F.—(1) A court—

(*a*) to which an application for an access order or any other application under this Part of this Act is made; or

(*b*) to which an appeal under this Part of this Act is brought,

shall regard the welfare of the child as the first and paramount consideration in determining the matter.

(2) In any proceedings before a court under this Part of this Act the court may, where it considers it necessary in order to safeguard the interests of the child, by order make the child a party to the proceedings.

(3) If the court makes the child a party to the proceedings, it shall in accordance with rules of court appoint a guardian ad litem of the child for the purposes of the proceedings unless it is satisfied that to do so is not necessary for safeguarding the interests of the child.

(4) A guardian ad litem appointed in pursuance of this section shall be under a duty to safeguard the interests of the child in the manner prescribed by rules of court.]

AMENDMENT
This section was inserted by the Health and Social Services and Social Security Adjudications Act 1983, s.6, Sched. 1.

[Code of practice

12G.—(1) The Secretary of State shall prepare, and from time to time revise, a code of practice with regard to access to children in care.

(2) Before preparing the code or making any alternation in it the Secretary of State shall consult such bodies as appear to him to be concerned.

(3) The Secretary of State shall lay copies of the code and of any alteration in the code before Parliament; and if either House of Parliament passes a resolution requiring the code or any alteration in it to be withdrawn the Secretary of State shall withdraw the code or alteration and, where he withdraws the code, shall prepare a code in substitution for the one which is withdrawn.

(4) No resolution shall be passed by either House of Parliament under subsection (3) above in respect of a code or alteration after the expiration of the period of 40 days beginning with the day on which a copy of the code or alteration was laid before the House; but for the purposes of this subsection no account shall be taken of any time during which Parliament is dissolved or prorogued or during which both Houses are adjourned for more than four days.

(5) The Secretary of State shall publish the code as for the time being in force.]

AMENDMENT
This section was inserted by the Health and Social Services and Social Security Adjudications Act 1983, s.6, Sched. 1.

PART II

ABSENCE FROM CARE

Provisions relating to children in care of local authorities under section 2

Penalty for assisting children in care under s.2 to run away etc.

13.—(1) Any person who—
  (*a*) knowingly assists or induces or persistently attempts to induce a child to whom this subsection applies to run away, or
  (*b*) without lawful authority takes away such a child, or
  (*c*) knowingly harbours or conceals such a child who has run away or who has been taken away or prevents him from returning,
shall be guilty of an offence and liable on summary conviction to a fine not exceeding £400 or to imprisonment for a term not exceeding three months or to both.

This subsection applies to any child in the care of a local authority under section 2 of this Act with respect to whom a resolution is in force under section 3 of this Act and for whom accommodation (whether in a home or otherwise) is being provided by the local authority in pursuance of Part III of this Act.

(2) Except in relation to an act done—

    (*a*) with the consent of the local authority or

    (*b*) by a parent or guardian of the child in relation to whom no resolution under section 3 of this Act is in force with respect to the child and who has given the local authority not less than 28 days' notice in writing of his intention to do it.]

subsection (1) above shall apply to a child in the care of a local authority under section 2 of this Act ([whether or not a] resolution is in force under section 3 of this Act with respect to the child) if he has been in the care of that local authority throughout the preceding six months; and for the purposes of the application of paragraph (*b*) of that subsection in such a case a parent or guardian of the child shall not be taken to have lawful authority to take him away.

(3) References in subsection (1) above to running away or taking away or to returning are references to running away or taking away from, or to returning to, a place where accommodation is or was being provided in pursuance of Part III of this Act by the local authority in whose care the child is.

(4) Where an order of any court is in force giving custody of a child to any person, this section shall have effect in relation to that child as if for references to a parent or guardian of the child there were substituted references to that person.

(5) The Secretary of State may by order a draft of which has been approved by each House of Parliament amend subsection (2) above by substituting a different period for the period of twenty-eight days or of six months mentioned in that subsection, or by substituting a different period for any period substituted by a previous order under this subsection.

AMENDMENT

    In subs. (2) the words in square brackets were substituted by the Health and Social Services and Social Security Adjudications Act 1983, s.9, Sched. 2, para. 48.

Harbouring or concealing child required to return to local authority

14. Where a local authority have, in accordance with section 21(2) of this Act, allowed any person to take charge of a child with respect to whom a resolution under section 3 of this Act is in force and have by notice in writing required that person to return the child at a time specified in the notice (which, if that person has been allowed to take charge of the child for a fixed period, shall not be earlier than the end of that period) any person who harbours or conceals the child after that time or prevents him from returning as required by the notice shall be guilty of an offence and liable on summary conviction to a fine not exceeding £100 or to imprisonment for a term not exceeding two months or to both.

Recovery of children in care under s.2

15.—(1) This section applies to a child—

    (*a*) who is in the care of a local authority under section 2 of this Act; and

    (*b*) with respect to whom there is in force a resolution under section 3 of this Act; and

    (*c*) who—

        (i) has run away from accommodation provided for him by the local authority under Part III of this Act; or

(ii) has been taken away from such accommodation contrary
to section 13(1) of this Act; or

(iii) has not been returned to the local authority as required by
a notice served under section 14 of this Act on a person
under whose charge and control the child was, in accordance with section 21(2) of this Act, allowed to be.

(2) If a justice of the peace is satisfied by information on oath that there
are reasonable grounds for believing that a person specified in the
information can produce a child to whom this section applies, he may issue a
summons directed to the person so specified and requiring him to attend and
produce the child before a magistrates' court acting for the same petty
sessions area as the justice.

(3) Without prejudice to the powers under subsection (2) above, if a
justice of the peace is satisfied by information on oath that there are
reasonable grounds for believing that a child to whom this section applies is
in premises specified in the information, he may issue a search warrant
authorising a person named in the warrant, being an officer of the local
authority in whose care the child is, to search the premises for the child; and
if the child is found, he shall be placed in such accommodation as the local
authority may provide for him under Part III of this Act.

(4) A person who, without reasonable excuse, fails to comply with a
summons under subsection (2) above shall, without prejudice to any liability
apart from this subsection, be guilty of an offence and liable on summary
conviction to a fine not exceeding £100.

*Provisions relating to children in care of local authorities by virtue of care order
etc.*

Recovery of children subject to care order etc.

    16.—(1) If any child.

(a) who is committed to the care of a local authority by a care order
or by a warrant under section 23(1) of the Children and Young
Persons Act 1969 (which relates to remands to the care of local
authorities); or

(b) who is in the care of a local authority in pursuance of
arrangements under section 29(3) of that Act (which relates to
the detention of arrested children),

is absent from the premises at which he is required by the local authority to
live at a time when he is not permitted by the local authority to be absent
from the premises, he may be arrested by a constable anywhere in the
United Kingdom or the Channel Islands without a warrant and shall if so
arrested be conducted, at the expense of the authority, to those premises or
such other premises as the authority may direct.

(2) If a magistrates' court is satisfied by information on oath that there are
reasonable grounds for believing that a person specified in the information
can produce a child who is absent as mentioned in subsection (1) above, the
court may issue a summons directed to the person so specified and requiring
him to attend and produce the absent child before the court; and a person
who without reasonable excuse fails to comply with any such requirement
shall, without prejudice to any liability apart from this subsection, be guilty
of an offence and liable on summary conviction to a fine not exceeding £100.

(3) Without prejudice to its powers under subsection (2) above a
magistrates' court may, if it is satisfied by information on oath that there are

reasonable grounds for believing that a child who is absent as mentioned in subsection (1) above is in premises specified in the information, issue a search warrant authorising a constable to search the premises for that child.

(4) A person who knowingly compels, persuades, incites or assists a child to become or continue to be absent as mentioned in subsection (1) above shall be guilty of an offence and liable on summary conviction to imprisonment for a term not exceeding six months or to a fine not exceeding £400 or to both.

(5) The reference to a constable in subsections (1) and (3) above includes a reference to a person who is a constable under the law of any part of the United Kingdom, to a member of the police in Jersey and to an officer of police within the meaning of section 43 of the Larceny (Guernsey) Law 1958 or any corresponding law for the time being in force.

(6) In the application of subsections (2) and (3) above to Northern Ireland, "magistrates' court" means a magistrates' court within the meaning of the Magistrates' Courts Act (Northern Ireland) 1964.

PART III

TREATMENT OF CHILDREN WHO ARE OR HAVE BEEN IN CARE OF LOCAL AUTHORITIES

Children to whom Part III applies

17. Except where the contrary intention appears, any reference in this Part of this Act to a child who is or was in the care of a local authority is a reference to a child who is or was in the care of the authority under section 2 of this Act or by virtue of a care order or a warrant under section 23(1) of the Children and Young Persons Act 1969 (which relates to remands to the care of local authorities).

General duty of local authority in relation to children in their care

18.—(1) In reaching any decision relating to a child in their care, a local authority shall give first consideration to the need to safeguard and promote the welfare of the child throughout his childhood; and shall so far as practicable ascertain the wishes and feelings of the child regarding the decision and give due consideration to them, having regard to his age and understanding.

(2) In providing for a child in their care a local authority shall make such use of facilities and services available for children in the care of their own parents as appears to the local authority reasonable in his case.

(3) If it appears to the local authority that it is necessary, for the purpose of protecting members of the public, to exercise their powers in relation to a particular child in their care in a manner which may not be consistent with their duty under subsection (1) above, the authority may, notwithstanding that duty, act in that manner.

Power of Secretary of State to give directions to local authority for protection of public

19. If the Secretary of State considers it necessary, for the purpose of protecting members of the public, to give directions to a local authority with respect to the exercise of their powers in relation to a particular child in their care, he may give such directions to the authority; and it shall be the duty of the authority, notwithstanding their general duty under section 18(1) of this Act, to comply with any such directions.

Review of care cases

20.—(1) Without prejudice to their general duty under section 18(1) of this Act, it shall be the duty of a local authority to review the case of each child in their care in accordance with regulations made under subsection (2) below.

(2) The Secretary of State may by regulations make provision as to—

(a) the manner in which cases are to be reviewed under this section;

(b) the considerations to which the local authority are to have regard in reviewing cases under this section; and

(c) the time when a child's case is first to be reviewed and the frequency of subsequent reviews under this section.

Provision of accommodation and maintenance for children in care

21.—(1) A local authority shall discharge their duty to provide accommodation and maintenance for a child in their care in such one of the following ways as they think fit, namely,—

(a) by boarding him out on such terms as to payment by the authority and otherwise as the authority may, subject to the provisions of this Act and regulations thereunder, determine; or

(b) by maintaining him in a community home or in any such home as is referred to in section 80 of this Act; or

(c) by maintaining him in a voluntary home (other than a community home) the managers of which are willing to receive him;

or by making such other arrangements as seem appropriate to the local authority [and shall secure, subject to section 18 of this Act, that any accommodation which they provide is, so far as practicable, near the child's home].

(2) Without prejudice to the generality of subsection (1) above [but subject to section 20A of the Children and Young Persons Act 1969 (power of court to add condition as to charge and control)], a local authority may allow a child in their care, either for a fixed period or until the local authority otherwise determine, to be under the charge and control of a parent, guardian, relative or friend.

(3) The terms, as to payment and other matters, on which a child may be accommodated and maintained in any such home as is referred to in section 80 of this Act shall be such as the Secretary of State may from time to time determine.

AMENDMENT

In subs. (1) the words in square brackets were added by the Health and Social Services and Social Security Adjudications Act 1983, s.9, Sched. 2, para. 49.

In subs. (2) the words in square brackets were substituted by the Criminal Justice Act 1982, Sched. 14, para. 45.

[Use of accommodation for restricting liberty

21A.—(1) Subject to the following provisions of this section, a child in the care of a local authority may not be placed, and, if placed, may not be kept, in accommodation provided for the purpose of restricting liberty unless it appears—

(*a*) that—
    (i) he has a history of absconding and is likely to abscond from any other description of accommodation; and
    (ii) if he absconds, it is likely that his physical, mental or moral welfare will be at risk; or
(*b*) that if he is kept in any other description of accommodation he is likely to injure himself or other persons.

(2) The Secretary of State may by regulations—
    (*a*) specify—
        (i) a maximum period beyond which a child may not be kept in such accommodation without the authority of a juvenile court; and
        (ii) a maximum period for which a juvenile court may authorise a child to be kept in such accommodation;
    (*b*) empower a juvenile court from time to time to authorise a child to be kept in such accommodation for such further period as the regulations may specify; and
    (*c*) provide that applications to a juvenile court under this section shall be made by local authorities.

(3) It shall be the duty of a juvenile court before which a child is brought by virtue of this section to determine whether any relevant criteria for keeping a child in accommodation provided for the purpose of restricting liberty are satisfied in his case; and if a court determines that any such criteria are satisfied, it shall make an order authorising the child to be kept in such accommodation and specifying the maximum period for which he may be so kept.

(4) On any adjournment of a hearing under subsection (3) above a juvenile court may make an interim order permitting the child to be kept during the period of the adjournment in accommodation provided for the purpose of restricting liberty.

(5) An appeal shall lie to the Crown Court from a decision of a juvenile court under this section.

(6) A juvenile court shall not exercise the powers conferred by this section in respect of a child who is not legally represented in that court unless either—
    (*a*) he applied for legal aid and the application was refused on the ground that it did not appear his means were such that he required assistance; or
    (*b*) having been so informed of his right to apply for legal aid and had the opportunity to do so, he refused or failed to apply.

(7) The Secretary of State may be regulations provide—
    (*a*) that this section shall or shall not apply to any description of children specified in the regulations;
    (*b*) that this section shall have effect in relation to children of a description specified in the regulations subject to such modifications as may be so specified.
    (*c*) that such other provisions as may be so specified shall have effect for the purpose of determining whether a child of a description specified in the regulations may be placed or kept in accommodation provided for the purpose of restricting liberty.

(8) The giving of an authorisation under this section shall not prejudice any power of any court in England and Wales or Scotland to give directions relating to the child to whom the authorisation relates.]

AMENDMENT
    This section was substituted by the Health and Social Services and Social Security Adjudications Act 1983, s.9, Sched. 2, para. 50.

Regulations as to boarding out

22.—(1) The Secretary of State may by regulations make provision for the welfare of children boarded out by local authorities under section 21(1)(*a*) of this Act.

(2) Without prejudice to the generality of subsection (1) above, regulations under this section may provide—

   (*a*) for the recording by local authorities of information relating to persons with whom children are boarded out under section 21(1)(*a*) of this Act and persons who are willing to have children so boarded out with them;

   (*b*) for securing that children shall not be boarded out in any household unless that household is for the time being approved by such local authority as may be prescribed by the regulations;

   (*c*) for securing that where possible the person with whom any child is to be boarded out is either of the same religious persuasion as the child or gives an undertaking that the child will be brought up in that religious persuasion;

   (*d*) for securing that children boarded out under section 21(1)(*a*) of this Act, and the premises in which they are boarded out, will be supervised and inspected by a local authority and that the children will be removed from those premises if their welfare appears to require it.

Power of local authority to guarantee apprenticeship deeds etc. of children in their care

23. While a child is in the care of a local authority under section 2 of this Act, the local authority may undertake any obligation by way of guarantee under any deed of apprenticeship or articles of clerkship entered into by that child; and where the local authority have undertaken any such obligation under any deed or articles they may at any time (whether or not the person concerned is still in their care) undertake the like obligation under any deed or articles supplemental thereto.

Power of local authorities to arrange for emigration of children

24.—(1) A local authority may, with the consent of the Secretary of State, procure or assist in procuring the emigration of any child in their care.

(2) Subject to subsection (3) below, the Secretary of State shall not give his consent under this section unless he is satisfied that emigration would benefit the child and that suitable arrangements have been or will be made for the child's reception and welfare in the country to which he is going, that the parents or guardians of the child have been consulted or that it is not practicable to consult them, and that the child consents.

(3) Where a child is too young to form or express a proper opinion on the matter, the Secretary of State may consent to his emigration notwithstanding that the child is unable to consent thereto in any case where the child is to emigrate in company with a parent, guardian [relative or friend] of his, or is to emigrate for the purpose of joining a parent, guardian, relative or friend.

(4) In subsection (2) above the reference to the parents or guardians of a child shall be construed as a reference to all the persons who are parents of the child or who are guardians of the child.

(5) Section 56 of the Adoption Act 1976 (which requires the authority of an order under section 55 of that Act or section 49 of the Adoption

(Scotland) Act 1978 for the taking or sending abroad for adoption of a child who is a British subject) shall not apply in the case of any child emigrating with the consent of the Secretary of State given under this section.

AMENDMENT
In subs. (3) the words in square brackets were substituted by the Health and Social Services and Social Security Adjudications Act 1983, s.9, Sched. 2, para.51.

Power of local authority to defray expenses of parents etc. visiting children or attending funerals

26. A local authority may make payments to any parent or guardian of, or other person connected with, a child in their care in respect of travelling, subsistence or other expenses incurred by the parent, guardian or other person in visiting the child or attending his funeral, if it appears to the authority that the parent, guardian or other person would not otherwise be able to visit the child or attend the funeral without undue hardship and that the circumstances warrant the making of the payments.

Financial assistance towards expenses of maintenance, education, or training of persons over seventeen

27.—(1) A local authority may make contributions to the cost of the accommodation and maintenance of any person to whom this subsection applies in any place near the place where he may be employed, or seeking employment, or in receipt of education or training.

This subsection applies to any person over compulsory school age but under the age of twenty-one who is, or has at any time after ceasing to be of compulsory school age been, in the care of a local authority being either—

(a) a person who has attained the age of seventeen but has not attained the age of eighteen and who has ceased to be in the care of a local authority; or

(b) a person who has attained the age of eighteen.

(2) A local authority may make grants to any person to whom this subsection applies to enable him to meet expenses connected with his receiving suitable education or training.

This subsection applies to any person who has attained the age of seventeen but has not attained the age of twenty-one and who at or after the time when he attained the age of seventeen was in the care of a local authority.

(3) Where a person—

(a) is engaged in a course of education or training at the time when he attains the age of twenty-one; or

(b) having previously been engaged in a course of education or training which has been interrupted by any circumstances, resumes the course as soon as practicable,

then, if a local authority, are at that time, or were at the time, when the course was interrupted, as the case may be, making any contributions or grants in respect of him under subsection (1) or (2) above, their powers under those subsections shall continue with respect to him until the completion of the course.

After-care of children formerly in care of local authorities under s.2

28.—(1) Where it comes to the knowledge of a local authority that there is in their area any child over compulsory school age who at the time when he ceased to be of that age or at any subsequent time was, but is no longer, in the care of a local authority under section 2 of this Act, then, unless the authority are satisfied that the welfare of the child does not require it, they shall be under a duty so long as he has not attained the age of eighteen to advise and befriend him.

(2) Where a child over compulsory school age ceases to be in the care of a local authority under section 2 of this Act and proposes to reside in the area of another local authority, the first mentioned local authority shall inform that other local authority.

(3) Where it comes to the knowledge of a local authority that a child whom they have been befriending in pursuance of this section proposes to transfer or has transferred his residence, to the area of another local authority, the first mentioned local authority shall inform that other local authority.

Power of local authority to visit and assist persons formerly in their care

29. Where a person was at or after the time when he attained the age of seventeen in the care of a local authority under section 2 of this Act but has ceased to be in their care, then, while he is under the age of twenty-one, the local authority, if so requested by him, may cause him to be visited, advised and befriended and, in exceptional circumstances, to be given financial assistance.

Allocation of functions as between local authority and local education authority

30. The Secretary of State for Social Services, the Secretary of State for Education and Science and the Secretary of State for Wales acting jointly may make regulations for providing, where a local authority under this Part of this Act and a local education authority as such have concurrent functions, by which authority the functions are to be exercised, and for determining as respects any functions of a local education authority specified in the regulations whether a child in the care of a local authority is to be treated as a child of parents of sufficient resources or a child of parents without resources.

   (*a*)   to an assisted community home; or
   (*b*)   to a controlled community home which, at any time before the instrument of management came into force, was an assisted community home,

then, on the home ceasing to be a community home, the voluntary organisation by which the home was provided or, as the case may be, the trustees of the home, shall pay to the Secretary of State a sum equal to that part of the value of the premises and any other property used for the purposes of the home which is attributable to the expenditure of money provided by way of grant under section 82 of this Act.

(5) Where an instrument of management has ceased to have effect as mentioned in subsection (1) above and the controlled or assisted community home to which it related was conducted in premises which formerly were used as an approved school were an approved probation hostel or home [. . .] then, on the home ceasing to be a community home, the voluntary organisation by which the home was provided or, as the case may be, the trustees of the home, shall pay to the Secretary of State a sum equal to that part of the value of the premises concerned and of any other property used for the purposes of the home and belonging to the voluntary organisation or the trustees of the home which is attributable to the expenditure—

(*a*) of sums paid towards the expenses of the managers of an approved school under section 104 of the Children and Young Persons Act 1933; or

(*b*) of sums paid under section 51(3)(*c*) of the Powers of Criminal Courts Act 1973 in relation to expenditure on approved probation hostels or homes.

(6) The amount of any sum payable under this section by the voluntary organisation by which a controlled or assisted community home was provided or by the trustees of the home shall be determined in accordance with such arrangements—

(*a*) as may be agreed between the voluntary organisation by which the home was provided and the local authority concerned or, as the case may be, the Secretary of State; or

(*b*) in default of agreement, as may be determined by the Secretary of State;

and with the agreement of the local authority concerned or the Secretary of State, as the case may be, the liability to pay any sum under this section may be discharged, in whole or in part, by the transfer of any premises or other property used for the purposes of the home in question.

(7) The provisions of this section shall have effect notwithstanding anything in any trust deed for a controlled or assisted community home and notwithstanding the provisions of any enactment or instrument governing the disposition of the property of a voluntary organisation.

(8) Any sums received by the Secretary of State under this section shall be paid into the Consolidated Fund.

AMENDMENTS

In subs. (5) the words omitted were repealed by the Health and Social Services and Social Security Adjudications Act 1983, s.30(1), Sched. 10, Pt. I.

In subs. (1) the words in square brackets were inserted by *ibid.*, s.9, Sched. 2, para. 53.

PART V

CONTRIBUTIONS TOWARDS MAINTENANCE OF CHILDREN IN CARE OF LOCAL AUTHORITIES

Liability for contributions in respect of children in care

45.—(1) Where—

(*a*) a child is in the care of a local authority under section 2 of this Act, or

(*b*) a child is in the care of a local authority by virtue of a care order (other than an interim order),

the following persons (and no others) shall be liable to make contributions in respect of the child, that is to say—

(i) [Subject to subsection (1A) below] if the child has not attained the age of sixteen, the father [and] mother of the child, and

(ii) if the child has attained the age of sixteen [. . .], the child himself.

[(1A)) A person shall not be liable under subsection (1)(i) above to make any contribution during any period when he is—

(*a*) in receipt of benefits under the Supplementary Benefits Act 1976; and

(*b*) in receipt of a family income supplement under the Family Income Supplements Act 1970.]

(2) Any contribution which any person is required to make under

subsection (1) above shall be payable to the local authority for the area in which that person is for the time being residing.

(3) Whether or not a contribution order has been made under section 47 of this Act in respect of any child in the care of a local authority, no contribution shall be payable in respect of him for any period during which he is allowed by the local authority to be under the charge and control of a parent, guardian, relative or friend, although remaining in the care of the local authority.

(4) Where a contribution order is made under section 47 of this Act requiring the father or mother of the child to make contributions in respect of the child, no payments shall be required to be made under the order in respect of any period after the child has attained the age of sixteen.

AMENDMENTS
In this section the words in square brackets were inserted and substituted, and the words omitted were repealed, by the Health and Social Services and Social Security Adjudications Act 1983, ss.9, 30(1), Sched. 2, para. 54, Sched. 10, Pt. I. Subs. (1A) was inserted by *ibid.* s.19(2).

Powers and duties of local authorities

Accommodation of persons over school age in convenient community home

72. A local authority may provide accommodation in a community home for any person who is over compulsory school age but has not attained the age of twenty-one if the community home is provided for children who are over compulsory school age and is near the place where that person is employed or seeking employment or receiving education or training.

Interpretation

87.—(1) In this Act, unless the context otherwise requires—
  "arrears order" has the meaning assigned to it by section 51 of this Act;
  "care order" has the meaning assigned to it by section 20 of the Children and Young Persons Act 1969;
  "child" means a person under the age of eighteen years and any person who has attained that age and is the subject of a care order;
  "commission area" has the same meaning as in section 1 of the Justices of the Peace Act 1979;
  "compulsory school age" has the same meaning as in the Education Act 1944;
  "contribution order" has the meaning assigned to it by section 47 of this Act;
  "functions" includes powers and duties;
  "guardian" means a person appointed by deed or will or by order of a court of competent jurisdiction to be the guardian of a child;
  "hospital" has the meaning assigned to it by section 128(1) of the National Health Service Act 1977;
  "instrument of management" means an instrument of management made under section 35 of this Act;
  "interim order", in relation to a care order, has the meaning assigned to it by section 20 of the Children and Young Persons Act 1969;
  "local authority" means the council of a county (other than a metropolitan county), of a metropolitan district or of a London borough or the Common Council of the City of London;
  "local education authority" means a local education authority for the purposes of the Education Act 1944;

"parent", in relation to a child who is illegitimate, means his mother, to the exclusion of his father;

[...];

[...];

"relative", in relation to a child, means a grand-parent, brother, sister, uncle or aunt, whether of the full blood, or the half blood, or by affinity, and includes, where the child is illegitimate, the father of the child and any person who would be a relative of the child within the meaning of this definition if the child were the legitimate child of his mother and father;

[...];

"supervision requirement" has the same meaning as in the Social Work (Scotland) Act 1968;

"trust deed" has the meaning assigned to it by section 36 of this Act;

"voluntary home" has the meaning assigned to it by section 56 of this Act;

"voluntary organisation" means a body the activities of which are carried on otherwise than for profit, but does not include any public or local authority.

(2) Any reference in this Act to an enactment of the Parliament of Northern Ireland shall be construed as a reference to that enactment as amended by any Act of that Parliament or by any Measure of the Northern Ireland Assembly, whether passed before or after this Act, and to any enactment of that Parliament or Assembly for the time being in force which re-enacts the said enactment with or without modifications.

AMENDMENT
In subs. (1) the words omitted were repealed by the Health and Social Services and Social Security Adjudications Act 1983, s.30(1), Sched. 10, Pt. I.

Magistrates Courts Act 1980

(C. 43)

Restriction on fines in respect of young persons

36.—(1) Where a person under 17 years of age is found guilty by a magistrates' court of an offence for which, apart from this section, the court would have power to impose a fine of an amount exceeding £200, the amount of any fine imposed by the court shall not exceed [£400].

(2) In relation to a person under the age of 14 subsection (1) above shall have effect as if for the words "[£400]", in both the places where they occur, there were substituted the words "[£100]"; but this subsection shall cease to have effect on the coming into force of section 4 of the Children and Young Persons Act 1969 (which prohibits criminal proceedings against children).

AMENDMENTS
In this section the figures in square brackets were substituted by S.I. 1984 No. 447, art. 2(1), Sched. 1.

Sums adjudged to be paid by a conviction

Enforcement of fines imposed on young offenders

81.—(1) Where a magistrates' court would, but for [section 1 of the Criminal Justice Act 1982], have power to commit to prison a person under the age of 17 for a default consisting in failure to pay, or want of sufficient distress to satisfy, a sum adjudged to be paid by a conviction, the court may, subject to the following provisions of this section, make—

(*a*) an order requiring the defaulter's parent or guardian to enter into a recognizance to ensure that the defaulter pays so much of that sum as remains unpaid; or

(*b*) an order directing so much of that sum as remains unpaid to be paid by the defaulter's parent or guardian instead of by the defaulter.

(2) An order under subsection (1) above shall not be made in respect of a defaulter—

(*a*) in pursuance of paragraph (*a*) of that subsection, unless the parent or guardian in question consents;

(*b*) in pursuance of paragraph (*b*) of that subsection, unless the court is satisfied in all the circumstances that it is reasonable to make the order.

(3) None of the following orders, namely—

(*a*) an order under section 19(1) of the Criminal Justice Act 1948 for attendance at an attendance centre; or

(*b*) any order under subsection (1) above,

shall be made by a magistrates' court in consequence of a default of a person under the age of 17 years consisting in failure to pay, or want of sufficient distress to satisfy, a sum adjudged to be paid by a conviction unless the court has since the conviction inquired into the defaulter's means in his presence on at least one occasion.

(4) An order under subsection (1) above shall not be made by a magistrates' court unless the court is satisfied that the defaulter has, or has had since the date on which the sum in question was adjudged to be paid, the means to pay the sum or any instalment of it on which he has defaulted, and refuses or neglects or, as the case may be, has refused or neglected, to pay it.

(5) An order under subsection (1) above may be made in pursuance of paragraph (*b*) of that subsection against a parent or guardian who, having been required to attend, has failed to do so; but, save as aforesaid, an order under that subsection shall not be made in pursuance of that paragraph without giving the parent or guardian an opportunity of being heard.

(6) A parent or guardian may appeal to the Crown Court against an order under subsection (1) above made in pursuance of paragraph (*b*) of that subsection.

(7) Any sum ordered under subsection (1)(*b*) above to be paid by a parent or guardian may be recovered from him in like manner as if the order had been made on the conviction of the parent or guardian of an offence.

(8) In this section—

"guardian", in relation to a person under the age of 17, means a person appointed, according to law, to be his guardian by deed or will, or by order of a court of competent jurisdiction;

[. . .];

"sum adjudged to be paid by a conviction" means any fine, costs, compensation or other sum adjudged to be paid by an order made on a finding of guilt, including an order made under section 35 of the Powers of Criminal Courts Act 1973 (compensation orders) as applied by section 3(6) of the Children and Young Persons Act 1969.

AMENDMENTS
 The words in subs. (1) were substituted, and the words omitted in subs. (8) were repealed, by the Criminal Justice Act 1982, Sched. 14, para. 51, and Sched. 16.

Criminal Justice Act 1982

(1982 c. 48)

An Act to make further provision as to the sentencing and treatment of offenders (including provision as to the enforcement of fines and the standardisation of fines and of certain other sums specified in enactments relating to the powers of criminal courts); to make provision for the prescribing of criteria for the placing and keeping of children in different descriptions of accommodation in community homes; to amend the law of Scotland relating to the mode of trial of certain offences and the recall of witnesses; to amend the law of England and Wales relating to the remand in custody of accused persons and to the grant of bail to persons convicted or sentenced in the Crown Court; to abolish (subject to savings) the right of a person accused in criminal proceedings under the law of England and Wales to make an unsworn statement; and for connected purposes.   [28th October 1982]

PART 1

TREATMENT OF YOUNG OFFENDERS

Custody and detention of persons under 21

General restriction on custodial sentences

1.—(1) Subject to subsection (2) below, no court shall pass a sentence of imprisonment on a person under 21 years of age or commit such a person to prison for any reason.

(2) Nothing in subsection (1) above shall prevent the committal to prison of a person under 21 years of age who is remanded in custody or committed in custody for trial or sentence.

(3) No court shall pass a sentence of Borstal training.

(4) Where a person under 21 years of age is convicted or found guilty of an offence, the court may not—

(a) make a detention centre order in respect of him under section 4 below;

(b) pass a youth custody sentence on him under section 6 below; or

(c) pass a sentence of custody for life on him under section 8(2) below,

unless it is of the opinion that no other method of dealing with him is appropriate because it appears to the court that he is unable or unwilling to respond to non-custodial penalties or because a custodial sentence is necessary for the protection of the public or because the offence was so serious that a non-custodial sentence cannot be justified.

(5) No court shall commit a person under 21 years of age to be detained under section 9 below unless it is of the opinion that no other method of dealing with him is appropriate.

(6) For the purposes of any provision of this Act which requires the determination of the age of a person by the court or the Secretary of State his age shall be deemed to be that which it appears to the court or the Secretary of State (as the case may be) to be after considering any available evidence.

Social inquiry reports etc.

2.—(1) For the purpose of determining whether there is any appropriate method of dealing with a person under 21 years of age other than a method whose use in the case of such a person is restricted by section 1(4) or (5) above the court shall obtain and consider information about the circumstances and shall take into account any information before the court which is relevant to his character and his physical and mental condition.

(2) Subject to subsection (3) below, the court shall in every case obtain a social inquiry report for the purpose of determining whether there is any appropriate method of dealing with a person other than a method whose use is restricted by section 1(4) above.

(3) Subsection (2) above does not apply if, in the circumstances of the case, the court is of the opinion that it is unnecessary to obtain a social inquiry report.

(4) Where a magistrates' court deals with a person under 21 years of age by a method whose use in the case of such a person is restricted by section 1(4) above, it shall state in open court the reason for its opinion that no other method of dealing with him is appropriate because it appears to the court that he is unable or unwilling to respond to non-custodial penalties or because a custodial sentence is necessary for the protection of the public or because the offence was so serious that a non-custodial sentence cannot be justified.

(5) Where a magistrates' court deals with a person under 21 years of age by a method whose use in the case of such a person is restricted by section 1(5) above, it shall state in open court the reason for its opinion that no other method of dealing with him is appropriate.

(6) Where a magistrates' court deals with a person under 21 years of age by a method whose use in the case of such a person is restricted by section 1(4) above without obtaining a social inquiry report, it shall state in open court the reason for its opinion that it was unnecessary to obtain such a report.

(7) A magistrates' court shall cause a reason stated under subsection (4),

(5) or (6) above to be specified in the warrant of commitment and to be entered in the register.

(8) No sentence or order shall be invalidated by the failure of a court to comply with subsection (2) above, but any other court on appeal from that court shall obtain a social inquiry report if none was obtained by the court below, unless it is of the opinion that in the circumstances of the case it is unnecessary to do so.

(9) In determining whether it should deal with the appellant by a method different from that by which the court below dealt with him the court hearing the appeal shall consider any social inquiry report obtained by it or by the court below.

(10) In this section "social inquiry report" means a report about a person and his circumstances made by a probation officer or by a social worker of a local authority social services department.

Restriction on imposing custodial sentences on persons under 21 not legally represented

3.—(1) A magistrates' court on summary conviction or the Crown Court on committal for sentence or on conviction on indictment shall not—

(*a*) make a detention centre order under section 4 below;

(*b*) pass a youth custody sentence under section 6 below;

(*c*) pass a sentence of custody for life under section 8(2) below; or

(*d*) make an order for detention under section 53(2) of the Children and Young Persons Act 1933,

in respect of or on a person who is not legally represented in that court, unless either—

(i) he applied for legal aid and the application was refused on the ground that it did not appear his means were such that he required assistance; or

(ii) having been informed of his right to apply for legal aid and had the opportunity to do so, he refused or failed to apply.

(2) For the purposes of this section a person is to be treated as legally represented in a court if, but only if, he has the assistance of counsel or a solicitor to represent him in the proceedings in that court at some time after he is found guilty and before he is sentenced, and in subsection (1)(i) and (ii) above "legal aid" means legal aid for the purposes of proceedings in that court, whether the whole proceedings or the proceedings on or in relation to sentence; but in the case of a person committed to the Crown Court for sentence or trial, it is immaterial whether he applied for legal aid in the Crown Court to, or was informed of his right to apply by, that court or the court which committed him.

Orders for detention of male offenders aged 14 to 20

4.—(1) Where—

(*a*) a male offender under 21 but not less than 14 years of age is convicted of an offence which is punishable with imprisonment in the case of a person aged 21 or over; and

(*b*) the court considers—

(i) that the only appropriate method of dealing with him is to pass a custodial sentence on him; but

(ii) that the term of such a sentence should be no more than 4 months,

the order that the court is to make, subject to the provisions of this section and to section 5(2) below, is an order for his detention in a detention centre for such period, not exceeding 4 months, as it considers appropriate.

(2) If the maximum term of imprisonment that a court could impose for an offence is less than 4 months, the maximum term of detention it may specify for that offence in a detention centre order is the same as the maximum term of imprisonment.

(3) Subject to subsection (4) below, no order may be made under this section for the detention of an offender in a detention centre for less than 21 days.

(4) A court may order the detention of an offender in a detention centre for less than 21 days for an offence under section 15(11) below.

(5) Subject to subsection (6) below, a court shall not make an order under this section for the detention of an offender in a detention centre—

(a) if it considers that his detention in such a centre would be unsuitable because of his mental or physical conditions; or

(b) if he is serving or has ever served a sentence—

(i) of imprisonment;

(ii) of detention under section 53 of the Children and Young Persons Act 1933 (detention on conviction of certain grave crimes);

(iii) of Borstal training;

(iv) of youth custody under section 6 below; or

(v) of custody for life under section 8 below.

(6) A court may make an order under this section for the detention in a detention centre of an offender who has served a sentence of a description specified in subsection (5)(b) above if it appears to the court that there are special circumstances (whether relating to the offence or to the offender) which warrant the making of such an order in his case.

(7) An order under this section is referred to in this Act as a "detention centre order".

Consecutive terms and aggregate periods of detention

5.—(1) Subject to the provisions of this section, any court which makes a detention centre order may direct that the term of detention under the order shall commence on the expiration of a term of detention under another detention centre order.

(2) No court shall—

(a) make a detention centre order in respect of an offender who is subject to another such order; or

(b) give a direction under subsection (1) above,

if the effect would be that the offender would be ordered to be detained in a detention centre for more than 4 months at a time.

(3) If a court makes such an order or gives such a direction in respect of an offender aged less than 15 years, so much of the aggregate of all the terms of detention in a detention centre to which he is subject as exceeds 4 months shall be treated as remitted.

(4) If a court makes such an order or gives such a direction in respect of an offender aged 15 years or over, he shall be treated for all purposes as if he had been sentenced to a term of youth custody equal to the aggregate of all the terms of detention in a detention centre to which he is subject.

(5) Where—

    (*a*) an offender not less than 15 years of age is serving a term of detention in a detention centre; and

    (*b*) on his conviction of an offence the court by which he is convicted considers that the only appropriate method of dealing with him is to pass a custodial sentence on him; and

    (*c*) the length of sentence which the court considers apppropriate is such that the period for which he would be ordered to be detained by virtue of the sentence, together with the period for which any detention centre order to which he is subject directed that he should be detained, would exceed 4 months,

the sentence that the court is to pass is a youth custody sentence for the term which it considers appropriate.

(6) Where a court passes a youth custody sentence on an offender under subsection (5) above, it shall direct that any detention centre order to which he is subject at the time of the conviction for which the youth custody sentence is imposed shall be treated for all purposes as if it had been a sentence of youth custody.

(7) Where a detention centre order is treated as a sentence of youth custody by virtue of this section, the portion of the term of detention imposed by the order which the offender has already served shall be deemed to have been a portion of a term of youth custody.

Youth custody: offenders aged 15 to 20

6.—(1) Subject to section 8 below and to section 53 of the Children and Young Persons Act 1933, where—

    (*a*) a person under 21 but not less than 15 years of age is convicted of an offence which is punishable with imprisonment in the case of a person aged 21 or over; and

    (*b*) the court considers for reasons which shall be stated in open court that the only appropriate method of dealing with the offender is to pass a custodial sentence; and

    (*c*) either—

        (i) the court considers that it would be appropriate to sentence the offender to a term of more than 4 months, or where the offender has been convicted of more than one offence, to terms of more than 4 months in the aggregate; or

        (ii) the case falls within subsection (2) or (4) below,

the sentence that the court is to pass is a sentence of youth custody.

(2) A case falls within this subsection where the offender is male and the court determines—

    (*a*) that a sentence of 4 months or less would be appropriate; but

    (*b*) that a detention centre order is precluded by section 4(5) above.

(3) If a court passes a sentence of youth custody on an offender because it considers that his detention in a detention centre would be unsuitable because of his mental condition, it shall certify in the warrant of commitment that it passed the sentence of youth custody for that reason.

(4) A case falls within this subsection if the offender is female and has attained the age of 17 years.

(5) A sentence under this section is referred to in this Act as a "youth custody sentence".

Youth custody: length of term

7.—(1) Subject to subsection (8) below, the maximum term of youth custody that a court may impose for an offence is the same as the maximum term of imprisonment that it may impose for that offence.

(2) Subject to subsection (8) below, where—

(*a*) an offender is convicted of more than one offence for which he is liable to a sentence of youth custody; or

(*b*) an offender who is serving a youth custody sentence is convicted of one or more further offences for which he is liable to such a sentence,

the court shall have the same power to pass consecutive youth custody sentences as if they were sentences of imprisonment.

(3) Where an offender who—

(*a*) is serving a youth custody sentence; and

(*b*) is aged over 21 years.

is convicted of one or more further offences for which he is liable to imprisonment, the court shall have the power to pass one or more sentences of imprisonment to run consecutively upon the youth custody sentence.

(4) Subject to subsections (6) and (7) below, a court shall not pass a youth custody sentence on an offender whose effect would be that he would be sentenced to a total term which is less than the usual term of youth custody.

(5) The usual term of youth custody is a term exceeding 4 months.

(6) If a case falls within section 6(2) or (4) above, the term of youth custody to which the offender is sentenced may be less than the usual term but not less than 21 days.

(7) A court may pass a sentence of youth custody for less than 21 days for an offence under section 15(11) below.

(8) An offender aged less than 17 years shall not be sentenced to a term of youth custody which exceeds 12 months at a time; and accordingly—

(*a*) a court shall not pass a youth custody sentence on such an offender whose effect would be that he would be sentenced to a total term which exceeds 12 months; and

(*b*) so much of any such term for which such an offender is sentenced as exceeds 12 months shall be treated as remitted.

(9) In subsections (4) and (8)(*a*) above "total term" means—

(*a*) in the case of an offender sentenced to two or more terms of youth custody which are consecutive or wholly or partly concurrent, the aggregate of those terms;

(*b*) in the case of any other offender, the term of the youth custody sentence in question.

Custody for life

8.—(1) Where a person under the age of 21 is convicted of murder or any other offence the sentence for which is fixed by law as imprisonment for life, the court shall sentence him to custody for life unless he is liable to be detained under section 53(1) of the Children and Young Persons Act 1933 (detention of persons under 18 convicted of murder).

(2) Where a person aged 17 years or over but under the age of 21 is convicted of any other offence for which a person aged 21 years or over

would be liable to imprisonment for life, the court shall, if it considers that a custodial sentence for life would be appropriate, sentence him to custody for life.

Attendance centre orders

17.—(1) Subject to subsections (3) and (4) below, where a court—

   (*a*) would have power, but for section 1 above, to pass a sentence of imprisonment on a person who is under 21 years of age or to commit such a person to prison in default of payment of any sum of money or for failing to do or abstain from doing anything required to be done or left undone; or

   (*b*) has power to deal with any such person under section 6 of the Powers of Criminal Courts Act 1973 for failure to comply with any of the requirements of a probation order,

the court may, if it has been notified by the Secretary of State that an attendance centre is available for the reception of persons of his description, order him to attend at such a centre, to be specified in the order, for such number of hours as may be so specified.

(2) An order under this section is referred to in this Act as an "attendance centre order".

(3) No attendance centre order shall be made in the case of an offender who has been previously sentenced—

   (*a*) to imprisonment;

   (*b*) to detention under section 53 of the Children and Young Persons Act 1933;

   (*c*) to Borstal training;

   (*d*) to youth custody or custody for life under this Act; or

   (*e*) to detention in a detention centre,

unless it appears to the court that there are special circumstances (whether relating to the offence or to the offender) which warrant the making of such an order in his case.

(4) The aggregate number of hours for which an attendance centre order may require an offender to attend at an attendance centre shall not be less than 12 except where he is under 14 years of age and the court is of opinion that 12 hours would be excessive, having regard to his age or any other circumstances.

(5) The aggregate number of hours shall not exceed 12 except where the court is of opinion, having regard to all the circumstances, that 12 hours would be inadequate, and in that case shall not exceed 24 where the offender is under 17 years of age, or 36 hours where the offender is under 21 but not less than 17 years of age.

(6) A court may make an attendance centre order in respect of an offender before a previous attendance centre order made in respect of him has ceased to have effect, and may determine the number of hours to be specified in the order without regard—

   (*a*) to the number specified in the previous order; or

   (*b*) to the fact that that order is still in effect.

(7) An attendance centre order shall not be made unless the court is satisfied that the attendance centre to be specified in it is reasonably accessible to the person concerned, having regard to his age, the means of access available to him and any other circumstances.

(8) The times at which an offender is required to attend at an attendance centre shall be such as to avoid interference, so far as practicable, with his school hours or working hours.

(9) The first such time shall be a time at which the centre is available for the attendance of the offender in accordance with the notification of the Secretary of State and shall be specified in the order.

(10) The subsequent times shall be fixed by the officer in charge of the centre, having regard to the offender's circumstances.

(11) An offender shall not be required under this section to attend at an attendance centre on more than one occasion on any day, or for more than three hours on any occasion.

(12) Where a court makes an attendance centre order, the clerk of the court shall deliver or send a copy of the order to the officer in charge of the attendance centre specified in it, and shall also deliver a copy to the offender or send a copy by registered post or the recorded delivery service addressed to the offender's last or usual place of abode.

(13) Where an offender has been ordered to attend at an attendance centre in default of the payment of any sum of money—

(a) on payment of the whole sum to any person authorised to receive it, the attendance centre order shall cease to have effect;

(b) on payment of a part of the sum to any such person, the total number of hours for which the offender is required to attend at the centre shall be reduced proportionately, that is to say by such number of complete hours as bears to the total number the proportion most nearly approximately to, without exceeding, the proportion which the part bears to the said sum.

MENTAL HEALTH ACT 1983

(1983 c. 20)

An Act to consolidate the law relating to mentally disordered persons.

[May 9, 1983]

PART I

APPLICATION OF ACT

Application of Act: "mental disorder"

1.—(1) The provisions of this Act shall have effect with respect to the reception, care and treatment of mentally disordered patients, the management of their property and other related matters.

(2) In this Act—

"mental disorder" means mental illness, arrested or incomplete development of mind, psychopathic disorder and any other disorder or disability of mind and "mentally disordered" shall be construed accordingly;

"severe mental impairment" means a state of arrested or incomplete development of mind which includes severe impairment of intelligence and social functioning and is associated with abnormally aggressive or seriously irresponsible conduct on the part of the person concerned and "severely mentally impaired" shall be construed accordingly;

"mental impairment" means a state of arrested or incomplete development of mind (not amounting to severe mental impairment) which includes significant impairment of intelligence and social functioning and is associated with abnormally aggressive or seriously irresponsible conduct on the part of the person concerned and "mentally impaired" shall be construed accordingly;

"psychopathic disorder" means a persistent disorder or disability of mind (whether or not including significant impairment of intelligence) which results in abnormally aggressive or seriously irresponsible conduct on the part of the person concerned;

and other expressions shall have the meanings assigned to them in section 145 below.

(3) Nothing in subsection (2) above shall be construed as implying that a person may be dealt with under this Act as suffering from mental disorder, or from any form of mental disorder described in this section, by reason only of promiscuity or other immoral conduct, sexual deviancy or dependence on alcohol or drugs.

PART II

COMPULSORY ADMISSION TO HOSPITAL AND GUARDIANSHIP

Procedure for hospital admission

Admission for assessment

2.—(1) A patient may be admitted to a hospital and detained there for the period allowed by subsection (4) below in pursuance of an application (in this Act referred to as "an application for admission for assessment") made in accordance with subsections (2) and (3) below.

(2) An application for admission for assessment may be made in respect of a patient on the grounds that—

(*a*) he is suffering from mental disorder of a nature or degree which warrants the detention of the patient in a hospital for assessment (or for assessment followed by medical treatment) for at least a limited period; and

(*b*) he ought to be so detained in the interests of his own health or safety or with a view to the protection of other persons.

(3) An application for admission for assessment shall be founded on the written recommendations in the prescribed form of two registered medical practitioners, including in each case a statement that in the opinion of the practitioner the conditions set out in subsection (2) above are complied with.

(4) Subject to the provisions of section 29(4) below, a patient admitted to hospital in pursuance of an application for admission for assessment may be detained for a period not exceeding 28 days beginning with the day on which he is admitted, but shall not be detained after the expiration of that period unless before it has expired he has become liable to be detained by virtue of a subsequent application, order or direction under the following provisions of this Act.

Admission for treatment

3.—(1) A patient may be admitted to a hospital and detained there for the period allowed by the following provisions of this Act in pursuance of an application (in this Act referred to as "an application for admission for treatment) made in accordance with this section.

(2) An application for admission for treatment may be made in respect of a patient on the grounds that—

(*a*) he is suffering from mental illness, severe mental impairment, psychopathic disorder or mental impairment and his mental disorder is of a nature or degree which makes it appropriate for him to receive medical treatment in a hospital; and

(*b*) in the case of psychopathic disorder or mental impairment, such treatment is likely to alleviate or prevent a deterioration of his condition; and

(*c*) it is necessary for the health or safety of the patient or for the protection of other persons that he should receive such treatment and it cannot be provided unless he is detained under this section.

(3) An application for admission for treatment shall be founded on the written recommendations in the prescribed form of two registered medical practitioners, including in each case a statement that in the opinion of the practitioner the conditions set out in subsection (2) above are complied with; and each such recommendation shall include—

(*a*) such particulars as may be prescribed of the grounds for that opinion so far as it relates to the conditions set out in paragraphs (*a*) and (*b*) of that subsection; and

(*b*) a statement of the reasons for that opinion so far as it relates to the conditions set out in paragraph (*c*) of that subsection, specifying whether other methods of dealing with the patient are available and, if so, why they are not appropriate.

Admission for assessment in cases of emergency

4.—(1) In any case of urgent necessity, an application for admission for assessment may be made in respect of a patient in accordance with the following provisions of this section, and any application so made is in this Act referred to as "an emergency application"

(2) An emergency application may be made either by an approved social worker or by the nearest relative of the patient; and every such application shall include a statement that it is of urgent necessity for the patient to be admitted and detained under section 2 above, and that compliance with the provisions of this Part of this Act relating to applications under that section would involve undesirable delay.

(3) An emergency application shall be sufficient in the first instance if founded on one of the medical recommendations required by section 2 above, given, if practicable, by a practitioner who has previous acquaintance with the patient and otherwise complying with the requirements of section 12 below so far as applicable to a single recommendation, and verifying the statement referred to in subsection (2) above.

(4) An emergency application shall cease to have effect on the expiration of a period of 72 hours from the time when the patient is admitted to the hospital unless—

(*a*) the second medical recommendation required by section 2 above is given and received by the managers within that period; and

(*b*) that recommendation and the recommendation referred to in subsection (3) above together comply with all the requirements of section 12 below (other than the requirement as to the time of signature of the second recommendation).

(5) In relation to an emergency application, section 11 below shall have effect as if in subsection (5) of that section for the words "the period of 14 days ending with the date of the application" there were substituted the words "the previous 24 hours".

Application in respect of patient already in hospital

5.—(1) An application for the admission of a patient to a hospital may be made under this Part of this Act notwithstanding that the patient is already an in-patient in that hospital or, in the case of an application for admission for treatment that the patient is for the time being liable to be detained in the hospital in pursuance of an application for admission for assessment; and where an application is so made the patient shall be treated for the purposes of this Part of this Act as if he had been admitted to the hospital at the time when that application was received by the managers.

(2) If, in the case of a patient who is an in-patient in a hospital, it appears to the registered medical practitioner in charge of the treatment of the patient that an application ought to be made under this Part of this Act for the admission of the patient to hospital, he may furnish to the managers a report in writing to that effect; and in any such case the patient may be detained in the hospital for a period of 72 hours from the time when the report is so furnished.

(3) The registered medical practitioner in charge of the treatment of a patient in a hospital may nominate one (but not more than one) other registered medical practitioner on the staff of that hospital to act for him under subsection (2) above in his absence.

(4) If, in the case of a patient who is receiving treatment for mental disorder as an in-patient in a hospital, it appears to a nurse of the prescribed class—

(*a*) that the patient is suffering from mental disorder to such a degree that it is necessary for his health or safety or for the protection of others for him to be immediately restrained from leaving the hospital; and

(*b*) that it is not practicable to secure the immediate attendance of a practitioner for the purpose of furnishing a report under subsection (2) above,

the nurse may record that fact in writing; and in that event the patient may be detained in the hospital for a period of six hours from the time when that fact is so recorded or until the earlier arrival at the place where the patient is detained of a practitioner having power to furnish a report under that subsection.

(5) A record made under subsection (4) above shall be delivered by the nurse (or by a person authorised by the nurse in that behalf) to the managers of the hospital as soon as possible after it is made; and where a record is made under that subsection the period mentioned in subsection (2) above shall begin at the time when it is made.

(6) The reference in subsection (1) above to an in-patient does not include an in-patient who is liable to be detained in pursuance of an application under this Part of this Act and the references in subsections (2) and (4) above do not include an in-patient who is liable to be detained in a hospital under this Part of this Act.

(7) In subsection (4) above "prescribed" means prescribed by an order made by the Secretary of State.

Effect of application for admission

6.—(1) An application for the admission of a patient to a hospital under this Part of this Act, duly completed in accordance with the provisions of this Part of this Act, shall be sufficient authority for the applicant, or any person authorised by the applicant, to take the patient and convey him to the hospital at any time within the following period, that is to say—

(*a*) in the case of an application other than an emergency application, the period of 14 days beginning with the date on which the patient was last examined by a registered medical practitioner before giving a medical recommendation for the purposes of the application;

(*b*) in the case of an emergency application, the period of 24 hours beginning at the time when the patient was examined by the practitioner giving the medical recommendation which is referred to in section 4(3) above, or at the time when the application is made, whichever is the earlier.

(2) Where a patient is admitted within the said period to the hospital specified in such an application as is mentioned in subsection (1) above, or, being within that hospital, is treated by virtue of section 5 above as if he had been so admitted, the application shall be sufficient authority for the managers to detain the patient in the hospital in accordance with the provisions of this Act.

(3) Any application for the admission of a patient under this Part of this Act which appears to be duly made and to be founded on the necessary medical recommendations may be acted upon without further proof of the signature or qualification of the person by whom the application or any such medical recommendation is made or given or of any matter of fact or opinion stated in it.

(4) Where a patient is admitted to a hospital in pursuance of an application for admission for treatment, any previous application under this Part of this Act by virtue of which he was liable to be detained in a hospital or subject to guardianship shall cease to have effect.

Guardianship

Application for guardianship

7.—(1) A patient who has attained the age of 16 years may be received into guardianship, for the period allowed by the following provisions of this Act, in pursuance of an application (in this Act referred to as "a guardianship application") made in accordance with this section.

(2) A guardianship application may be made in respect of a patient on the grounds that—

(*a*) he is suffering from mental disorder, being mental illness, severe mental impairment, psychopathic disorder or mental impairment and his mental disorder is of a nature or degree which warrants his reception into guardianship under this section; and

(*b*) it is necessary in the interests of the welfare of the patient or for the protection of other persons that the patient should be so received.

(3) A guardianship application shall be founded on the written recommendations in the prescribed form of two registered medical practitioners, including in each case a statement that in the opinion of the

practitioner the conditions set out in subsection (2) above are complied with; and each such recommendation shall include—

(*a*) such particulars as may be prescribed of the grounds for that opinion so far as it relates to the conditions set out in paragraph (*a*) of that subsection; and

(*b*) a statement of the reasons for that opinion so far as it relates to the conditions set out in paragraph (*b*) of that subsection.

(4) A guardianship application shall state the age of the patient or, if his exact age is not known to the applicant, shall state (if it be the fact) that the patient is believed to have attained the age of 16 years.

(5) The person named as guardian in a guardianship application may be either a local social services authority or any other person (including the applicant himself); but a guardianship application in which a person other than a local social services authority is named as guardian shall be of no effect unless it is accepted on behalf of that person by the local social services authority for the area in which he resides, and shall be accompanied by a statement in writing by that person that he is willing to act as guardian.

Effect of guardianship application, etc.

8.—(1) Where a guardianship application, duly made under the provisions of this Part of this Act and forwarded to the local social services authority within the period allowed by subsection (2) below is accepted by that authority, the application shall, subject to regulations made by the Secretary of State, confer on the authority or person named in the application as guardian, to the exclusion of any other person—

(*a*) the power to require the patient to reside at a place specified by the authority or person named as guardian;

(*b*) the power to require the patient to attend at places and times so specified for the purpose of medical treatment, occupation, education or training;

(*c*) the power to require access to the patient to be given, at any place where the patient is residing, to any registered medical practitioner, approved social worker or other person so specified.

(2) The period within which a guardianship application is required for the purposes of this section to be forwarded to the local social services authority is the period of 14 days beginning with the date on which the patient was last examined by a registered medical practitioner before giving a medical recommendation for the purposes of the application.

(3) A guardianship application which appears to be duly made and to be founded on the necessary medical recommendations may be acted upon without further proof of the signature or qualification of the person by whom the application or any such medical recommendation is made or given, or of any matter of fact or opinion stated in the application.

(4) If within the period of 14 days beginning with the day on which a guardianship application has been accepted by the local social services authority the application, or any medical recommendation given for the purposes of the application, is found to be in any respect incorrect or defective, the application or recommendation may, within that period and with the consent of that authority, be amended by the person by whom it was signed; and upon such amendment being made the application or recommendation shall have effect and shall be deemed to have had effect as if it had been originally made as so amended.

(5) Where a patient is received into guardianship in pursuance of a

guardianship application, any previous application under this Part of this Act by virtue of which he was subject to guardianship or liable to be detained in a hospital shall cease to have effect.

Regulations as to guardianship

9.—(1) Subject to the provisions of this Part of this Act, the Secretary of State may make regulations—
  (a) for regulating the exercise by the guardians of patients received into guardianship under this Part of this Act of their powers as such; and
  (b) for imposing on such guardians, and upon local social services authorities in the case of patients under the guardianship of persons other than local social services authorities, such duties as he considers necessary or expedient in the interests of the patients.

(2) Regulations under this section may in particular make provision for requiring the patients to be visited, on such occasions or at such intervals as may be prescribed by the regulations, on behalf of such local social services authorities as may be so prescribed, and shall provide for the appointment, in the case of every patient subject to the guardianship of a person other than a local social services authority, of a registered medical practitioner to act as the nominated medical attendant of the patient.

Transfer of guardianship in case of death, incapacity, etc., of guardian

10.—(1) If any person (other than a local social services authority) who is the guardian of a patient received into guardianship under this Part of this Act—
  (a) dies; or
  (b) gives notice in writing to the local social services authority that he desires to relinquish the functions of guardian,
the guardianship of the patient shall thereupon vest in the local social services authority, but without prejudice to any power to transfer the patient into the guardianship of another person in pursuance of regulations under section 19 below.

(2) If any such person, not having given notice under subsection (1)(b) above, is incapacitated by illness or any other cause from performing the functions of guardian of the patient, those functions may, during his incapacity, be performed on his behalf by the local social services authority or by any other person approved for the purposes by that authority.

(3) If it appears to the county court, upon application made by an approved social worker, that any person other than a local social services authority having the guardianship of a patient received into guardianship under this Part of this Act has performed his functions negligently or in a manner contrary to the interests of the welfare of the patient, the court may order that the guardianship of the patient be transferred to the local social services authority or to any other person approved for the purpose by that authority.

(4) Where the guardianship of a patient is transferred to a local social services authority or other person by or under this section, subsection (2)(c) of section 19 below shall apply as if the patient had been transferred into the guardianship of that authority or person in pursuance of regulations under that section.

General provisions as to applications and recommendations

General provisions as to applications

11.—(1) Subject to the provisions of this section, an application for admission for assessment, an application for admission for treatment and a guardianship application may be made either by the nearest relative of the patient or by an approved social worker; and every such application shall specify the qualification of the applicant to make the application.

(2) Every application for admission shall be addressed to the managers of the hospital to which admission is sought and every guardianship application shall be forwarded to the local social services authority named in the application as guardian, or, as the case may be, to the local social services authority for the area in which the person so named resides.

(3) Before or within a reasonable time after an application for the admission of a patient for assessment is made by an approved social worker, that social worker shall take such steps as are practicable to inform the person (if any) appearing to be the nearest relative of the patient that the application is to be or has been made and of the power of the nearest relative under section 23(2)(*a*) below.

(4) Neither an application for admission for treatment nor a guardianship application shall be made by an approved social worker if the nearest relative of the patient has notified that social worker, or the local social services authority by whom that social worker is appointed, that he objects to the application being made and, without prejudice to the foregoing provision, no such application shall be made by such a social worker except after consultation with the person (if any) appearing to be the nearest relative of the patient unless it appears to that social worker that in the circumstances such consultation is not reasonably practicable or would involve unreasonable delay.

(4) None of the applications mentioned in subsection (1) above shall be made by any person in respect of a patient unless that person has personally seen the patient within the period of 14 days ending with the date of the application.

(6) An application for admission for treatment or a guardianship application, and any recommendation given for the purposes of such an application, may describe the patient as suffering from more than one of the following forms of mental disorder, namely mental illness, severe mental impairment, psychopathic disorder or mental impairment; but the application shall be of no effect unless the patient is described in each of the recommendations as suffering from the same form of mental disorder, whether or not he is also described in either of those recommendations as suffering from another form.

(7) Each of the applications mentioned in subsection (1) above shall be sufficient if the recommendations on which it is founded are given either as separate recommendations, each signed by a registered medical practitioner, or as a joint recommendation signed by two such practitioners.

General provisions as to medical recommendations

12.—(1) The recommendations required for the purposes of an application for the admission of a patient under this Part of this Act (in this Act referred to as "medical recommendations") shall be signed on or before the date of the application, and shall be given by practitioners who have personally examined the patient either together or separately, but where they have examined the patient separately not more than five days must have elapsed between the days on which the separate examinations took place.

(2) Of the medical recommendations given for the purposes of any such application, one shall be given by a practitioner approved for the purposes of this section by the Secretary of State as having special experience in the diagnosis or treatment of mental disorder; and unless that practitioner has previous acquaintance with the patient, the other such recommendation shall, if practicable, be given by a registered medical practitioner who has such previous acquaintance.

(3) Subject to subsection (4) below, where the application is for the admission of the patient to a hospital which is not a mental nursing home, one (but not more than one) of the medical recommendations may be given by a practitioner on the staff of that hospital, except where the patient is proposed to be accommodated under section 65 or 66 of the National Health Service Act 1977 (which relate to accommodation for private patients).

(4) Subsection (3) above shall not preclude both the medical recommendations being given by practitioners on the staff of the hospital in question if—

(*a*) compliance with that subsection would result in delay involving serious risk to the health or safety of the patient; and

(*b*) one of the practitioners giving the recommendations works at the hospital for less than half of the time which he is bound by contract to devote to work in the health service; and

(*c*) where one of those practitioners is a consultant, the other does not work (whether at the hospital or elsewhere) in a grade in which he is under that consultant's directions.

(5) A medical recommendation for the purposes of an application for the admission of a patient under this Part of this Act shall not be given by—

(*a*) the applicant;

(*b*) a partner of the applicant or of a practitioner by whom another medical recommendation is given for the purposes of the same application;

(*c*) a person employed as an assistant by the applicant or by any such practitioner;

(*d*) a person who receives or has an interest in the receipt of any payments made on account of the maintenance of the patient; or

(*e*) except as provided by subsection (3) or (4) above, a practitioner on the staff of the hospital to which the patient is to be admitted,

or by the husband, wife, father, father-in-law, mother, mother-in-law, son, son-in-law, daughter, daughter-in-law, brother, brother-in-law, sister or sister-in-law of the patient, or of any person mentioned in paragraphs (*a*) to (*e*) above, or of a practitioner by whom another medical recommendation is given for the purposes of the same application

(6) A general practitioner who is employed part-time in a hospital shall not for the purposes of this section be regarded as a practitioner on its staff.

(7) Subsections (1), (2) and (5) above shall apply to applications for guardianship as they apply to applications for admission but with the substitution for paragraph (*e*) of subsection (5) above of the following paragraph—

"(*e*) the person named as guardian in the application.".

Duty of approved social workers to make applications for admission or guardianship

13.—(1) It shall be the duty of an approved social worker to make an application for admission to hospital or a guardianship application in respect of a patient within the area of the local social services authority by which that officer is appointed in any case where he is satisfied that such an application ought to be made and is of the opinion, having regard to any wishes expressed by relatives of the patient or any other relevant circumstances, that it is necessary or proper for the application to be made by him.

(2) Before making an application for the admission of a patient to hospital an approved social worker shall interview the patient in a suitable manner and satisfy himself that detention in a hospital is in all the circumstances of the case the most appropriate way of providing the care and medical treatment of which the patient stands in need.

(3) An application under this section by an approved social worker may be made outside the area of the local social services authority by which he is appointed.

(4) It shall be the duty of a local social services authority, if so required by the nearest relative of a patient residing in their area, to direct an approved social worker as soon as practicable to take the patient's case into consideration under subsection (1) above with a view to making an application for his admission to hospital; and if in any such case that approved social worker decides not to make an application he shall inform the nearest relative of his reasons in writing.

(5) Nothing in this section shall be construed as authorising or requiring an application to be made by an approved social worker in contravention of the provisions of section 11(4) above, or as restricting the power of an approved social worker to make any application under this Act.

Social reports

14. Where a patient is admitted to a hospital in pursuance of an application (other than an emergency application) made under this Part of this Act by his nearest relative, the managers of the hospital shall as soon as practicable give notice of that fact to the local social services authority for the area in which the patient resided immediately before his admission; and that authority shall as soon as practicable arrange for a social worker of their social services department to interview the patient and provide the managers with a report on his social circumstances.

Rectification of applications and recommendations

15.—(1) If within the period of 14 days beginning with the day on which a patient has been admitted to a hospital in pursuance of an application for admission for assessment or for treatment the application, or any medical recommendation given for the purposes of the application, is found to be in any respect incorrect or defective, the application or recommendation may, within that period and with the consent of the managers of the hospital, be amended by the person by whom it was signed; and upon such amendment being made the application or recommendation shall have effect and shall be deemed to have had effect as if it had been originally made as so amended.

(2) Without prejudice to subsection (1) above, if within the period mentioned in that subsection it appears to the managers of the hospital that one of the two medical recommendations on which an application for the admission of a patient is founded is insufficient to warrant the detention of the patient in pursuance of the application, they may, within that period,

give notice in writing to that effect to the applicant; and where any such notice is given in respect of a medical recommendation, that recommendation shall be disregarded, but the application shall be, and shall be deemed always to have been, sufficient if—

(a) a fresh medical recommendation complying with the relevant provisions of this Part of this Act (other than the provisions relating to the time of signature and the interval between examinations) is furnished to the managers within that period; and

(b) that recommendation, and the other recommendation on which the application is founded, together comply with those provisions.

(3) Where the medical recommendations upon which an application for admission is founded are, taken together, insufficient to warrant the detention of the patient in pursuance of the application, a notice under subsection (2) above may be given in respect of either of those recommendations; but this subsection shall not apply in a case where the application is of no effect by virtue of section 11(6) above.

(4) Nothing in this section shall be construed as authorising the giving of notice in respect of an application made as an emergency application, or the detention of a patient admitted in pursuance of such an application, after the period of 72 hours referred to in section 4(4) above, unless the conditions set out in paragraphs (a) and (b) of that section are complied with or would be complied with apart from any error or defect to which this section applies.

Position of patients subject to detention or guardianship

Reclassification of patients

16.—(1) If in the case of a patient who is for the time being detained in a hospital in pursuance of an application for admission for treatment, or subject to guardianship in pursuance of a guardianship application, it appears to the appropriate medical officer that the patient is suffering from a form of mental disorder other than the form or forms specified in the application, he may furnish to the managers of the hospital, or to the guardian, as the case may be, a report to that effect; and where a report is so furnished, the application shall have effect as if that other form of mental disorder were specified in it.

(2) Where a report under subsection (1) above in respect of a patient detained in a hospital is to the effect that he is suffering from psychopathic disorder or mental impairment but not from mental illness or severe mental impairment the appropriate medical officer shall include in the report a statement of his opinion whether further medical treatment in hospital is likely to alleviate or prevent a deterioration of the patient's condition; and if he states that in his opinion such treatment is not likely to have that effect the authority of the managers to detain the patient shall cease.

(3) Before furnishing a report under subsection (1) above the appropriate medical officer shall consult one or more other persons who have been professionally concerned with the patient's medical treatment.

(4) Where a report is furnished under this section in respect of a patient, the managers or guardian shall cause the patient and the nearest relative to be informed.

(5) In this section "appropriate medical officer" means—

(a) in the case of a patient who is subject to the guardianship of a person other than a local social services authority, the nominated medical attendant of the patient; and

(b) in any other case, the responsible medical officer.

Leave of absence from hospital

17.—(1) The responsible medical officer may grant to any patient who is for the time being liable to be detained in a hospital under this Part of this Act leave to be absent from the hospital subject to such conditions (if any) as that officer considers necessary in the interests of the patient or for the protection of other persons.

(2) Leave of absence may be granted to a patient under this section either indefinitely or on specified occasions or for any specified period; and where leave is so granted for a specified period, that period may be extended by further leave granted in the absence of the patient.

(3) Where it appears to the responsible medical officer that it is necessary so to do in the interests of the patient or for the protection of other persons, he may, upon granting leave of absence under this section, direct that the patient remain in custody during his absence; and where leave of absence is so granted the patient may be kept in the custody of any officer on the staff of the hospital, or of any other person authorised in writing by the managers of the hospital or, if the patient is required in accordance with conditions imposed on the grant of leave of absence to reside in another hospital, of any officer on the staff of that other hospital.

(4) In any case where a patient is absent from a hospital in pursuance of leave of absence granted under this section, and it appears to the responsible medical officer that it is necessary so to do in the interests of the patient's health or safety or for the protection of other persons, that officer may, subject to subsection (5) below, by notice in writing given to the patient or to the person for the time being in charge of the patient, revoke the leave of absence and recall the patient to the hospital.

(5) A patient to whom leave of absence is granted under this section shall not be recalled under subsection (4) above after he has ceased to be liable to be detained under this Part of this Act; and without prejudice to any other provision of this Part of this Act any such patient shall cease to be so liable at the expiration of the period of six months beginning with the first day of his absence on leave unless either—

(a) he has returned to the hospital, or has been transferred to another hospital under the following provisions of this Act, before the expiration of that period; or

(b) he is absent without leave at the expiration of that period.

Return and readmission of patients absent without leave

18.—(1) Where a patient who is for the time being liable to be detained under this Part of this Act in a hospital—

(a) absents himself from the hospital without leave granted under section 17 above; or

(b) fails to return to the hospital on any occasion on which, or at the expiration of any period for which, leave of absence was granted to him under that section, or upon being recalled under that section; or

(c) absents himself without permission from any place where he is required to reside in accordance with conditions imposed on the grant of leave of absence under that section,

he may, subject to the provisions of this section, be taken into custody and returned to the hospital or place by any approved social worker, by any officer on the staff of the hospital, by any constable, or by any person authorised in writing by the managers of the hospital.

(2) Where the place referred to in paragraph (c) of subsection (1) above is

a hospital other than the one in which the patient is for the time being liable to be detained, the references in that subsection to an officer on the staff of the hospital and the managers of the hospital shall respectively include references to an officer on the staff of the first-mentioned hospital and the managers of that hospital.

(3) Where a patient who is for the time being subject to guardianship under this Part of this Act absents himself without the leave of the guardian from the place at which he is required by the guardian to reside, he may, subject to the provisions of this section, be taken into custody and returned to that place by any officer on the staff of a local social services authority, by any constable, or by any person authorised in writing by the guardian or a local social services authority.

(4) A patient shall not be taken into custody under this section after the expiration of the period of 28 days beginning with the first day of his absence without leave; and a patient who has not returned or been taken into custody under this section within the said period shall cease to be liable to be detained or subject to guardianship, as the case may be, at the expiration of that period.

(5) A patient shall not be taken into custody under this section if the period for which he is liable to be detained is that specified in section 2(4), 4(4) or 5(2) or (4) above and that period has expired.

(6) In this Act "absent without leave" means absent from any hospital or other place and liable to be taken into custody and returned under this section, and related expressions shall be construed accordingly.

Regulations as to transfer of patients

19.—(1) In such circumstances and subject to such conditions as may be prescribed by regulations made by the Secretary of State—

  (*a*) a patient who is for the time being liable to be detained in a hospital by virtue of an application under this Part of this Act may be transferred to another hospital or into the guardianship of a local social services authority or of any person approved by such an authority;

  (*b*) a patient who is for the time being subject to the guardianship of a local social services authority or other person by virtue of an application under this Part of this Act may be transferred into the guardianship of another local social services authority or person, or be transferred to a hospital.

(2) Where a patient is transferred in pursuance of regulations under this section, the provisions of this Part of this Act (including this subsection) shall apply to him as follows, that is to say—

  (*a*) in the case of a patient who is liable to be detained in a hospital by virtue of an application for admission for assessment or for treatment and is transferred to another hospital, as if the application were an application for admission to that other hospital and as if the patient had been admitted to that other hospital at the time when he was originally admitted in pursuance of the application;

  (*b*) in the case of a patient who is liable to be detained in a hospital by virtue of such an application and is transferred into guardianship, as if the application were a guardianship application duly accepted at the said time;

  (*c*) in the case of a patient who is subject to guardianship by virtue of a guardianship application and is transferred into the guardianship of another authority or person, as if the application were for his reception into the guardianship of that authority or person and had been accepted at the time when it was originally accepted;

(*d*) in the case of a patient who is subject to guardianship by virtue of a guardianship application and is transferred to a hospital, as if the guardianship application were an application for admission to that hospital for treatment and as if the patient had been admitted to the hospital at the time when the application was originally accepted.

(3) Without prejudice to subsections (1) and (2) above, any patient, who is for the time being liable to be detained under this Part of this Act in a hospital vested in the Secretary of State for the purposes of his functions under the National Health Service Act 1977 or any accommodation used under Part I of that Act by the managers of such a hospital, may at any time be removed to any other such hospital or accommodation for which the managers of the first-mentioned hospital are also the managers; and paragraph (*a*) of subsection (2) above shall apply in relation to a patient so removed as it applies in relation to a patient transferred in pursuance of regulations made under this section.

(4) Regulations made under this section may make provision for regulating the conveyance to their destination of patients authorised to be transferred or removed in pursuance of the regulations or under subsection (3) above.

Duration of detention or guardianship and discharge

Duration of authority

20.—(1) Subject to the following provisions of this Part of this Act, a patient admitted to hospital in pursuance of an application for admission for treatment, and a patient placed under guardianship in pursuance of a guardianship application, may be detained in a hospital or kept under guardianship for a period not exceeding six months beginning with the day on which he was so admitted, or the day on which the guardianship application was accepted, as the case may be, but shall not be so detained or kept for any longer period unless the authority for his detention or guardianship is renewed under this section.

(2) Authority for the detention or guardianship of a patient may, unless the patient has previously been discharged, be renewed—

(*a*) from the expiration of the period referred to in subsection (1) above, for a further period of six months;

(*b*) from the expiration of any period of renewal under paragraph (*a*) above, for a further period of one year,

and so on for periods of one year at a time.

(3) Within the period of two months ending on the day on which a patient who is liable to be detained in pursuance of an application for admission for treatment would cease under this section to be so liable in default of the renewal of the authority for his detention, it shall be the duty of the responsible medical officer—

(*a*) to examine the patient; and

(*b*) if it appears to him that the conditions set out in subsection (4) below are satisfied, to furnish to the managers of the hospital where the patient is detained a report to that effect in the prescribed form;

and where such a report is furnished in respect of a patient the managers shall, unless they discharge the patient, cause him to be informed.

(4) The conditions referred to in subsection (3) above are that—

    (*a*) the patient is suffering from mental illness, severe mental impairment, psychopathic disorder or mental impairment, and his mental disorder is of a nature or degree which makes it appropriate for him to receive medical treatment in a hospital; and

    (*b*) such treatment is likely to alleviate or prevent a deterioration of his condition; and

    (*c*) it is necessary for the health or safety of the patient or for the protection of other persons that he should receive such treatment and that it cannot be provided unless he continues to be detained;

but, in the case of mental illness or severe mental impairment, it shall be an alternative to the condition specified in paragraph (*b*) above that the patient, if discharged, is unlikely to be able to care for himself, to obtain the care which he needs or to guard himself against serious exploitation.

(5) Before furnishing a report under subsection (3) above the responsible medical officer shall consult one or more other persons who have been professionally concerned with the patient's medical treatment.

(6) Within the period of two months ending with the day on which a patient who is subject to guardianship under this Part of this Act would cease under this section to be so liable in default of the renewal of the authority for his guardianship, it shall be the duty of the appropriate medical officer—

    (*a*) to examine the patient; and

    (*b*) if it appears to him that the conditions set out in subsection (7) below are satisfied, to furnish to the guardian and, where the guardian is a person other than a local social services authority, to the responsible local social services authority a report to that effect in the prescribed form;

and where such a report is furnished in respect of a patient, the local social services authority shall, unless they discharge the patient, cause him to be informed.

(7) The conditions referred to in subsection (6) above are that—

    (*a*) the patient is suffering from mental illness, severe mental impairment, psychopathic disorder or mental impairment and his mental disorder is of a nature or degree which warrants his reception into guardianship; and

    (*b*) it is necessary in the interests of the welfare of the patient or for the protection of other persons that the patient should remain under guardianship.

(8) Where a report is duly furnished under subsection (3) or (6) above, the authority for the detention or guardianship of the patient shall be thereby renewed for the period prescribed in that case by subsection (2) above.

(9) Where the form of mental disorder specified in a report furnished under subsection (3) or (6) above is a form of disorder other than that specified in the application for admission for treatment or, as the case may be, in the guardianship application, that application shall have effect as if that other form of mental disorder were specified in it; and where on any occasion a report specifying such a form of mental disorder is furnished under either of those subsections the appropriate medical officer need not on that occasion furnish a report under section 16 above.

(10) In this section "appropriate medical officer" has the same meaning as in section 16(5) above.

Special provisions as to patients absent without leave

21.—(1) If on the day on which, apart from this section, a patient would cease to be liable to be detained or subject to guardianship under this Part of this Act or, within the period of one week ending with that day, the patient is absent without leave, he shall not cease to be so liable or subject—

(a) in any case, until the expiration of the period during which he can be taken into custody under section 18 above or the day on which he is returned or returns himself to the hospital or place where he ought to be, whichever is the earlier; and

(b) if he is so returned or so returns himself within the period first mentioned in paragraph (a) above, until the expiration of the period of one week beginning with the day on which he is so returned or so returns.

(2) Where the period for which a patient is liable to be detained or subject to guardianship is extended by virtue of this section, any examination and report to be made and furnished under section 20(3) or (6) above may be made and furnished within that period as so extended.

(3) Where the authority for the detention or guardianship of a patient is renewed by virtue of this section after the day on which, apart from this section, that authority would have expired under section 20, above, the renewal shall take effect as from that day.

Special provisions as to patients sentenced to imprisonment, etc.

22.—(1) Where a patient who is liable to be detained by virtue of an application for admission for treatment or is subject to guardianship by virtue of a guardianship application is detained in custody in pursuance of any sentence or order passed or made by a court on the United Kingdom (including an order committing or remanding him in custody), and is so detained for a period exceeding, or for successive periods exceeding in the aggregate, six months, the application shall cease to have effect at the expiration of that period.

(2) Where any such patient is so detained in custody but the application does not cease to have effect under subsection (1) above, then—

(a) if apart from this subsection the patient would have ceased to be liable to be so detained or subject to guardianship on or before the day on which he is discharged from custody, he shall not cease and shall be deemed not to have ceased to be so liable or subject until the end of that day; and

(b) in any case, sections 18 and 21 above shall apply in relation to the patient as if he had absented himself without leave on that day.

Discharge of patients

23.—(1) Subject to the provisions of this section and section 25 below, a patient who is for the time being liable to be detained or subject to guardianship under this Part of this Act shall cease to be so liable or subject if an order in writing discharging him from detention or guardianship (in this Act referred to as "an order for discharge") is made in accordance with this section.

(2) An order for discharge may be made in respect of a patient—

(a) where the patient is liable to be detained in a hospital in pursuance of an application for admission for assessment or for treatment by the responsible medical officer, by the managers or by the nearest relative of the patient;

(b) where the patient is subject to guardianship, by the responsible medical officer, by the responsible local social services authority or by the nearest relative of the patient.

(3) Where the patient is liable to be detained in a mental nursing home in pursuance of an application for admission for assessment or for treatment, an order for his discharge may, without prejudice to subsection (2) above, be made by the Secretary of State and, if the patient is maintained under a contract with a Regional Health Authority, District Health Authority or special health authority, by that authority.

(4) The powers conferred by this section on any authority or body of persons may be exercised by any three or more members of that authority or body authorised by them in that behalf or by three or more members of a committee or sub-committee of that authority or body which has been authorised by them in that behalf.

Visiting and examination of patients

24.—(1) For the purpose of advising as to the exercise by the nearest relative of a patient who is liable to be detained or subject to guardianship under this Part of this Act of any power to order his discharge, any registered medical practitioner authorised by or on behalf of the nearest relative of the patient may, at any reasonable time, visit the patient and examine him in private.

(2) Any registered medical practitioner authorised for the purposes of subsection (1) above to visit and examine a patient may require the production of and inspect any records relating to the detention or treatment of the patient in any hospital.

(3) Where application is made by the Secretary of State or a Regional Health Authority, District Health Authority or special health authority to exercise, in respect of a patient liable to be detained in a mental nursing home, any power to make an order for his discharge, the following persons, that is to say—

(a) any registered medical practitioner authorised by the Secretary of State or, as the case may be, that authority; and

(b) any other person (whether a registered medical practitioner or not) authorised under [Part II of the Registered Homes Act 1984] to inspect the home,

may at any reasonable time visit the patient and interview him in private.

(4) Any person authorised for the purposes of subsection (3) above to visit a patient may require the production of and inspect any documents constituting or alleged to constitute the authority for the detention of the patient under this Part of this Act; and any person so authorised, who is a registered medical practitioner, may examine the patient in private, and may require the production of and inspect any other records relating to the treatment of the patient in the home.

AMENDMENT

In subs. (3)(b) the words in square brackets were substituted by the Registered Homes Act 1984, s.57(1), Sched. 1, para. 9.

Restrictions on discharge by nearest relative

25.—(1) An order for the discharge of a patient who is liable to be detained in a hospital shall not be made by his nearest relative except after giving not less than 72 hours' notice in writing to the managers of the hospital; and if, within 72 hours after such notice has been given, the responsible medical officer furnishes to the managers a report certifying that in the opinion of that officer the patient, if discharged, would be likely to act in a manner dangerous to other persons or to himself—

(a) any order for the discharge of the patient made by that relative in pursuance of the notice shall be of no effect; and

(b) no further order for the discharge of the patient shall be made by that relative during the period of six months beginning with the date of the report.

(2) In any case where a report under subsection (1) above is furnished in respect of a patient who is liable to be detained in pursuance of an application for admission for treatment the managers shall cause the nearest relative of the patient to be informed.

Functions of relatives of patients

Definition of "relative" and "nearest" relative

26.—(1) In this Part of this Act "relative" means any of the following persons:—

(a) husband or wife;

(b) son or daughter;

(c) father or mother;

(d) brother or sister;

(e) grandparent;

(f) grandchild;

(g) uncle or aunt;

(h) nephew or niece.

(2) In deducing relationships for the purposes of this section, any relationship of the half-blood shall be treated as a relationship of the whole blood, and an illegitimate person shall be treated as the legitimate child of his mother.

(3) In this Part of this Act, subject to the provisions of this section and to the following provisions of this Part of this Act, the "nearest relative" means the person first described in subsection (1) above who is for the time being surviving, relatives of the whole blood being preferred to relatives of the same description of the half-blood and the elder or eldest of two or more relatives described in any paragraph of that subsection being preferred to the other or others of those relatives, regardless of sex.

(4) Subject to the provisions of this section and to the following provisions of this Part of this Act, where the patient ordinarily resides with or is cared for by one or more of his relatives (or, if he is for the time being an in-patient in a hospital, he last ordinarily resided with or was cared for by one or more of his relatives) his nearest relative shall be determined—

(a) by giving preference to that relative or those relatives over the other or others; and

(b) as between two or more such relatives, in accordance with subsection (3) above.

(5) Where the person who, under subsection (3) or (4) above, would be the nearest relative of a patient—

(a) in the case of a patient ordinarily resident in the United Kingdom, the Channel Islands or the Isle of Man, is not so resident; or

(b) is the husband or wife of the patient, but is permanently separated from the patient, either by agreement or under an order of a court, or has deserted or has been deserted by the patient for a period which has not come to an end; or

(c) is a person other than the husband, wife, father or mother of the patient, and is for the time being under 18 years of age; or

(d) is a person against whom an order divesting him of authority over the patient has been made under section 38 of the Sexual Offences Act 1956 (which relates to incest with a person under eighteen) and has not been rescinded,

the nearest relative of the patient shall be ascertained as if that person were dead.

(6) In this section "husband" and "wife" include a person who is living with the patient as the patient's husband or wife, as the case may be (or, if the patient is for the time being an in-patient in a hospital, was so living until the patient was admitted), and has been or had been so living for a period of not less than six months; but a person shall not be treated by virtue of this subsection as the nearest relative of a married patient unless the husband or wife of the patient is disregarded by virtue of paragraph (b) of subsection (5) above.

(7) A person, other than a relative, with whom the patient ordinarily resides (or, if the patient is for the time being an in-patient in a hospital, last ordinarily resided before he was admitted), and with whom he has or had been ordinarily residing for a period of not less than five years, shall be treated for the purposes of this Part of this Act as if he were a relative but—

(a) shall be treated for the purposes of subsection (3) above as if mentioned last in subsection (1) above; and

(b) shall not be treated by virtue of this subsection as the nearest relative of a married patient unless the husband or wife of the patient is disregarded by virtue of paragraph (b) of subsection (5) above.

Children and young persons in care of local authority

27. In any case where the rights and powers of a parent of a patient, being a child or young person, are vested in a local authority or other person by virtue of—

(a) section 3 of the Child Care Act 1980 (which relates to the assumption by a local authority of parental rights and duties in relation to a child in their care);

(b) section 10 of that Act (which relates to the powers and duties of local authorities with respect to persons committed to their care under the Children and Young Persons Act 1969); or

(c) section 17 of the Social Work (Scotland) Act 1968 (which makes corresponding provision for Scotland),

that authority or person shall be deemed to be the nearest relative of the patient in preference to any person except the patient's husband or wife (if any) and except, in a case where the said rights and powers are vested in a local authority by virtue of subsection (1) of the said section 3, any parent of the patient not being the person on whose account the resolution mentioned in that subsection was passed.

Nearest relative of minor under guardianship, etc.

28.—(1) Where a patient who has not attained the age of 18 years—

(a) is, by virtue of an order made by a court in the exercise of jurisdiction (whether under any enactment or otherwise) in respect of the guardianship of minors (including an order under section 38 of the Sexual Offences Act 1956), or by virtue of a deed or will executed by his father or mother, under the guardianship of a person who is not his nearest relative under the foregoing provisions of this Act, or is under the joint guardianship of two persons of whom one is such a person; or

(b) is, by virtue of an order made by a court in the exercise of such jurisdiction or in matrimonial proceedings, or by virtue of a separation agreement between his father and mother, in the custody of any such person,

the person or persons having the guardianship or custody of the patient shall, to the exclusion of any other person, be deemed to be his nearest relative.

(2) Subsection (5) of section 26 above shall apply in relation to a person who is, or who is one of the persons, deemed to be the nearest relative of a patient by virtue of this section as it applies in relation to a person who would be the nearest relative under subsection (3) of that section.

(3) A patient shall be treated for the purposes of this section as being in the custody of another person if he would be in that other person's custody apart from section 8 above.

(4) In this section "court" includes a court in Scotland or Northern Ireland, and "enactment" includes an enactment of the Parliament of Northern Ireland, a Measure of the Northern Ireland Assembly and an Order in Council under Schedule 1 of the Northern Ireland Act 1974.

Appointment by court of acting nearest relative

29.—(1) The county court may, upon application made in accordance with the provisions of this section in respect of a patient, by order direct that the functions of the nearest relative of the patient under this Part of this Act and sections 66 and 69 below shall, during the continuance in force of the order, be exercisable by the applicant, or by any other person specified in the application, being a person who, in the opinion of the court, is a proper person to act as the patient's nearest relative and is willing to do so.

(2) An order under this section may be made on the application of—

(a) any relative of the patient;

(b) any other person with whom the patient is residing (or, if the patient is then an in–patient in a hospital, was last residing before he was admitted); or

(c) an approved social worker;

but in relation to an application made by such a social worker, subsection (1) above shall have effect as if for the words "the applicant" there were substituted the words "the local social services authority."

(3) An application for an order under this section may be made upon any of the following grounds, that is to say—

(a) that the patient has no nearest relative within the meaning of this Act, or that it is not reasonably practicable to ascertain whether he has such a relative, or who that relative is;

(b) that the nearest relative of the patient is incapable of acting as such by reason of mental disorder or other illness;

(c) that the nearest relative of the patient unreasonably objects to the making of an application for admission for treatment or a guardianship application in respect of the patient; or

(d) that the nearest relative of the patient has exercised without due regard to the welfare of the patient or the interests of the public his power to discharge the patient from hospital or guardianship under this Part of this Act, or is likely to do so.

(4) If, immediately before the expiration of the period for which a patient is liable to be detained by virtue of an application for admission for assessment, an application under this section, which is an application made on the ground specified in subsection (3)(*c*) or (*d*) above, is pending in respect of the patient, that period shall be extended—

  (*a*) in any case, until the application under this section has been finally disposed of; and

  (*b*) if an order is made in pursuance of the application under this section, for a further period of seven days;

and for the purposes of this subsection an application under this section shall be deemed to have been finally disposed of at the expiration of the time allowed for appealing from the decision of the court or, if notice of appeal has been given within that time, when the appeal has been heard or withdrawn, and "pending" shall be construed accordingly.

(5) An order made on the ground specified in subsection (3)(*a*) or (*b*) above may specify a period for which it is to continue in force unless previously discharged under section 30 below.

(6) While an order made under this section is in force, the provisions of this Part of this Act (other than this section and section 30 below) and sections 66, 69, 132(4) and 133 below shall apply in relation to the patient as if for any reference to the nearest relative of the patient there were substituted a reference to the person having the functions of that relative and (without prejudice to section 30 below) shall so apply notwithstanding that the person who was the patient's nearest relative when the order was made is no longer his nearest relative; but this subsection shall not apply to section 66 below in the case mentioned in paragraph (*h*) of subsection (1) of that section.

Discharge and variation of orders under s.29

30.—(1) An order made under section 29 above in respect of a patient may be discharged by the county court upon application made—

  (*a*) in any case, by the person having the functions of the nearest relative of the patient by virtue of the order;

  (*b*) where the order was made on the ground specified in paragraph (*a*) or paragraph (*b*) of section 29(3) above, or where the person who was the nearest relative of the patient when the order was made has ceased to be his nearest relative, on the application of the nearest relative of the patient.

(2) An order made under section 29 above in respect of a patient may be varied by the county court, on the application of the person having the functions of the nearest relative by virtue of the order or on the application of an approved social worker, by substituting for the first–mentioned person a local social services authority or any other person who in the opinion of the court is a proper person to exercise those functions, being an authority or person who is willing to do so.

(3) If the person having the functions of the nearest relative of a patient by virtue of an order under section 29 above dies—

  (*a*) subsections (1) and (2) above shall apply as if for any reference to that person there were substituted a reference to any relative of the patient, and

  (*b*) until the order is discharged or varied under those provisions the functions of the nearest relative under this Part of this Act and sections 66 and 69 below shall not be exercisable by any person.

(4) An order under section 29 above shall, unless previously discharged under subsection (1) above, cease to have effect at the expiration of the period, if any, specified under subsection (5) of that section or, where no such period is specified—

(*a*) If the patient was on the date of the order liable to be detained in pursuance of an application for admission for treatment or by virtue of an order or direction under Part III of this Act (otherwise than under section 35, 36 or 38) or was subject to guardianship under this Part of this Act or by virtue of such an order or direction, or becomes so liable or subject within the period of three months beginning with that date, when he ceases to be so liable or subject (otherwise than on being transferred in pursuance of regulations under section 19 above);

(*b*) if the patient was not on the date of the order, and has not within the said period become, so liable or subject, at the expiration of that period.

(5) The discharge or variation under this section of an order made under section 29 above shall not affect the validity of anything previously done in pursuance of the order.

Special provisions as to wards of court

33.—(1) An application for the admission to hospital of a minor who is a ward of court may be made under this Part of this Act with the leave of the court; and section 11(4) above shall not apply in relation to an application so made.

(2) Where a minor who is a ward of court is liable to be detained in a hospital by virtue of an application for admission under this Part of this Act, any power exercisable under this Part of this Act or under section 66 below in relation to the patient by his nearest relative shall be exercisable by or with the leave of the court.

(3) Nothing in this Part of this Act shall be construed as authorising the making of a guardianship application in respect of a minor who is a ward of court, or the transfer into guardianship of any such minor.

Interpretation of Part II

34.—(1) In this Part of this Act—

"the nominated medical attendant", in relation to a patient who is subject to the guardianship of a person other than a local social services authority, means the person appointed in pursuance of regulations made under section 9(2) above to act as the medical attendant of the patient;

"the responsible medical officer" means—

(*a*) in relation to a patient liable to be detained by virtue of an application for admission for assessment or an application for admission for treatment, the registered medical practitioner in charge of the treatment of the patient;

(*b*) in relation to a patient subject to guardianship, the medical officer authorised by the local social services authority to act (either generally or in any particular case or for any particular purpose) as the responsible medical officer.

(2) Except where otherwise expressly provided, this Part of this Act applies in relations to a mental nursing home, being a home in respect of which the particulars of registration are for the time being entered in the

separate part of the register kept for the purposes of section [23(5)(*b*) of the Registered Homes Act 1984] as it applies in relation to a hospital, and references in this Part of this Act to a hospital, and any reference in this Act to a hospital to which this Part of this Act applies, shall be construed accordingly.

(3) In relation to a patient who is subject to guardianship in pursuance of a guardianship application, any reference in this Part of this Act to the responsible local social services authority is a reference—

(*a*) where the patient is subject to the guardianship of a local social services authority, to that authority;

(*b*) where the patient is subject to the guardianship of a person other than a local social services authority, to the local social services authority for the area in which that person resides.

AMENDMENT
In subs. (2) the words in square brackets were substituted by the Registered Homes Act 1984, s.57(1), Sched. 1 para. 10.

Hospital and guardianship orders

Powers of courts to order hospital admission or guardianship

37.—(1) Where a person is convicted before the Crown Court of an offence punishable with imprisonment other than an offence the sentence for which is fixed by law, or is convicted by a magistrates' court of an offence punishable on summary conviction with imprisonment, and the conditions mentioned in subsection (2) below are satisfied, the court may by order authorise his admission to and detention in such hospital as may be specified in the order or, as the case may be, place him under the guardianship of a local social services authority or of such other person approved by a local social services authority as may be so specified.

(2) The conditions referred to in subsection (1) above are that—

(*a*) the court is satisfied, on the written or oral evidence of two registered medical practitioners, that the offender is suffering from mental illness, psychopathic disorder, severe mental impairment or mental impairment and that either—

(i) the mental disorder from which the offender is suffering is of a nature or degree which makes it appropriate for him to be detained in a hospital for medical treatment and, in the case of psychopathic disorder or mental impairment, that such treatment is likely to alleviate or prevent a deterioration of his condition; or

(ii) in the case of an offender who has attained the age of 16 years, the mental disorder is of a nature or degree which warrants his reception into guardianship under this Act; and

(*b*) the court is of the opinion, having regard to all the circumstances including the nature of the offence and the character and antecedents of the offender, and to the other available methods of dealing with him, that the most suitable method of disposing of the case is by means of an order under this section.

(3) Where a person is charged before a magistrates' court with any act or omission as an offence and the court would have power, on convicting him of that offence, to make an order under subsection (1) above in his case as being a person suffering from mental illness or severe mental impairment, then, if the court is satisfied that the accused did the act or made the omission charged, the court may, if it thinks fit, make such an order without convicting him.

(4) An order for the admission of an offender to a hospital (in this Act referred to as "a hospital order") shall not be made under this section unless the court is satisfied on the written or oral evidence of the registered medical practitioner who would be in charge of his treatment or of some other person representing the managers of the hospital that arrangements have been made for his admission to that hospital in the event of such an order being made by the court, and for his admission to it within the period of 28 days beginning with the date of the making of such an order; and the court may, pending his admission within that period, give such directions as it thinks fit for his conveyance to and detention in a place of safety.

(5) If within the said period of 28 days it appears to the Secretary of State that by reason of an emergency or other special circumstances it is not practicable for the patient to be received into the hospital specified in the order, he may give directions for the admission of the patient to such other hospital as appears to be appropriate instead of the hospital so specified; and where such directions are given—

(*a*) the Secretary of State shall cause the person having the custody of the patient to be informed, and

(*b*) the hospital order shall have effect as if the hospital specified in the directions were substituted for the hospital specified in the order.

(6) An order placing an offender under the guardianship of a local social services authority or of any other person (in this Act referred to as "a guardianship order") shall not be made under this section unless the court is satisfied that that authority or person is willing to receive the offender into guardianship.

(7) A hospital order or guardianship order shall specify the form or forms of mental disorder referred to in subsection (2)(*a*) above from which, upon the evidence taken into account under that subsection, the offender is found by the court to be suffering; and no such order shall be made unless the offender is described by each of the practitioners whose evidence is taken into account under that subsection as suffering from the same one of those forms of mental disorder, whether or not he is also described by either of them as suffering from another of them.

(8) Where an order is made under this section, the court shall not pass sentence of imprisonment or impose a fine or make a probation order in respect of the offence or make any such order as is mentioned in paragraph (*b*) or (*c*) of section 7(7) of the Children and Young Persons Act 1969 in respect of the offender, but may make any other order which the court has power to make apart from this section; and for the purposes of this subsection "sentence of imprisonment" includes any sentence or order for detention.

Effect of hospital orders, guardianship orders and interim hospital orders

40.—(1) A hospital order shall be sufficient authority—

(*a*) for a constable, an approved social worker or any other person directed to do so by the court to convey the patient to the hospital specified in the order within a period of 28 days; and

(*b*) for the managers of the hospital to admit him at any time within that period and thereafter detain him in accordance with the provisions of this Act.

(2) A guardianship order shall confer on the authority or person named in the order as guardian the same powers as a guardianship application made and accepted under Part II of this Act.

(3) Where an interim hospital order is made in respect of an offender—

    (*a*) a constable or any other person directed to do so by the court shall convey the offender to the hospital specified in the order within the period mentioned in section 38(4) above; and

    (*b*) the managers of the hospital shall admit him within that period and thereafter detain him in accordance with the provisions of section 38 above.

(4) A patient who is admitted to a hospital in pursuance of a hospital order, or placed under guardianship by a guardianship order, shall, subject to the provisions of this subsection, be treated for the purposes of the provisions of this Act mentioned in Part I of Schedule 1 to this Act as if he had been so admitted or placed on the date of the order in pursuance of an application for admission for treatment or a guardianship application, as the case may be, duly made under Part II of this Act, but subject to any modifications of those provisions specified in that Part of that Schedule.

(5) Where a patient is admitted to a hospital in pursuance of a hospital order, or placed under guardianship by a guardianship order, any previous application, hospital order or guardianship order by virtue of which he was liable to be detained in a hospital or subject to guardianship shall cease to have effect; but if the first-mentioned order, or the conviction on which it was made, is quashed on appeal, this subsection shall not apply and section 22 above shall have effect as if during any period for which the patient was liable to be detained or subject to guardianship under the order, he had been detained in custody as mentioned in that section.

Restriction orders

Power of higher courts to restrict discharge from hospital

41.—(1) Where a hospital order is made in respect of an offender by the Crown Court, and it appears to the court, having regard to the nature of the offence, the antecedents of the offender and the risk of his committing further offences if set at large, that it is necessary for the protection of the public from serious harm so to do, the court may, subject to the provisions of this section, further order that the offender shall be subject to the special restrictions set out in this section, either without limit of time or during such period as may be specified in the order; and an order under this section shall be known as "a restriction order".

(2) A restriction order shall not be made in the case of any person unless at least one of the registered medical practitioners whose evidence is taken into account by the court under section 37(2)(*a*) above has given evidence orally before the court.

(3) The special restrictions applicable to a patient in respect of whom a restriction order is in force are as follows—

    (*a*) none of the provisions of Part II of this Act relating to the duration, renewal and expiration of authority for the detention of patients shall apply, and the patient shall continue to be liable to be detained by virtue of the relevant hospital order until he is duly discharged under the said Part II or absolutely discharged under section 42, 73, 74 or 75 below;

    (*b*) no application shall be made to a Mental Health Review Tribunal in respect of a patient under section 66 or 69(1) below;

(*c*) the following powers shall be exercisable only with the consent of the Secretary of State, namely—

    (i) power to grant leave of absence to the patient under section 17 above;

    (ii) power to transfer the patient in pursuance of regulations under section 19 above; and

    (iii) power to order the discharge of the patient under section 23 above;

and if leave of absence is granted under the said section 17 power to recall the patient under that section shall vest in the Secretary of State as well as the responsible medical officer; and

(*d*) the power of the Secretary of State to recall the patient under the said section 17 and power to take the patient into custody and return him under section 18 above may be exercised at any time;

and in relation to any such patient section 40(4) above shall have effect as if it referred to Part II of Schedule 1 to this Act instead of Part I of that Schedule.

(4) A hospital order shall not cease to have effect under section 40(5) above if a restriction order in respect of the patient is in force at the material time.

(5) Where a restriction order in respect of a patient ceases to have effect while the relevant hospital order continues in force, the provisions of section 40 above and Part I of Schedule 1 to this Act shall apply to the patient as if he had been admitted to the hospital in pursuance of a hospital order (without a restriction order) made on the date on which the restriction order ceased to have effect.

(6) While a person is subject to a restriction order the responsible medical officer shall at such intervals (not exceeding one year) as the Secretary of State may direct examine and report to the Secretary of State on that person; and every report shall contain such particulars as the Secretary of State may require.

Powers of Secretary of State in respect of patients subject to restriction orders

42.—(1) If the Secretary of State is satisfied that in the case of any patient a restriction order is no longer required for the protection of the public from serious harm, he may direct that the patient shall cease to be subject to the special restrictions set out in section 41(3) above; and where the Secretary of State so directs, the restriction order shall cease to have effect, and section 41(5) above shall apply accordingly.

(2) At any time while a restriction order is in force in respect of a patient, the Secretary of State may, if he thinks fit, by warrant discharge the patient from hospital, either absolutely or subject to conditions; and where a person is absolutely discharged under this subsection, he shall thereupon cease to be liable to be detained by virtue of the relevant hospital order, and the restriction order shall cease to have effect accordingly.

(3) The Secretary of State may at any time during the continuance in force of a restriction order in respect of a patient who has been conditionally discharged under subsection (2) above by warrant recall the patient to such hospital as may be specified in the warrant.

(4) Where a patient is recalled as mentioned in subsection (3) above—

    (*a*) if the hospital specified in the warrant is not the hospital from which the patient was conditionally discharged, the hospital order and the restriction order shall have effect as if the hospital specified in the warrant were substituted for the hospital specified in the hospital order;

(b) in any case, the patient shall be treated for the purposes of section 18 above as if he had absented himself without leave from the hospital specified in the warrant, and, if the restriction order was made for a specified period, that period shall not in any event expire until the patient returns to the hospital or is returned to the hospital under that section.

(5) If a restriction order in respect of a patient ceases to have effect after the patient has been conditionally discharged under this section, the patient shall, unless previously recalled under subsection (3) above, be deemed to be absolutely discharged on the date when the order ceases to have effect, and shall cease to be liable to be detained by virtue of the relevant hospital order accordingly.

(6) The Secretary of State may, if satisfied that the attendance at any place in Great Britain of a patient who is subject to a restriction order is desirable in the interests of justice or for the purposes of any public inquiry, direct him to be taken to that place; and where a patient is directed under this subsection to be taken to any place he shall, unless the Secretary of State otherwise directs, be kept in custody while being so taken, while at that place and while being taken back to the hospital in which he is liable to be detained.

Transfer to hospital of prisoners, etc.

Removal to hospital of persons serving sentences of imprisonment, etc.

47.—(1) If in the case of a person serving a sentence of imprisonment the Secretary of State is satisfied, by reports from at least two registered medical practitioners—

(a) that the said person is suffering from mental illness, psychopathic disorder, severe mental impairment or mental impairment; and

(b) that the mental disorder from which that person is suffering is of a nature or degree which makes it appropriate for him to be detained in a hospital for medical treatment and, in the case of psychopathic disorder or mental impairment, that such treatment is likely to alleviate or prevent a deterioration of his condition;

the Secretary of State may, if he is of the opinion having regard to the public interest and all the circumstances that it is expedient so to do, by warrant direct that that person be removed to and detained in such hospital (not being a mental nursing home) as may be specified in the direction; and a direction under this section shall be known as "a transfer direction".

(2) A transfer direction shall cease to have effect at the expiration of the period of 14 days beginning with the date on which it is given unless within that period the person with respect to whom it was given has been received into the hospital specified in the direction.

(3) A transfer direction with respect to any person shall have the same effect as a hospital order made in his case.

(4) A transfer direction shall specify the form or forms of mental disorder referred to in paragraph (a) of subsection (1) above from which, upon the reports taken into account under that subsection, the patient is found by the Secretary of State to be suffering; and no such direction shall be given unless the patient is described in each of those reports as suffering from the same

form of disorder, whether or not he is also described in either of them as suffering from another form.

(5) References in this Part of this Act to a person serving a sentence of imprisonment include references—

> (*a*) to a person detained in pursuance of any sentence or order for detention made by a court in criminal proceedings (other than an order under any enactment to which section 46 above applies);
>
> (*b*) to a person committed to custody under section 115(3) of the Magistrates' Courts Act 1980 (which relates to persons who fail to comply with an order to enter into recognisances to keep the peace or be of good behaviour); and
>
> (*c*) to a person committed by a court to a prison or other institution to which the Prison Act 1952 applies in default of payment of any sum adjudged to be paid on his conviction.

PART IV

CONSENT TO TREATMENT

Patients to whom Part IV applies

56.—(1) This Part of this Act applies to any patient liable to be detained under this Act except—

> (*a*) a patient who is liable to be detained by virtue of an emergency application and in respect of whom the second medical recommendation referred to in section 4(4)(*a*) above has not been given and received;
>
> (*b*) a patient who is liable to be detained by virtue of section 5(2) or (4) or 35 above or section 135 or 136 below or by virtue of a direction under section 37(4) above; and
>
> (*c*) a patient who has been conditionally discharged under section 42(2) above or section 73 or 4 below and has not been recalled to hospital.

(2) Section 57 and, so far as relevant to that section, sections 59, 60 and 62 below, apply also to any patient who is not liable to be detained under this Act.

Treatment requiring consent and a second opinion

57.—(1) This section applies to the following forms of medical treatment for mental disorder—

> (*a*) any surgical operation for destroying brain tissue or for destroying the functioning of brain tissue; and
>
> (*b*) such other forms of treatment as may be specified for the purposes of this section by regulations made by the Secretary of State.

(2) Subject to section 62 below, a patient shall not be given any form of treatment to which this section applies unless he has consented to it and—

> (*a*) a registered medical practitioner appointed for the purposes of this Part of this Act by the Secretary of State (not being the responsible medical officer) and two other persons appointed for the purposes of this paragraph by the Secretary of State (not being registered medical practitioners) have certified in writing that the patient is capable of understanding the nature, purpose and likely effects of the treatment in question and has consented to it; and
>
> (*b*) the registered medical practitioner referred to in paragraph (*a*) above

has certified in writing that, having regard to the likelihood of the treatment alleviating or preventing a deterioration of the patient's condition, the treatment should be given.

(3) Before giving a certificate under subsection (2)(*b*) above the registered medical practitioner concerned shall consult two other persons who have been professionally concerned with the patient's medical treatment, and of those persons one shall be a nurse and the other shall be neither a nurse nor a registered medical practitioner.

(4) Before making any regulations for the purpose of this section the Secretary of State shall consult such bodies as appear to him to be concerned.

Treatment requiring consent or a second opinion

58.—(1) This section applies to the following forms of medical treatment for mental disorder—

(*a*) such forms of treatment as may be specified for the purposes of this section by regulations made by the Secretary of State;

(*b*) the administration of medicine to a patient by any means (not being a form of treatment specified under paragraph (*a*) above or section 57 above) at any time during a period for which he is liable to be detained as a patient to whom this Part of this Act applies if three months or more have elapsed since the first occasion in that period when medicine was administered to him by any means for this mental disorder.

(2) The Secretary of State may by order vary the length of the period mentioned in subsection (1)(*b*) above.

(3) Subject to section 62 below, a patient shall not be given any form of treatment to which this section applies unless—

(*a*) he has consented to that treatment and either the responsible medical officer or a registered medical practitioner appointed for the purposes of this Part of this Act by the Secretary of State has certified in writing that the patient is capable of understanding its nature, purpose and likely effect and has consented to it; or

(*b*) a registered medical practitioner appointed as aforesaid (not being the responsible medical officer) has certified in writing that the patient is not capable of understanding the nature, purpose and likely effects of that treatment or has not consented to it but that, having regard to the likelihood of its alleviating or preventing a deterioration of his condition, the treatment should be given.

(4) Before giving a certificate under subsection (3)(*b*) above the registered medical practitioner concerned shall consult two other persons who have been professionally concerned with the patient's medical treatment, and of those persons one shall be a nurse and the other shall be neither a nurse nor a registered medical practitioner.

(5) Before making any regulations for the purposes of this section the Secretary of State shall consult such bodies as appear to him to be concerned.

Plans of treatment

59. Any consent or certificate under section 57 or 58 above may relate to a plan of treatment under which the patient is to be given (whether within a specified period or otherwise) one or more of the forms of treatment to which that section applies.

Withdrawal of consent

60.—(1) Where the consent of a patient to any treatment has been given for the purpose of section 57 or 58 above, the patient may, subject to section 62 below, at any time before the completion of the treatment withdraw his consent, and those sections shall then apply as if the remainder of the treatment were a separate form of treatment.

(2) Without prejudice to the application of subsection (1) above to any treatment given under the plan of treatment to which a patient has consented, a patient who has consented to such a plan may, subject to section 62 below, at any time withdraw his consent to further treatment, or to further treatment of any description, under the plan.

Review of treatment

61.—(1) Where a patient is given treatment in accordance with section 57(2) or 58(3)(*b*) above a report on the treatment and the patient's condition shall be given by the responsible medical officer to the Secretary of State—

    (*a*) on the next occasion on which the responsible medical officer furnishes a report in respect of the patient under section 20(3) above; and

    (*b*) at any other time if so required by the Secretary of State.

(2) In relation to a patient who is subject to a restriction order or restriction direction subsection (1) above shall have effect as if paragraph (*a*) required the report to be made—

    (*a*) in the case of treatment in the period of six months beginning with the date of the order or direction, at the end of that period;

    (*b*) in the case of treatment at any subsequent time, on the next occasion on which the responsible medical officer makes a report in respect of the patient under section 41(6) or 49(3) above.

(3) The Secretary of State may at any time give notice to the responsible medical officer directing that, subject to section 62 below, a certificate given in respect of a patient under section 57(2) or 58(3)(*b*) above shall not apply to treatment given to him after a date specified in the notice and sections 57 and 58 above shall then apply to any such treatment as if that certificate had not been given.

Urgent treatment

62.—(1) Sections 57 and 58 above shall not apply to any treatment—

    (*a*) which is immediately necessary to save the patient's life; or

    (*b*) which (not being irreversible) is immediately necessary to prevent a serious deterioration of his condition; or

    (*c*) which (not being irreversible or hazardous) is immediately necessary to alleviate serious suffering by the patient; or

    (*d*) which (not being irreversible or hazardous) is immediately necessary and represents the minimum interference necessary to prevent the patient from behaving violently or being a danger to himself or to others.

(2) Sections 60 and 61(3) above shall not preclude the continuation of any treatment or of treatment under any plan pending compliance with section 57 or 58 above if the responsible medical officer considers that the discontinuance of the treatment or of treatment under the plan would cause serious suffering to the patient.

(3) For the purposes of this section treatment is irreversible if it has

unfavourable irreversible physical or psychological consequences and hazardous if it entails significant physical hazard.

Treatment not requiring consent

63. The consent of a patient shall not be required for any medical treatment given to him for the mental disorder from which he is suffering, not being treatment falling within section 57 or 58 above, if the treatment is given by or under the direction of the responsible medical officer.

Applications and references concerning Part II patients

Applications to tribunals

66.—(1) Where—
- (*a*) a patient is admitted to a hospital in pursuance of an application for admission for assessment; or
- (*b*) a patient is admitted to a hospital in pursuance of an application for admission for treatment; or
- (*c*) a patient is received into guardianship in pursuance of a guardianship application; or
- (*d*) a report is furnished under section 16 above in respect of a patient; or
- (*e*) a patient is transferred from guardianship to a hospital in pursuance of regulations made under section 19 above; or
- (*f*) a report is furnished under section 20 above in respect of a patient and the patient is not discharged; or
- (*g*) a report is furnished under section 25 above in respect of a patient who is detained in pursuance of an application for admission for treatment; or
- (*h*) an order is made under section 29 above in respect of a patient who is or subsequently becomes liable to be detained or subject to guardianship under Part II of this Act,

an application may be made to a Mental Health Review Tribunal within the relevant period—
- (i) by the patient (except in the cases mentioned in paragraphs (*g*) and (*h*) above) or, in the case mentioned in paragraph (*d*) above, by his nearest relative, and
- (ii) in the cases mentioned in paragraphs (*g*) and (*h*) above, by his nearest relative.

(2) In subsection (1) above "the relevant period" means—
- (*a*) in the case mentioned in paragraph (*a*) of that subsection, 14 days beginning with the day on which the patient is admitted as so mentioned;
- (*b*) in the case mentioned in paragraph (*b*) of that subsection, six months beginning with the day on which the patient is admitted as so mentioned;
- (*c*) in the case mentioned in paragraph (*c*) of that subsection, six months beginning with the day on which the application is accepted;
- (*d*) in the cases mentioned in paragraphs (*d*) and (*g*) of that subsection, 28 days beginning with the day on which the applicant is informed that the report has been furnished;
- (*e*) in the case mentioned in paragraph (*e*) of that subsection, six

months beginning with the day on which the patient is transferred;

(*f*) in the case mentioned in paragraph (*f*) of that subsection, the period for which authority for the patient's detention or guardianship is renewed by virtue of the report;

(*g*) in the case mentioned in paragraph (*h*) of that subsection, 12 months beginning with the date of the order, and in any subsequent period of 12 months during which the order continues in force.

(3) Section 32 above shall apply for the purposes of this section as it applies for the purposes of Part II of this Act.

Duty of managers of hospitals to refer cases to tribunal

68.—(1) Where a patient who is admitted to a hospital in pursuance of an application for admission for treatment or a patient who is transferred from guardianship to hospital does not exercise his right to apply to a Mental Health Review Tribunal under section 66(1) above by virtue of his case falling within paragraph (*b*) or, as the case may be, paragraph (*e*) of that section, the managers of the hospital shall at the expiration of the period for making such an application refer the patient's case to such a tribunal unless an application or reference in respect of the patient has then been made under section 66(1) above by virtue of his case falling within paragraph (*d*), (*g*) or (*h*) of that section or under section 67(1) above.

(2) If the authority for the detention of a patient in a hospital is renewed under section 20 above and a period of three years (or, if the patient has not attained the age of sixteen years, one year) has elapsed since his case was last considered by a Mental Health Review Tribunal, whether on his own application or otherwise, the managers of the hospital shall refer his case to such a tribunal.

(3) For the purpose of furnishing information for the purpose of any reference under this section, any registered medical practitioner authorised by or on behalf of the patient may at any reasonable time visit and examine the patient in private and require the production of and inspect any records relating to the detention or treatment of the patient in any hospital.

(4) The Secretary of State may by order vary the length of the periods mentioned in subsection (2) above.

(5) For the purposes of subsection (1) above a person who applies to a tribunal but subsequently withdraws his application shall be treated as not having exercised his right to apply, and where a person withdraws his application on a date after the expiration of the period mentioned in that subsection, the managers shall refer the patient's case as soon as possible after that date.

Applications and references concerning Part III patients

Applications to tribunals concerning patients subject to hospital and guardianship orders

69.—(1) Without prejudice to any provision of section 66(1) above as applied by section 40(4) above, an application to a Mental Health Review Tribunal may also be made—

(*a*) in respect of a patient admitted to a hospital in pursuance of a hospital order, by the nearest relative of the patient in the period between the expiration of six months and the expiration of 12 months beginning with the date of the order and in any subsequent period of 12 months; and

(*b*) in respect of a patient placed under guardianship by a guardianship order—

    (i) by the patient, within the period of six months beginning with the date of the order;

    (ii) by the nearest relative of the patient, within the period of 12 months beginning with the date of the order and in any subsequent period of 12 months.

(2) Where a person detained in a hospital—

    (*a*) is treated as subject to a hospital order or transfer direction by virtue of section 41(5) above, 82(2) or 85(2) below, [section 77(2) of the Mental Health (Scotland) Act 1984] or section 5(1) of the Criminal Procedure (Insanity) Act 1964; or

    (*b*) is subject to a direction having the same effect as a hospital order by virtue of section 46(3), 47(3) or 48(3) above,

then, without prejudice to any provision of Part II of this Act as applied by section 40 above, that person may make an application to a Mental Health Review Tribunal in the period of six months beginning with the date of the order or direction mentioned in paragraph (*a*) above or, as the case may be, the date of the direction mentioned in paragraph (*b*) above.

AMENDMENT

In subs. (2) the words in square brackets were substituted by the Mental Health (Scotland) Act 1984, s.127(1), Sched. 3, para. 49.

Applications to tribunals concerning restricted patients

70. A patient who is a restricted patient within the meaning of section 79 below and is detained in a hospital may apply to a Mental Health Review Tribunal—

    (*a*) in the period between the expiration of six months and the expiration of 12 months beginning with the date of the relevant hospital order or transfer direction; and

    (*b*) in any subsequent period of 12 months.

Discharge of patients

Powers of tribunals

72.—(1) Where application is made to a Mental Health Review Tribunal by or in respect of a patient who is liable to be detained under this Act, the tribunal may in any case direct that the patient be discharged, and—

    (*a*) the tribunal shall direct the discharge of a patient liable to be detained under section 2 above if they are satisfied—

        (i) that he is not then suffering from mental disorder or from mental disorder of a nature or degree which warrants his detention in a hospital for assessment (or for assessment followed by a medical treatment) for at least a limited period; or

        (ii) that his detention as aforesaid is not justified in the interests of his own health or safety or with a view to the protection of other persons;

    (*b*) the tribunal shall direct the discharge of a patient liable to be detained otherwise than under section 2 above if they are satisfied—

        (i) that he is not then suffering from mental illness, psychopathic disorder, severe mental impairment or mental impairment or from any of those forms of disorder of a nature or degree which makes it appropriate for him to be liable to be detained in a hospital for medical treatment; of

    (ii) that it is not necessary for the health or safety of the patient or for the protection of other persons that he should receive such treatment; or

    (iii) in the case of an application by virtue of paragraph (*g*) of section 66(1) above, that the patient, if released, would not be likely to act in a manner dangerous to other persons or to himself.

(2) In determining whether to direct the discharge of a patient detained otherwise than under section 2 above in a case not falling within paragraph (*b*) of subsection (1) above, the tribunal shall have regard—

    (*a*) to the likelihood of medical treatment alleviating or preventing a deterioration of the patient's condition; and

    (*b*) in the case of a patient suffering from mental illness or severe mental impairment, to the likelihood of the patient, if discharged, being able to care for himself, to obtain the care he needs or to guard himself against serious exploitation.

(3) A tribunal may under subsection (1) above direct the discharge of a patient on a future date specified in the direction; and where a tribunal do not direct the discharge of a patient under that subsection the tribunal may—

    (*a*) with a view to facilitating his discharge on a future date, recommend that he be granted leave of absence or transferred to another hospital or into guardianship; and

    (*b*) further consider his case in the event of any such recommendation not being complied with.

(4) Where application is made to a Mental Health Review Tribunal by or in respect of a patient who is subject to guardianshp under this Act, the tribunal may in any case direct that the patient be discharged, and shall so direct if they are satisfied—

    (*a*) that he is not then suffering from mental illness, psychopathic disorder, severe mental impairment or mental impairment; or

    (*b*) that it is not necessary in the interests of the welfare of the patient, or for the protection of other persons, that the patient should remain under such guardianship.

(5) Where application is made to a Mental Health Review Tribunal under any provision of this Act by or in respect of a patient and the tribunal do not direct that the patient be discharged, the tribunal may, if satisfied that the patient is suffering from a form of mental disorder other than the form specified in the application, order or direction relating to him, direct that that application, order or direction be amended by substituting for the form of mental disorder specified in it such other form of mental disorder as appears to the tribunal to be appropriate.

(6) Subsections (1) to (5) above apply in relation to references to a Mental Health Review Tribunal as they apply in relation to applications made to such a tribunal by or in respect of a patient.

(7) Subsection (1) above shall not apply in the case of a restricted patient except as provided in sections 73 and 74 below.

Power to discharge restricted patients

73.—(1) Where an application to a Mental Health Review Tribunal is made by a restricted patient who is subject to a restriction order, or where the case of such a patient is referred to such a tribunal, the tribunal shall direct the absolute discharge of the patient if satisfied—

    (*a*) as to the matters mentioned in paragraph (*b*)(i) or (ii) of section 72(1) above; and (*b*) that it is not appropriate for the patient to remain liable to be recalled to hospital for further treatment.

(2) Where in the case of any such patient as is mentioned in subsection (1) above the tribunal are satisfied as to the matters referred to in paragraph (*a*) of that subsection but not as to the matter referred to in paragraph (*b*) of that subsection the tribunal shall direct the conditional discharge of the patient.

(3) Where a patient is absolutely discharged under this section he shall thereupon cease to be liable to be detained by virtue of the relevant hospital order, and the restriction order shall cease to have effect accordingly.

(4) Where a patient is conditionally discharged under this section—

    (*a*) he may be recalled by the Secretary of State under subsection (3) of section 42 above as if he had been conditionally discharged under subsection (2) of that section; and

    (*b*) the patient shall comply with such conditions (if any) as may be imposed at the time of discharge by the tribunal or at any subsequent time by the Secretary of State.

(5) The Secretary of State may from time to time vary any condition imposed (whether by the tribunal or by him) under subsection (4) above.

(6) Where a restriction order in respect of a patient ceases to have effect after he has been conditionally discharged under this section the patient shall, unless previously recalled, be deemed to be absolutely discharged on the date when the order ceases to have effect and shall cease to be liable to be detained by virtue of the relevant hospital order.

(7) A tribunal may defer a direction for the conditional discharge of a patient until such arrangements as appear to the tribunal to be necessary for that purpose have been made to their satisfaction; and where by virtue of any such deferment no direction has been given on an application or reference before the time when the patient's case comes before the tribunal on a subsequent application or reference, the previous application or reference shall be treated as one on which no direction under this section can be given.

(8) This section is without prejudice to section 42 above.

Part VIII

Miscellaneous Functions of Local Authorities and the Secretary of State

Approved social workers

Appointment of approved social workers

114.—(1) A local social services authority shall appoint a sufficient number of approved social workers for the purpose of discharging the functions conferred on them by this Act.

(2) No person shall be appointed by a local social services authority as an approved social worker unless he is approved by the authority as having appropriate competence in dealing with persons who are suffering from mental disorder.

(3) In approving a person for appointment as an approved social worker a local social services authority shall have regard to such matters as the Secretary of State may direct.

Powers of entry and inspection

115. An approved social worker of a local social services authority may at all reasonable times after producing, if asked to do so, some duly authenticated document showing that he is such a social worker, enter and inspect any premises (not being a hospital) in the area of that authority in which a mentally disordered patient is living, if he has reasonable cause to believe that the patient is not under proper care.

Visiting patients

Welfare of certain hospital patients

116.—(1) Where a patient to whom this section applies is admitted to a hospital or nursing home in England and Wales (whether for treatment for mental disorder or for any other reason) then, without prejudice to their duties in relation to the patient apart from the provisions of this section, the authority shall arrange for visits to be made to him on behalf of the authority, and shall take such other steps in relation to the patient while in the hospital or nursing home as would be expected to be taken by his parents.

(2) This section applies to—

    (*a*) a child or young person in respect of whom the rights and powers of a parent are vested in a local authority by virtue of—

        (i) section 3 of the Child Care Act 1980 (which relates to the assumption by a local authority of parental rights and duties in relation to a child in their care),

        (ii) section 10 of that Act (which relates to the powers and duties of local authorities with respect to persons committed to their care under the Children and Young Persons Act 1969), or

        (iii) section 17 of the Social Work (Scotland) Act 1968 (which makes corresponding provisions for Scotland);

    (*b*) a person who is subject to the guardianship of a local social services authority under the provisions of this Act or the [Mental Health (Scotland) Act 1984] or

    (*c*) a person the functions of whose nearest relative under this Act or under the [Mental Health (Scotland) Act 1984] are for the time being transferred to a local social services authority.

AMENDMENTS

In subs. (2) the words in square brackets were substituted by the Mental Health (Scotland) Act 1984, s.127(1), Sched. 3, para. 55.

After-care

After-care

117.—(1) This section applies to persons who are detained under section 3 above, or admitted to a hospital in pursuance of a hospital order made under section 37 above, or transferred to a hospital in pursuance of a transfer direction made under section 47 or 48 above, and then cease to be detained and leave hospital.

(2) It shall be the duty of the District Health Authority and of the local social services authority to provide, in co-operation with relevant voluntary agencies, after-care services for any person to whom this section applies until such time as the District Health Authority and the local social services authority are satisfied that the person concerned is no longer in need of such services.

(3) In this section "the District Health Authority" means the District Health Authority for the district, and "the local social services authority" means the local social services authority for the area in which the person concerned is resident or to which he is sent on discharge by the hospital in which he was detained.

Functions of the Secretary of State

Code of practice

118.—(1) The Secretary of State shall prepare, and from time to time revise, a code of practice—

(*a*) for the guidance of registered medical practitioners, managers and staff of hospitals and mental nursing homes and approved social workers in relation to the admission of patients to hospitals and mental nursing homes under this Act; and

(*b*) for the guidance of registered medical practitioners and members of other professions in relation to the medical treatment of patients suffering from mental disorder.

(2) The code shall, in particular, specify forms of medical treatment in addition to any specified by regulations made for the purposes of section 57 above which in the opinion of the Secretary of State give rise to special concern and which should accordingly not be given by a registered medical practitioner unless the patient has consented to the treatment (or to a plan of treatment including that treatment) and a certificate in writing as to the matters mentioned in subsection (2)(*a*) and (*b*) of that section has been given by another registered medical practitioner, being a practitioner appointed for the purposes of this section by the Secretary of State.

(3) Before preparing the code or making any alteration in it the Secretary of State shall consult such bodies as appear to him to be concerned.

(4) The Secretary of State shall lay copies of the code and of any alteration in the code before Parliament; and if either House of Parliament passes a resolution requiring the code or any alteration in it to be withdrawn the Secretary of State shall withdraw the code or alteration and, where he withdraws the code, shall prepare a code in substitution for the one which is withdrawn.

(5) No resolution shall be passed by either House of Parliament under subsection (4) above in respect of a code or alteration after the expiration of the period of 40 days beginning with the day on which a copy of the code or alteration was laid before that House; but for the purposes of this subsection no account shall be taken of any time during which Parliament is dissolved or prorogued or during which both Houses are adjourned for more than four days.

(6) The Secretary of State shall publish the code as for the time being in force.

General protection of detained patients

120.—(1) The Secretary of State shall keep under review the exercise of the powers and the discharge of the duties conferred or imposed by this Act so far as relating to the detention of patients or to patients liable to be detained under this Act and shall make arrangements for persons authorised by him in that behalf—

(*a*) to visit and interview in private patients detained under this Act in hospitals and mental nursing homes; and

(*b*) to investigate—

(i) any complaint made by a person in respect of a matter that occurred while he was detained under this Act in a hospital or mental nursing home and which he considers has not been satisfactorily dealt with by the managers of that hospital or mental nursing home; and

(ii) any other complaint as to the exercise of the powers or the discharge of the duties conferred or imposed by this Act in respect of a person who is or has been so detained.

(2) The arrangements made under this section in respect of the investigation of complaints may exclude matters from investigation in specified circumstances and shall not require any person exercising functions under the arrangements to undertake or continue with any investigation where he does not consider it appropriate to do so.

(3) Where any such complaint as is mentioned in subsection (1)(*b*)(ii) above is made by a Member of Parliament and investigated under the arrangements made under this section the results of the investigation shall be reported to him.

(4) For the purpose of any such review as is mentioned in subsection (1) above or of carrying out his functions under arrangements made under this section any person authorised in that behalf by the Secretary of State may at any reasonable time—

(*a*) visit and interview and, if he is a registered medical practitioner, examine in private any patient in a mental nursing home; and

(*b*) require the production of and inspect any records relating to the detention or treatment of any person who is or has been detained in a mental nursing home.

(5) The matters in respect of which regulations may be made under section 6 of the Nursing Homes Act 1975 shall include the keeping of records relating to the detention and treatment of persons detained under this Act in a mental nursing home.

(6) The Secretary of State may make such provision as he may with the approval of the Treasury determine for the payment of remuneration allowances, pensions or gratuities to or in respect of persons exercising functions in relation to any such review as is mentioned in subsection (1) above or functions under arrangements made under this section.

(7) The powers and duties referred to in subsection (1) above do not include any power or duty conferred or imposed by Part VII of this Act.

Mental Health Act Commission

121.—(1) Without prejudice to section 126(3) of the National Health Service Act 1977 (power to vary or revoke orders or directions) there shall continue to be a special health authority known as the Mental Health Act Commission established under section 11 of that Act.

(2) Without prejudice to the generality of his powers under section 13 of that Act, the Secretary of State shall direct the Commission to perform on his behalf—

(*a*) the function of appointing registered medical practitioners for the purposes of Part IV of this Act and section 118 above and of appointing other persons for the purposes of section 57(2)(*a*) above; and

(*b*) the functions of the Secretary of State under sections 61 and 120(1) and (4) above.

(3) The registered medical practitioners and other persons appointed for

the purposes mentioned in subsection (2)(*a*) above may include members of the Commission.

(4) The Secretary of State may, at the request of or after consultation with the Commission and after consulting such other bodies as appear to him to be concerned, direct the Commission to keep under review the care and treatment, or any aspect of the care and treatment, in hospitals and mental nursing homes of patients who are not liable to be detained under this Act.

(5) For the purpose of any such review as is mentioned in subsection (4) above any person authorised in that behalf by the Commission may at any reasonable time—

 (*a*) visit and interview and, if he is a registered medical practitioner, examine in private any patient in a mental nursing home; and

 (*b*) require the production of and inspect any records relating to the treatment of any person who is or has been a patient in a mental nursing home.

(6) The Secretary of State may make such provision as he may with the approval of the Treasury determine for the payment of remuneration, allowances, pensions or gratuities to or in respect of persons exercising functions in relation to any such review as is mentioned in subsection (4) above.

(7) The Commission shall review any decision to withhold a postal packet (or anything contained in it) under subsection (1)(*b*) or (2) of section 134 below if an application in that behalf is made—

 (*a*) in a case under subsection (1)(*b*), by the patient; or

 (*b*) in a case under subsection (2), either by the patient or by the person by whom the postal packet was sent;

and any such application shall be made within six months of the receipt by the applicant of the notice referred to in subsection (6) of that section.

(8) On an application under subsection (7) above the Commission may direct that the postal packet which is the subject of the application (or anything contained in it) shall not be withheld and the manager in question shall comply with any such direction.

(9) The Secretary of State may by regulations make provision with respect to the making and determination of applications under subsection (7) above, including provision for the production to the Commission of any postal packet which is the subject of such an application.

(10) The Commission shall in the second year after its establishment and subsequently in every second year publish a report on its activities; and copies of every such report shall be sent by the Commission to the Secretary of State who shall lay a copy before each House of Parliament.

(11) Paragraph 9 of Schedule 5 to the said Act of 1977 (pay and allowances for chairmen and members of health authorities) shall have effect in relation to the Mental Health Act Commission as if references in sub-paragraphs (1) and (2) to the Chairman included references to any member and as if sub-paragraphs (4) and (5) were omitted.

Obstruction

129.—(1) Any person who without reasonable cause—

 (*a*) refuses to allow the inspection of any premises; or

 (*b*) refuses to allow the visiting, interviewing or examination of any person by a person authorised in that behalf by or under this Act; or

 (*c*) refuses to produce for the inspection of any person so authorised any document or record the production of which is duly required by him; or

(*d*) otherwise obstructs any such person in the exercise of his functions,

shall be guilty of an offence.

(2) Without prejudice to the generality of subsection (1) above, any person who insists on being present when required to withdraw by a person authorised by or under this Act to interview or examine a person in private shall be guilty of an offence.

(3) Any person guilty of an offence under this section shall be liable on summary conviction to imprisonment for a term not exceeding three months or to a fine not exceeding level 4 on the standard scale or to both.

PART X

MISCELLANEOUS AND SUPPLEMENTARY

Miscellaneous provisions

Informal admission of patients

131.—(1) Nothing in this Act shall be construed as preventing a patient who requires treatment for mental disorder from being admitted to any hospital or mental nursing home in pursuance of arrangements made in that behalf and without any application, order or direction rendering him liable to be detained under this Act, or from remaining in any hospital or mental nursing home in pursuance of such arrangements after he has ceased to be so liable to be detained.

(2) In the case of a minor who has attained the age of 16 years and is capable of expressing his own wishes, any such arrangements as are mentioned in subsection (1) above may be made, carried out and determined notwithstanding any right of custody or control vested by law in his parent or guardian.

Duty of managers of hospitals to give information to detained patients

132.—(1) The managers of a hospital or mental nursing home in which a patient is detained under this Act shall take such steps as are practicable to ensure that the patient understands—

(*a*) under which of the provisions of this Act he is for the time being detained and the effect of that provision; and

(*b*) what rights of applying to a Mental Health Review Tribunal are available to him in respect of his detention under that provision;

and those steps shall be taken as soon as practicable after the commencement of the patient's detention under the provision in question.

(2) The managers of a hospital or mental nursing home in which a patient is detained as aforesaid shall also take such steps as are practicable to ensure that the patient understands the effect, so far as relevant in his case, of sections 23, 25, 56 to 64, 66(1)(*g*), 118 and 120 above and section 134 below; and those steps shall be taken as soon as practicable after the commencement of the patient's detention in the hospital or nursing home.

(3) The steps to be taken under subsections (1) and (2) above shall include giving the requisite information both orally and in writing.

(4) The managers of a hospital or mental nursing home in which a patient

is detained as aforesaid shall, except where the patient otherwise requests, take such steps as are practicable to furnish the person (if any) appearing to them to be his nearest relative with a copy of any information given to him in writing under subsections (1) and (2) above; and those steps shall be taken when the information is given to the patient or within a reasonable time thereafter.

Duty of managers of hospitals to inform nearest relatives of discharge

133.—(1) Where a patient liable to be detained under this Act in a hospital or mental nursing home is to be discharged otherwise than by virtue of an order for discharge made by his nearest relative, the managers of the hospital or mental nursing home shall, subject to subsection (2) below, take such steps as are practicable to inform the person (if any) appearing to them to be the nearest relative of the patient; and that information shall, if practicable, be given at least seven days before the date of discharge.

(2) Subsection (1) above shall not apply if the patient or his nearest relative has requested that information about the patient's discharge should not be given under this section.

Correspondence of patients

134.—(1) A postal packet addressed to any person by a patient detained in a hospital under this Act and delivered by the patient for dispatch may be withheld from the Post Office—
- (*a*) if that person has requested that communications addressed to him by the patient should be withheld; or
- (*b*) subject to subsection (3) below, if the hospital is a special hospital and the managers of the hospital consider that the postal packet is likely—
  - (i) to cause distress to the person to whom it is addressed or to any other person (not being a person on the staff of the hospital); or
  - (ii) to cause danger to any person;

and any request for the purposes of paragraph (*a*) above shall be made by a notice in writing given to the managers of the hospital, the registered medical practitioner in charge of the treatment of the patient or the Secretary of State.

(2) Subject to subsection (3) below, a postal packet addressed to a patient detained in a special hospital under this Act may be withheld from the patient if, in the opinion of the managers of the hospital, it is necessary to do so in the interests of the safety of the patient or for the protection of other persons.

(3) Subsections (1)(*b*) and (2) above do not apply to any postal packet addressed by a patient to, or sent to a patient by or on behalf of—
- (*a*) any Minister of the Crown or Member of either House of Parliament;
- (*b*) the Master or any other officer of the Court of Protection or any of the Lord Chancellor's Visitors;
- (*c*) the Parliamentary Commissioner for Administration, the Health Service Commissioner for England, the Health Service Commissioner for Wales or a Local Commissioner within the meaning of Part III of the Local Government Act 1974;
- (*d*) a Mental Health Review Tribunal;
- (*e*) a health authority within the meaning of the National Health Service Act 1977, a local social services authority, a Community Health Council or a probation and after-care committee appointed under

paragraph 2 of Schedule 3 to the Powers of Criminal Courts Act 1973;

(f) the managers of the hospital in which the patient is detained;

(g) any legally qualified person instructed by the patient to act as his legal adviser; or

(h) the European Commission of Human Rights or the European Court of Human Rights.

(4) The managers of a hospital may inspect and open any postal packet for the purposes of determining—

(a) whether it is one to which subsection (1) or (2) applies, and

(b) in the case of a postal packet to which subsection (1) or (2) above applies, whether or not it should be withheld under that subsection;

and the power to withhold a postal packet under either of those subsections includes power to withhold anything contained in it.

(5) Where a postal packet or anything contained in it is withheld under subsection (1) or (2) above the managers of the hospital shall record that fact in writing.

(6) Where a postal packet or anything contained in it is withheld under subsection (1)(b) or (2) above the managers of the hospital shall within seven days give notice of that fact to the patient and, in the case of a packet withheld under subsection (2) above, to the person (if known) by whom the postal packet was sent; and any such notice shall be given in writing and shall contain a statement of the effect of section 121(7) and (8) above.

(7) The functions of the managers of a hospital under this section shall be discharged on their behalf by a person on the staff of the hospital appointed by them for that purpose and different persons may be appointed to discharge different functions.

(8) The Secretary of State may make regulations with respect to the exercise of the powers conferred by this section.

(9) In this section "hospital" has the same meaning as in Part II of this Act, "postal packet" has the same meaning as in the Post Office Act 1953 and the provisions of this section shall have effect notwithstanding anything in section 56 of that Act.

Warrant to search for and remove patients

135.—(1) If it appears to a justice of the peace, on information on oath laid by an approved social worker, that there is reasonable cause to suspect that a person believed to be suffering from mental disorder—

(a) has been, or is being, ill-treated, neglected or kept otherwise than under proper control, in any place within the jurisdiction of the justice, or

(b) being unable to care for himself, is living alone in any such place,

the justice may issue a warrant authorising any constable named in the warrant to enter, if need be by force, any premises specified in the warrant in which that person is believed to be, and, if thought fit, to remove him to a place of safety with a view to the making of an application in respect of him under Part II of this Act, or of other arrangements for his treatment or care.

(2) If it appears to a justice of the peace, on information on oath laid by any constable or other person who is authorised by or under this Act or under section 83 of the [Mental Health (Scotland) Act 1984] to take a patient to any place, or to take into custody or retake a patient who is liable under this Act or under the said section 83 to be so taken or retaken—

(a) that there is reasonable cause to believe that the patient is to be found on premises within the jurisdiction of the justice; and (*b*) that admission to the premises has been refused or that a refusal of such admission is apprehended,

the justice may issue a warrant authorising any constable named in the warrant to enter the premises, if need be by force, and remove the patient.

(3) A patient who is removed to a place of safety in the execution of a warrant issued under this section may be detained there for a period not exceeding 72 hours.

(4) In the execution of a warrant issued under subsection (1) above, the constable to whom it is addressed shall be accompanied by an approved social worker and by a registered medical practitioner, and in the execution of a warrant issued under subsection (2) above the constable to whom it is addressed may be accompanied—

(*a*) by a registered medical practitioner;

(*b*) by any person authorised by or under this Act or under section 83 of the [Mental Health (Scotland) Act 1984] to take or retake the patient.

(5) It shall not be necessary in any information or warrant under subsection (1) above to name the patient concerned.

(6) In this section "place of safety" means residential accommodation provided by a local social services authority under Part III of the National Assistance Act 1948 or under paragraph 2 of Schedule 8 to the National Health Service Act 1977, a hospital as defined by this Act, a police station, a mental nursing home or residential home for mentally disordered persons or any other suitable place the occupier of which is willing temporarily to receive the patient.

AMENDMENT

In subss. (2) and (4) the words in square brackets were substituted by the Mental Health (Scotland) Act 1984, s.127(1), Sched. 3, para. 56.

Mentally disordered persons found in public places

136.—(1) If a constable finds in a place to which the public have access a person who appears to him to be suffering from mental disorder and to be in immediate need of care or control, the constable may, if he thinks it necessary to do so in the interests of that person or for the protection of other persons, remove that person to a place of safety within the meaning of section 135 above.

(2) A person removed to a place of safety under this section may be detained there for a period not exceeding 72 hours for the purpose of enabling him to be examined by a registered medical practitioner and to be interviewed by an approved social worker and of making any necessary arrangements for his treatment or care.

Provisions as to custody, conveyance and detention

137.—(1) Any person required or authorised by or by virtue of this Act to be conveyed to any place or to be kept in custody or detained in a place of safety or at any place to which he is taken under section 42(6) above shall, while being so conveyed, detained or kept, as the case may be, be deemed to be in legal custody.

(2) A constable or any other person required or authorised by or by virtue of this Act to take any person into custody, or to convey or detain any person shall, for the purposes of taking him into custody or conveying or detaining him, have all the powers, authorities, protection and privileges which a constable has within the area for which he acts as constable.

(3) In this section "convey" includes any other expression denoting removal from one place to another.

Retaking of patients escaping from custody

138.—(1) If any person who is in legal custody by virtue of section 137 above escapes, he may, subject to the provisions of this section, be retaken—

  (*a*) in any case, by the person who had his custody immediately before the escape, or by any constable or approved social worker;

  (*b*) if at the time of the escape he was liable to be detained in a hospital within the meaning of Part II of this Act, or subject to guardianship under this Act, by any other person who could take him into custody under section 18 above if he had absented himself without leave.

(2) A person to whom paragraph (*b*) of subsection (1) above applies shall not be retaken under this section after the expiration of the period within which he could be retaken under section 18 above if he had absented himself without leave on the day of the escape unless he is subject to a restriction order under Part III of this Act or an order or direction having the same effect as such an order; and subsection (4) of the said section 18 shall apply with the necessary modifications accordingly.

(3) A person who escapes while being taken to or detained in a place of safety under section 135 or 136 above shall not be retaken under this section after the expiration of the period of 72 hours beginning with the time when he escapes or the period during which he is liable to be so detained, whichever expires first.

(4) This section, so far as it relates to the escape of a person liable to be detained in a hospital within the meaning of Part II of this Act, shall apply in relation to a person who escapes—

  (*a*) while being taken to or from such a hospital in pursuance of regulations under section 19 above, or of any order, direction or authorisation under Part III or VI of this Act (other than under section 35, 36, 38, 53, 83 or 85) or under section 123 above; or

  (*b*) while being taken to or detained in a place of safety in pursuance of an order under Part III of this Act (other than under section 35, 36 or 38 above) pending his admission to such a hospital,

as if he were liable to be detained in that hospital and, if he had not previously been received in that hospital, as if he had been so received.

(5) In computing for the purposes of the power to give directions under section 37(4) above and for the purposes of sections 37(5) and 40(1) above the period of 28 days mentioned in those sections, no account shall be taken of any time during which the patient is at large and liable to be retaken by virtue of this section.

(6) Section 21 above shall, with any necessary modifications, apply in relation to a patient who is at large and liable to be retaken by virtue of this section as it applies in relation to a patient who is absent without leave and references in that section to section 18 above shall be construed accordingly.

Protection for acts done in pursuance of this Act

139.—(1) No person shall be liable, whether on the ground of want of jurisdiction or on any other ground, to any civil or criminal proceedings to which he would have been liable apart from this section in respect of any act purporting to be done in pursuance of this Act or any regulations or rules made under this Act, or in, or in pursuance of anything done in, the discharge of functions conferred by any other enactment on the authority having jurisdiction under Part VII of this Act, unless the act was done in bad faith or without reasonable care.

(2) No civil proceedings shall be brought against any person in any court

in respect of any such act without the leave of the High Court; and no criminal proceedings shall be brought against any person in any court in respect of any such act except by or with the consent of the Director of Public Prosecutions.

(3) This section does not apply to proceedings for an offence under this Act, being proceedings which, under any other provision of this Act, can be instituted only by or with the consent of the Director of Public Prosecutions.

(4) This section does not apply to proceedings against the Secretary of State or against a health authority within the meaning of the National Health Service Act 1977.

(5) In relation to Northern Ireland the reference in this section to the Director of Public Prosecutions shall be construed as a reference to the Director of Public Prosecutions for Northern Ireland.

Interpretation

145.—(1) In this Act, unless the context otherwise requires—

"absent without leave" has the meaning given to it by section 18 above and related expressions shall be construed accordingly;

"application for admission for assessment" has the meaning given in section 2 above;

"application for admission for treatment" has the meaning given in section 3 above;

"approved social worker" means an officer of a local social services authority appointed to act as an approved social worker for the purposes of this Act;

"hospital" means—

    (*a*) any health service hospital within the meaning of the National Health Service Act 1977; and

    (*b*) any accommodation provided by a local authority and used as a hospital or on behalf of the Secretary of State under that Act;

and "hospital within the meaning of Part II of this Act" has the meaning given in section 34 above;

"hospital order" and "guardianship order" have the meanings respectively given in section 37 above;

"interim hospital order" has the meaning given in section 38 above;

"local social services authority" means a council which is a local authority for the purpose of the Local Authority Social Services Act 1970;

"the managers" means—

    (*a*) in relation to a hospital vested in the Secretary of State for the purposes of his functions under the National Health Service Act 1977, and in relation to any accommodation provided by a local authority and used as a hospital by or on behalf of the Secretary of State under that Act, the District Health Authority or special health authority responsible for the administration of the hospital;

    (*b*) in relation to a special hospital, the Secretary of State;

    (*c*) in relation to a mental nursing home registered in pursuance of the [Registered Homes Act 1984] the person or persons registered in respect of the home;

and in this definition "hospital" means a hospital within the meaning of Part II of this Act;

"medical treatment" includes nursing, and also includes care, habilitation and rehabilitation under medical supervision;

"mental disorder", "severe mental impairment", "mental impairment" and "psychopathic disorder" have the meanings given in section 1 above;

"mental nursing home" has the same meaning as in the Nursing Homes Act 1975;

"nearest relative", in relation to a patient, has the meaning given in Part II of this Act;

"patient" (except in Part VII of this Act) means a person suffering or appearing to be suffering from mental disorder;

"restriction direction" has the meaning given to it by section 49 above;

"restriction order" has the meaning given to it by section 41 above;

"special hospital" has the same meaning as in the National Health Service Act 1977;

"standard scale" has the meaning given in section 75 of the Criminal Justice Act 1982;

"transfer direction" has the meaning given to it by section 47 above.

(2) "Statutory maximum" has the meaning given in section 74 of the Criminal Justice Act 1982 and for the purposes of section 128(4)(*a*) above—

(*a*) subsection (1) of section 74 shall have effect as if after the words "England and Wales" there were inserted the words "or Northern Ireland"; and

(*b*) section 32 of the Magistrates' Courts Act 1980 shall extend to Northern Ireland.

(3) In relation to a person who is liable to be detained or subject to guardianship by virtue of an order or direction under Part III of this Act (other than under section 35, 36, or 38), any reference in this Act to any enactment contained in Part II of this Act or in section 66 or 67 above shall be construed as a reference to that enactment as it applies to that person by virtue of Part III of this Act.

AMENDMENT

In subs. (1) the words in square brackets were substituted by the Registered Homes Act 1984, s.57(1), Sched. 1, para. 11.

REGISTERED HOMES ACT 1984

(1984 c. 23)

An Act to consolidate certain enactments relating to residential care homes and nursing homes and Registered Homes Tribunals, with amendments to give effect to recommendations of the Law Commission.

[26th June 1984]

PART I

RESIDENTIAL CARE HOMES

Registration and conduct of residential care homes

Requirement of registration

1.—(1) Subject to the following provisions of this section, registration under this Part of this Act is required in respect of any establishment which provides or is intended to provide, whether for reward or not, residential personal care by reason of old age, disablement, past or present dependence on alcohol or drugs, or past or present mental disorder.

(2) Such an establishment is referred to in this Part of this Act as a "residential care home".

(3) Registration under this Part of this Act does not affect any requirement to register under Part II of this Act.

(4) Registration under this Part of this Act is not required in respect of an establishment which provides or is intended to provide residential accommodation with both board and personal care for fewer than 4 persons, excluding persons carrying on or intending to carry on the home or employed or intended to be employed there and their relatives.

(5) Registration under this Part of this Act is not required in respect of any of the following—

(a) any establishment which is used, or is intended to be used, solely as a nursing home or mental nursing home;

(b) any hospital as defined in section 128 of the National Health Service Act 1977 which is maintained in pursuance of an Act of Parliament;

(c) any hospital as defined in section 145(1) of the Mental Health Act 1983;

(d) any voluntary home or community home within the meaning of the Child Care Act 1980;

(e) any children's home to which the Children's Homes Act 1982 applies;

(f) subject to subsection (6) below, any school, as defined in section 114 of the Education Act 1944;

(g) subject to subsection (7) below, any establishment to which the Secretary of State has made a payment of maintenance grant under regulations made by virtue of section 100(1)(b) of the Education Act 1944;

(h) any university or university college or college, school or hall of a university;

(j) any establishment managed or provided by a government department or local authority or by any authority or body constituted by an Act of Parliament or incorporated by Royal Charter.

(6) An independent school within the meaning of the Education Act 1944 is not excluded by subsection (5) above if the school provides accommodation for 50 or less children under the age of 18 years and is not for the time being approved by the Secretary of State under section 11(3)(a) of the Education Act 1981.

(7) An establishment to which the Secretary of State has made a payment of maintenance grant under regulations made by virtue of section 100(1)(b) of the Education Act 1944 is only excluding by subsection (5) above until the end of the period of 12 months from the date on which the Secretary of State made the payment.

Offence of carrying on home without registration

2. If any person carries on a residential care home without being registered under this Part of this Act in respect of it, he shall be guilty of an offence.

Registration of managers etc., and persons in control

3. Where the manager or intended manager of a residential care home is not in control of it (whether as owner or otherwise) both the manager or intended manager and the person in control are to be treated as carrying on or intending to carry on the home and accordingly as requiring to be registered under this Part of this Act.

Optional registration

4.—(1) A person who—
  (*a*) is registered under Part II of this Act in respect of any premises; and
  (*b*) would be required to be registered in respect of them under this Part of this Act but for section 1(4) above,
may apply to be registered under this Part of this Act in respect of those premises.

(2) If he does so apply, this Part of this Act shall have effect in relation to him as if he required to be registered under this Part of this Act in respect of those premises.

Refusal of registration

9. The registration authority may refuse to register an applicant for registration in respect of a residential care home if they are satisfied—
  (*a*) that he or any other person concerned or intended to be concerned in carrying on the home is not a fit person to be concerned in carrying on a residential care home;
  (*b*) that for reasons connected with their situation, construction, state of repair, accommodation, staffing, or equipment, the premises used or intended to be used for the purposes of the home, or any other premises used or intended to be used in connection with it, are not fit to be used; or
  (*c*) that the way in which it is intended to carry on the home is such as not to provide services or facilities reasonably required.

Cancellation of registration

10. The registration authority may cancel the registration of a person in respect of a residential care home—
  (*a*) on any ground which would entitle them to refuse an application for his registration in respect of it;
  (*b*) on the ground that the annual fee in respect of the home has not been paid on or before the due date; or
  (*c*) on the ground—
    (i) that he has been convicted of an offence under this Part of this Act or any regulations made under it in respect of that or any other residential care home;
    (ii) that any other person has been convicted of such an offence in respect of that home; or
    (iii) that any condition for the time being in force in respect of the home by virtue of this Part of this Act has not been complied with.

Urgent procedure for cancellation of registration etc.

11.—(1) If—
  (*a*) the registration authority apply to a justice of the peace for an order—
    (i) cancelling the registration of a person in respect of a residential care home;

    (ii) varying any condition for the time being in force in respect of a home by virtue of this Part of this Act; or

    (iii) imposing an additional condition; and

  (*b*) it appears to the justice of the peace that there will be a serious risk to the life, health or well-being of the residents in the home unless the order is made,

he may make the order, and the cancellation, variation or imposition shall have effect from the date on which the order is made.

(2) An application under subsection (1) above may be made ex parte and shall be supported by a written statement of the registration authority's reasons for making the application.

(3) An order under subsection (1) above shall be in writing.

(4) Where such an order is made, the registration authority shall serve on any person registered in respect of the home, as soon as practicable after the making of the order,—

  (*a*) notice of the making of the order and of its terms; and

  (*b*) a copy of the statement of the authority's reasons which supported their application for the order.

Appeals

15.—(1) An appeal against—

  (*a*) a decision of a registration authority; or

  (*b*) an order made by a justice of the peace under section 11 above,

shall lie to a Registered Homes Tribunal.

(2) An appeal shall be brought by notice in writing given to a registration authority.

(3) No appeal against a decision or order may be brought by a person more than 28 days after service on him of notice of the decision or order.

(4) On an appeal against a decision of a registration authority the tribunal may confirm the decision or direct that it shall not have effect.

(5) On an appeal against an order made by a justice of the peace the tribunal may confirm the order or direct that it shall cease to have effect.

(6) A tribunal shall also have power on an appeal against a decision or order—

  (*a*) to vary any condition for the time being in force in respect of the home to which the appeal relates by virtue of this Part of this Act;

  (*b*) to direct that any such condition shall cease to have effect; or

  (*c*) to direct that any such condition as it thinks fit shall have effect in respect of the home.

(7) A registration authority shall comply with any direction given by a tribunal under this section.

Inspection of homes

17.—(1) Any person authorised in that behalf by the Secretary of State may at all times enter and inspect any premises which are used, or which that person has reasonable cause to believe to be used, for the purposes of a residential care home.

(2) Any person authorised in that behalf by a registration authority may at all times enter and inspect any premises in the area of the authority which are used, or which that person has reasonable cause to believe to be used, for those purposes.

(3) The powers of inspection conferred by subsections (1) and (2) above shall include power to inspect any records required to be kept in accordance with regulations under this Part of this Act.

(4) The Secretary of State may by regulations require that residential care homes shall be inspected on such occasions or at such intervals as the regulations may prescribe.

(5) A person who proposes to exercise any power of entry or inspection conferred by this section shall if so required produce some duly authenticated document showing his authority to exercise the power.

(6) Any person who obstructs the exercise of any such power shall be guilty of an offence.

General interpretation

20.—(1) In this Part of this Act—

"disablement", in relation to persons, means that they are blind, deaf or dumb or substantially and permanently handicapped by illness, injury or congenital deformity or any other disability prescribed by the Secretary of State;

"personal care" means care which includes assistance with bodily functions where such assistance is required;

"prescribed" means prescribed by regulations under this Part of this Act;

"registration authority", in relation to a residential care home, means, subject to subsection (2) below, the local social services authority for the area in which the home is situated.

(2) The Council of the Isles of Scilly is the registration authority in relation to a residential care home in the Isles.

PART II

NURSING HOMES AND MENTAL NURSING HOMES

Interpretation

Meaning of "nursing home"

21.—(1) In this Act "nursing home" means, subject to subsection (3) below—

(a) any premises used, or intended to be used, for the reception of, and the provision of nursing for, persons suffering from any sickness, injury or infirmity;

(b) any premises used, or intended to be used, for the reception of pregnant women, or of women immediately after childbirth (in this Act referred to as a "maternity home"); and

(c) any premises not falling within either of the preceding paragraphs which are used, or intended to be used, for the provision of all or any of the following services, namely—

(i) the carrying out of surgical procedures under anaesthesia;

(ii) the termination of pregnancies;

(iii) endoscopy;

(iv) haemodialysis or peritoneal dialysis;

(v) treatment by specially controlled techniques.

(2) In subsection (1) above "specially controlled techniques" means techniques specified under subsection (4) below as subject to control for the purposes of this Part of this Act.

(3) The definition in subsection (1) above does not include—

(*a*) any hospital or other premises maintained or controlled by a government department or local authority or any other authority or body instituted by special Act of Parliament or incorporated by Royal Charter;

(*b*) any mental nursing home;

(*c*) any sanatorium provided at a school or educational establishment and used, or intended to be used, solely by persons in attendance at, or members of the staff of, that school or establishment or members of their families;

(*d*) any first aid or treatment room provided at factory premises, at premises to which the Offices, Shops and Railways Premises Act 1963 applies or at a sports ground, show ground or place of public entertainment;

(*e*) any premises used, or intended to be used, wholly or mainly—

(i) by a medical practitioner for the purpose of consultations with his patients;

(ii) by a dental practitioner or chiropodist for the purpose of treating his patients; or

(iii) for the provision of occupational health facilities,

unless they are used, or intended to be used, for the provision of treatment by specially controlled techniques and are not excepted by regulations under paragraph (*g*) below;

(*f*) any premises used, or intended to be used, wholly or mainly as a private dwelling; or

(*g*) any other premises excepted from that definition by regulations made by the Secretary of State.

(4) The Secretary of State may by regulations specify as subject to control for the purposes of this Part of this Act any technique of medicine or surgery (including cosmetic surgery) as to which he is satisfied that its use may create a hazard for persons treated by means of it or for the staff of any premises where the technique is used.

(5) Without prejudice to the generality of section 56 below, regulations under subsection (4) above may define a technique by reference to any criteria which the Secretary of State considers appropriate.

(6) In this section "treatment" includes diagnosis and "treated" shall be construed accordingly.

Meaning of "mental nursing home"

22.—(1) In this Act "mental nursing home" means, subject to subsection (2) below, any premises used, or intended to be used, for the reception of, and the provision of nursing or other medical treatment (including care, habilitation and rehabilitation under medical supervision) for, one or more mentally disordered patients (meaning persons suffering, or appearing to be suffering, from mental disorder), whether exclusively or in common with other persons.

(2) In this Act "mental nursing home" does not include any hospital as defined in subsection (3) below, or any other premises managed by a government department or provided by a local authority.

(3) In subsection (2) above, "hospital" means—

(a) any health service hospital within the meaning of the National Health Service Act 1977; and

(b) any accommodation provided by a local authority and used as a hospital by or on behalf of the Secretary of State under that Act.

Registration and conduct of nursing homes and mental nursing homes

Registration of nursing homes and mental nursing homes

23.—(1) Any person who carries on a nursing home or a mental nursing home without being registered under this Part of this Act in respect of that home shall be guilty of an offence.

(2) Registration under this Part of this Act does not affect any requirement to register under Part I of this Act.

(3) An application for registration under this Part of this Act—

(a) shall be made to the Secretary of State;

(b) shall be accompanied by a fee of such amount as the Secretary of State may by regulations prescribe;

(c) in the case of a mental nursing home, shall specify whether or not it is proposed to receive in the home patients who are liable to be detained under the provisions of the Mental Health Act 1983.

(4) Subject to section 25 below, the Secretary of State shall, on receiving an application under subsection (3) above, register the applicant in respect of the home named in the application, and shall issue to the applicant a certificate of registration.

(5) Where a person is registered in pursuance of an application stating that it is proposed to receive in the home such patients as are described in subsection (3)(c) above—

(a) that fact shall be specified in the certificate of registration; and

(b) the particulars of the registration shall be entered by the Secretary of State in a separate part of the register.

(6) The certificate of registration issued under this Part of this Act in respect of any nursing home or mental nursing home shall be kept affixed in a conspicuous place in the home, and if default is made in complying with this subsection, the person carrying on the home shall be guilty of an offence.

Prohibition of holding out premises as nursing home, maternity home or mental nursing home

24.—(1) A person who, with intent to deceive any person,—

(a) applies any name to premises in England or Wales; or

(b) in any way so describes such premises or holds such premises out, as to indicate, or reasonably be understood to indicate, that the premises are a nursing home or maternity home, shall be guilty of an offence unless registration has been effected under this Part of this Act in respect of the premises as a nursing home.

(2) A person who, with intent to deceive any person,—

(a) applies any name to premises in England or Wales; or

(b) in any way so describes such premises or holds such premises out, as to indicate, or reasonably be understood to indicate, that the premises are a mental nursing home, shall be guilty of an offence, unless registration has been effected under this Part of this Act in respect of the premises as a mental nursing home.

INDEX